Business Result

SECOND EDITION

Intermediate *Student's Book* with Online practice

OXFORD
UNIVERSITY PRESS

John Hughes & Jon Naunton

Contents

Introduction

Welcome to *Business Result Second Edition Intermediate*. In this book you will find:

- 15 units
- 5 Viewpoint video lessons
- Practice files
- Communication activities
- Audio scripts
- Access to the Online practice

What's in a unit?

Starting point
- an introduction to the theme of the unit
- discussion questions

Working with words
- reading and listening about a work-related topic
- focus on key words and phrases
- practise the new words in speaking activities

Language at work
- grammar presented in authentic work contexts
- *Language point* box focuses on the key grammar points
- practise using the language in real work situations

Practically speaking
- focus on an aspect of everyday communication at work
- helps you to sound more natural when speaking
- practise speaking in real work situations

Business communication
- key expressions for authentic work contexts
- improve your communication skills for meetings, presentations, socializing, and phone calls
- *Key expressions* list in every unit

Talking point
- focus on interesting business topics and concepts
- improve your fluency with *Discussion* and *Task* activities
- *Discussion* and *Task* allow you to apply the topic to your own area of work

What's in the *Communication activities*?

- roles and information for pair and group activities
- extra speaking practice for the main sections of each unit

What's in the *Viewpoint* lessons?

The *Viewpoints* are video lessons, which appear after every three units. The topics of the *Viewpoint* lessons relate to a theme from the main units and include:
- interviews with expert speakers
- case studies of real companies

Each *Viewpoint* is divided into three or four sections, with a number of short video clips in each lesson. A *Viewpoint* lesson usually includes:
- A focus to introduce the topic. This contains a short video showing people discussing the topic.
- Key vocabulary and phrases which appear in the videos.
- Main video sections which develop listening and note-taking skills, and build confidence in listening to authentic language in an authentic context.
- Activities which provide speaking practice about the topic of the lesson.

All of the videos in the *Viewpoint* lessons can be streamed or downloaded from the *Online practice*.

What's in the *Practice files*?

Written exercises to practise the key language in:
- *Working with words*
- *Business communication*
- *Language at work*

Use the *Practice files*:
- in class to check your understanding
- out of class for extra practice or homework

The *Practice files* include a *Grammar reference* section with more detailed explanations of the grammar from each unit.

Follow the links (as shown below) to the *Practice file* in each unit.

>> For more exercises, go to **Practice file 6** on page 116

>> For more information, go to **Grammar reference** on page 117

What's in the *Online practice*?

- practice exercises for each *Working with words*, *Language at work*, and *Business communication* section
- unit tests
- email exercises for each unit
- automatic marking for instant answers
- gradebook to check your scores and progress

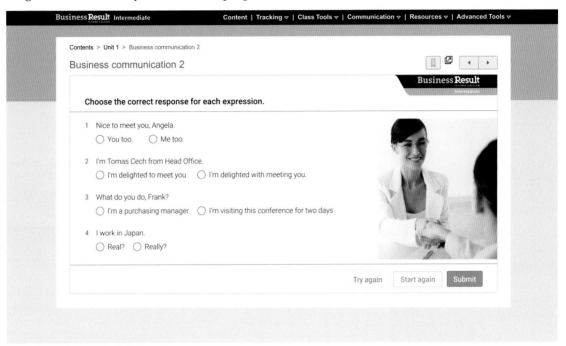

Additional resources

- watch and download all of the *Viewpoint* videos
- listen to and download all of the class audio
- sample emails for each unit

How to access your *Online practice*

To access your *Online practice*, you will find an access card on the inside cover of your Student's Book. This contains an access code to unlock all the content in the *Online practice*.

Go to **www.oxfordlearn.com** and activate your code, and then follow the instructions online to access the content.

1 Working life

Starting point

1 What kind of business or organization do you work for?

2 Where do you spend most of your working day? At your desk, in meetings or somewhere else?

3 How much of your time is spent working on your own, with colleagues or with clients?

Working with words | Describing work

1 What kind of information do these places have about you and your job?
- A company website
- A personal webpage
- A social media site such as Facebook or LinkedIn
- A brochure or publication such as a conference programme

2 Read these profiles about people from a training company website and answer the questions.
  1 What is the name of the company? What kinds of training courses does it provide?
  2 Which people work full-time for the company?
  3 Which people are freelance and sometimes work for the company?

HOWARD BRIGHT

I'm the Director of In-balance, which I set up in 1996. We offer high quality training services throughout the UK. I'm mainly **in charge of** planning and coordinating our courses. I **work with** a team of full-time office staff and freelance trainers.

EMRANN BHATT

I **work as** a trainer for In-balance and run regular courses on using mobile technologies in marketing. I'm also a marketing consultant with my own agency. I **specialize in** online marketing and a large part of my work involves developing marketing strategies for small-to-medium sized business owners.

TASIA CLIFFORD

I work part-time for In-balance and I **am responsible for** running their courses on employment law and health and safety. For the rest of the time, I'm a business lawyer with experience in the fields of employment law and health and safety. Most of my work **consists of** advising managers and businesses in these two areas. My clients come from a range of businesses and organizations.

FEY DE BOUTILIER

I **work in** customer services for In-balance. As the customer service representative, I mainly **deal with** enquiries and bookings from a variety of clients ranging from multinational corporations to individual customers.

3 Complete this table with information about Tasia, Emrann and Fey from their profiles in **2**.

	Job(s)	Colleagues and clients	Main area(s) of business	Workplace activities
Howard	*Director*	*office staff and freelance trainers*	*training*	*planning and coordinating courses*
Tasia				
Emrann				
Fey				

4 Discuss with a partner. How many full-time, part-time and freelance staff do you have in your company?

5 Complete the verb phrases in these sentences with a preposition. Check your answers by looking for the same verb phrases in **bold** in the profiles in **2**.
   1 I work _____ a large group of people. We make a great team.
   2 I'm responsible _____ planning and budgeting.
   3 My job consists _____ advising businesses and organizations on employment law.
   4 I'm in charge _____ coordinating sales teams across the region.
   5 I specialize _____ workplace motivation.
   6 I work _____ a receptionist in a large multinational.
   7 I work _____ the areas of finance and accounting.
   8 I deal _____ after-sales enquiries.

6 Which of the categories a–d do sentences 1–8 refer to? (Some of the sentences can refer to more than one category.)
   a Job   ___
   b Colleagues and clients   _1_
   c Areas of business   ___
   d Workplace activities   ___

   » For more exercises, go to **Practice file 1** on page 106.

7 Work with a partner. Tell your partner about your job. Use the verb phrases from **5**.

8 Write a profile about yourself and your job for your company website.

> **About yourself**
>
> _____
> _____
> _____
> _____
> _____

Tip | *mainly*
You can use the adverb *mainly* to emphasize your main workplace activities. Notice the position is after the verb *to be* but before the main verb:
*I'm **mainly** responsible for planning.*
*I **mainly** deal with taking bookings.*

Language at work | Present simple and present continuous

1 In what situations do you have to give a short personal presentation about yourself and your work?

2 ▶ 1.1 Listen to a conversation between Emrann Bhatt and Veronique Denvir and answer the questions.

1 What is the course? *Online mkting*
2 What does Emrann ask everyone to do? *short presentation*
3 What kind of charity does Veronique work for? *medical*
4 What is she responsible for? *advertising, fund raising*
5 Where is she mainly based? *Paris*
6 What is her reason for taking the course? *needs to learn new mkting techniques*

30s **3** ▶ 1.1 Listen again and write the missing verbs in these sentences.

1 I ___work___ for a medical charity.
2 In my job, I often __deal__ with fundraising projects and advertising campaigns.
3 I __am__ currently __running__ a campaign to raise over a million euros.
4 I __m diving__ and __working__ in London for three months.
5 Why __are__ you __talking__ this course today?
6 My organization usually _____ in traditional media.
7 These days, more and more people __are really__ text and __watching__ video online.
8 I __don't know__ enough about online marketing.

4 Answer the questions in the *Language point*.

LANGUAGE POINT

Complete explanations a–f with *simple* or *continuous*. Then match the sentences in **3** to each explanation.

a We use the present ___simple___ to talk about regular or repeated actions.
  ___Sentences 2 and 6___

b We use the present _____ to talk about actions happening now and current projects. _____

c We use the present _____ to talk about general facts. _____

d We use the present _____ to talk about trends and changing situations. _____

e We use the present _____ to talk about temporary situations. _____

f We use the present _____ with state verbs such as *understand, know, like,* etc. _____

We often use adverbs with the present simple and present continuous. Find four adverbs in the sentences in **3** and add them to these categories:
Adverbs of frequency (How often?):
  always, sometimes, never, _____, _____
Adverbs of time (When?): *now, at the moment,* _____, _____

Tip | Adverb position

Adverbs of frequency can go before the main verb or after *be*:
*I **always** work from an office.*
*I'm **always** on time.*
Adverbs of time often go at the beginning or the end of a sentence:
***These days**, I'm working online.*
*I'm working online **these days**.*
The adverb of time *currently* is an exception:
*I'm **currently** working from home.*

» For more information, go to **Grammar reference** on page 107.

5 Underline the correct tense in *italics* and add the adverb in brackets where given.

1 What *do you work / are you working* on? (at the moment)
2 We *have / are having* offices in over 20 countries.
3 More and more of our customers *order / are ordering* our goods online. (these days)
4 I'*m responsible / 'm being responsible* for everyone else's travel arrangements. (normally)
5 We *don't do / aren't doing* any business in Brazil until we can all speak Portuguese.
6 Overall, the economic climate *improves / is improving*.
7 My company *tries / is trying* to increase its trade in China. (currently)
8 I *do / 'm doing* this course because I *don't understand / 'm not understanding* Excel software.
9 *Do you give / Are you giving* presentations in your job? (often)

>> For more exercises, go to **Practice file 1** on page 107.

6 Prepare a short personal presentation using the present simple and present continuous. Use adverbs where appropriate. Talk about:
• your job and your responsibilities
• a current project at work
• your reasons for taking this English course

7 Take turns to give your personal presentations to the class. When you listen to a presenter, take notes and ask follow-up questions at the end of their presentation.

Practically speaking | How to show interest

1 When you listen to someone, how can you show interest?

2 ▶ 1.2 Listen to a conversation between Veronique and Joel. Match sentences 1–3 to responses a–c.
1 But at the moment, I'm doing a lot of work in the USA. ___
2 It's a project for a pharmaceutical company. ___
3 This one gives money to charities and non-profit organizations. ___

a **Is that right?** My company works with pharmaceutical companies, too.
b **Really?** How often do you travel there?
c **That sounds interesting!** It would be good to keep in contact.

3 ▶ 1.3 The expressions in **bold** show the speaker's interest. Listen to the intonation and repeat the expressions.

4 Which other technique does each speaker use in a–c in **2** to show more interest?
1 Suggesting keeping in contact. ___
2 Finding a connection. ___
3 Asking a question. ___

5 Work with a partner. Write five sentences about your working life. Take turns to tell each other the information and respond by showing interest using an expression from **2** and a technique from **4**.

> *Example:* **A** *I'm developing a new product at the moment.*
> **B** *That sounds interesting! What type of product is it?*

Business communication | Networking

1 Discuss questions 1–3 with a partner.

1 Do you ever attend networking events?

2 How important is networking in your job?

3 In what other situations do you need to network with people?

2 ▶ 1.4 The Culham Health Trust is holding an event for its key personnel, staff and fundraisers. Listen to the extracts from two different conversations. Write notes about the jobs and responsibilities for these people.

Luc Akele: _____

Jo Johansson: _____

Walter Mayer: _____

3 ▶ 1.4 Listen to the conversations again. Tick (✓) the person who says each expression.

Conversation 1	Hannah	Jo	Luc
1 I want you to meet …			
2 Nice to meet you.			
3 What do you do, exactly?			
4 I'm afraid I have to go now.			
5 It was nice meeting you, too.			
6 I'd like to keep in contact.			
7 Do you have a card?			

Conversation 2	Dr Mayer	Hiroko
8 Let me introduce myself.		
9 I'm delighted to meet you.		
10 Please, call me Walter.		
11 I'm very pleased to meet you, too.		
12 Here's my card.		
13 Which part of Japan are you from?		
14 It was nice meeting you.		
15 I look forward to hearing from you.		

4 Which conversation is more formal? Give reasons for your answer.

» For more exercises, go to **Practice file 1** on page 106.

5 Work with a partner. Practise a networking conversation with your own jobs and responsibilities using this flow chart.

```
Introduce yourself. ┄┄> Exchange greetings. ┄┄> Ask about
                                                  personal details.
                                                         ┊
                                                         ∨
End the          <┄┄  Agree to keep
conversation.           in contact.
```

6 Stand up with your partner from **5** and meet other students in the class. Introduce your partner to other students and continue networking.

Key expressions

Introducing yourself
Hi / Hello / Good evening.
I'm …
Let me introduce myself.
I don't think we've met
(before). I'm …
Please, call me (Walter).

Exchanging greetings
Nice to meet you, (too).
I'm very pleased to meet you. /
I'm delighted to meet you.

Introducing other people
I want you to meet …
This is …
I'd like to introduce you to …

Asking about personal details
What do you do, exactly?
Where are you from?
Which part of … are you from?

Keeping in contact
Do you have a card?
Here's my card.
I'd like to keep in contact.

Ending the conversation
I'm afraid I have to go now.
It was very nice to meet you.
It was nice meeting you, (too).
I look forward to hearing
from you.

TALKING POINT

Speed networking

Contact25 organizes business-to-business speed networking events. At these events, participants have a series of mini-meetings with new contacts. The idea is that within a few minutes of talking to someone, they will know whether it is possible to do business with them. This makes it a very efficient form of business networking. Each meeting lasts five minutes.

You have:

- two minutes to talk about yourself, your company or organization
- two minutes to listen to your partner describe their company or organization
- 30 seconds to score your partner, and note future action
- 30 seconds to move to the next meeting

Contact25 estimates that each participant creates around €5,000 worth of new business at each event.

Discussion

1 What are the advantages of speed networking? Can you think of any disadvantages?

2 Would speed networking be useful in your job/company? Why/Why not?

Task

1 You are going to attend a speed networking event with Contact25. You can be yourself or you can choose a person from the role cards on page 136. Prepare what you are going to say about:
- yourself and what you do
- the company or organization you represent
- why you are at this event

2 Follow the rules of speed networking. Meet and talk to one person (two minutes for you to talk and two minutes for them to talk). Then give that person points out of three using the scorecard below and write your reasons.

1 point = I have no reason to contact this person again.
2 points = I might contact this person again but I need more information.
3 points = I definitely want to contact this person again.

	Person 1	Person 2	Person 3
Name and company			
Points (1, 2 or 3?)			
Reason			

3 Next, meet and network with another person for four minutes and score them. Then network with a third person and complete the scorecard.

4 Tell the class about your most useful contact and give your reasons.

2 Work–life balance

Starting point

1 What is 'work–life' balance?

2 Is there a 'long-hours' working culture in your country?

Working with words | Work–life balance

1 Why should employers care about their employees' work–life balance?

2 Read the extract of a company's terms and conditions for its employees. Choose the correct heading for each section.
- Family and health
- Working hours
- Holiday

Terms and conditions of employment

1 _____

The company operates a system of flexitime. All employees must be at work during the core hours of between 10 a.m. and 4 p.m. but they can start and finish work between the hours of 8 a.m. and 6 p.m. Employees must take their lunch break anytime between midday and 2 p.m. and this should not be less than 30 minutes long. Paid overtime must be done outside of the flexible working hours (e.g. before 8 a.m. or after 6 p.m.) and agreed in writing by your manager. The company also allows home-working (where appropriate to the employee's roles and responsibilities) for up to a maximum of eight hours on one day a week. Requests to work from home must be made in writing to your manager.

2 _____

Full-time employees receive 25 working days' holiday (not including public holidays) in a calendar year. Annual leave for part-time staff is calculated according to the number of days worked per year. After five years of service, an employee can take an extra two days' leave per year. Managers may accept requests for additional leave depending on your circumstances.

3 _____

Expectant mothers can take up to 52 weeks' maternity leave at the following rates: 12 weeks of full pay, 27 weeks of statutory pay and an additional 13 weeks of unpaid leave. Fathers can take two weeks off for paternity leave at any time between the child's birth until eight weeks afterwards.

For sick leave, employees receive full pay for a short-term illness up to 28 days. For longer-term illness, employees with over 24 months' service will receive full pay for up to six months. Employees with under 24 months' service receive statutory pay after 28 days. A medical certificate is required from your doctor if you are absent for more than five days.

---

3 Do you think these terms and conditions provide a good work–life balance for employees? Why/Why not?

4 Look for compound words in the text and match them to definitions 1–10.
   1 A system of working a particular number of hours each week or month but choosing when you start and finish. _____*flexitime*_____
   2 The times when you always have to work. _____
   3 Time at work in addition to your normal hours. _____
   4 Not working in your office but at your house. _____
   5 The number of days off for holidays per year. _____
   6 Extra days off. _____
   7 An official rate of pay according to the law. _____
   8 Time off with no money. _____
   9 Time off for men to spend time with a new baby. _____
   10 All your normal salary. _____

5 Read a new employee's questions to their manager. Using the terms and conditions in the text in **2**, what will the manager reply?
   1 Can I start work earlier in the day so I finish by five o'clock?
   2 I'd like to finish work every day at three-thirty. Is that possible?
   3 How long can I take for lunch?
   4 I worked until eight last night. Do I get paid anything extra?
   5 January 1st is a public holiday, but is it part of my normal holiday?
   6 Does everyone get the same amount of annual leave?
   7 My wife is having a baby next month. Can I take some time off when it's born?
   8 Sorry I was off sick yesterday. Do I still get paid?

6 Work with a partner.
   Student A: You are a new employee at Student B's company.
   Ask the questions in **5**.
   Student B: Student A is a new employee at your company.
   Answer their questions with true answers for your company.

7 Now change roles and repeat **6**. Afterwards, compare your answers.

   » For more exercises, go to **Practice file 2** on page 108.

8 ▶ 2.1 Listen to two people talking about their company and their work–life balance. Make notes on each question in the table.

What is good about the work–life balance at your company?
Speaker 1:
Speaker 2:
What don't you like about the system?
Speaker 1:
Speaker 2:
What would you change about it?
Speaker 1:
Speaker 2:

9 Work with a partner. Discuss the three questions in **8** for you and your company.

Language at work | *to* + infinitive and *-ing* form

1 Take this quiz to find out if you have a good work–life balance.

FIND OUT YOUR WORK–LICE BALANCE

Write 2 if the statement is true for you, 1 if it's mostly true and 0 if it's not true.

1 I **enjoy doing** exercise and **playing** sport. ___

2 I never think **about checking** work emails in my free time. ___

3 This year, I **intend to take** all my annual leave. ___

4 I always leave work on time **to make sure** I have free time in the evening. ___

5 I think it's **important to take** an hour for lunch. ___

Now add up your score and find out what it means:

0–4 Your life is out of balance. Put less emphasis on your job and give more time to family, friends and leisure.

5–8 Your work–life balance is OK, but be careful. You need to spend more time relaxing.

9–10 You have a great work–life balance. Don't change it!

2 Do you agree with your quiz results? Do you think you have a good work–life balance?

3 Look at the verb patterns in **bold** in the quiz in 1. Choose the correct words in *italics* to complete the explanations a–e in the *Language point*. Then write the sentence number from the quiz that matches each explanation.

> **LANGUAGE POINT**
>
> a We use *to + infinitive / the -ing form* when it follows an adjective. ___
>
> b We use *to + infinitive / the -ing form* when it follows a preposition. ___
>
> c We use *to + infinitive / the -ing form* to express purpose. ___
>
> d *To + infinitive / The -ing form* often comes after verbs about likes and dislikes. ___
>
> e *To + infinitive / The -ing form* often comes after verbs about making plans and decisions. ___

4 Which of these common verbs and phrases are usually followed by …?

to + infinitive _____

the *-ing* form _____

want   agree   responsible for   it's difficult   look forward to   involve   would like   plan   interested in   I'm pleased   enjoy   decide

≫ For more information, go to **Grammar reference** on page 109.

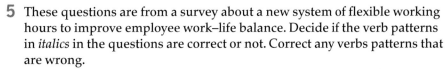

Tip | *to*: infinitive or preposition?

The *infinitive* form is *to* + base form of the verb: **to** *do*, **to** *go*, **to** *make*. When 'to' is a preposition after a verb, remember to use the *-ing* form:

*I **look forward to** meeting you.*

5 These questions are from a survey about a new system of flexible working hours to improve employee work–life balance. Decide if the verb patterns in *italics* in the questions are correct or not. Correct any verbs patterns that are wrong.

1 How difficult is it *to balance* your current job with your home-life?
2 Do you like *working* at the same times every day?
3 What percentage of your time consists of *to work* in teams and what percentage on your own?
4 Do you often stay late *to finish* what you are working on, or do you leave it until the next day?
5 Do you plan *taking* unpaid leave at any time in the next three years?
6 In your position, is it easy *to take* time off for childcare or to care for a sick or elderly relative?
7 Would you like *managing* your own working hours?
8 If you had flexitime, would you decide *starting* work earlier or later in the day?

>> For more exercises, go to **Practice file 2** on page 109.

6 Work with a partner. Ask and answer the questions in **5** about your own working hours. Give reasons for your answers.

7 Imagine your company wants to survey its own employees' opinions on their work–life balance. Write three questions it should ask. Then ask your partner.

Practically speaking | How to say 'yes'

1 When your boss or colleagues ask you to do something, do you always say 'yes'? How difficult is it to say 'no'?

2 ▶ 2.2 Listen to four conversations. Match each conversation to the requests in a–d.

Conversation 1: ___	a to work late
Conversation 2: ___	b to do some paid overtime
Conversation 3: ___	c to take a day off next week
Conversation 4: ___	d to work during the lunch break

3 ▶ 2.2 Each person answers 'yes' in different ways. Listen again and match these answers to requests a–d.
1 Yes, absolutely! ___
2 Yes, no problem. ___
3 Yes, I suppose so. ___
4 Yes, sure. ___

4 Which response in **3** is less positive? In which situations and with whom would you normally use this response?

5 Work with a partner. Practise these conversations by making the request and answering 'yes' in different ways.
- A manager asks you to work this weekend and offers a bonus.
- A manager asks you to work on your day off. Three other employees are off sick today so they need help.
- A colleague asks you to help him during the lunch break.
- A manager asks you to work late this evening because no one else is available to help.

Business communication | Exchanging contact details

1 How much information do you keep about your work contacts? Tick (✓) the type of information you keep.

___ Email	___ Website	___ Work address
___ Home address	___ Mobile number	___ Office number
___ Home number	___ Picture	___ Name of spouse
___ Name(s) of children	___ Birthday	___ Other?

2 How difficult is it to organize contact information these days? Why?

3 ▶ 2.3 Listen to a phone conversation between two colleagues, Raul and Mirella. Complete the missing information from a business card.

Name: Leif _____

Office: _____

Email: _____

Company website: _____

4 ▶ 2.3 Match expressions 1–8 to responses a–h. Then listen again and check.

1 Could you give me his details? ___
2 Can I have his number? ___
3 Sorry, can you repeat that? ___
4 So that's 96 7 55 6745. ___
5 And do you spell his last name with one N or double N? ___
6 Sorry, was that E-R or A-R? ___
7 Do you have his email? ___
8 What's his company's web address? ___

a A as in apple. So it's Gunnarson.
b Yes, it's double 0 46 for Sweden. And then 967 double 5 6745.
c It's www.SBNshipping.se/sales. The SBN is in upper case letters.
d Double N. So that's G-U-N-N-A-R-S-O-N.
e Yes, that's it.
f It's leif.gunnarson@sbnshipping.se
g Yes, sure.
h His mobile or his office?

》 For more exercises, go to **Practice file 2** on page 108.

5 Prepare for a similar conversation with your partner. Write down a last name, a phone number, email and company web address.

6 Take turns to ask for and give the contact details using these prompts. Afterwards, check the information is correct.

1 Can / last name?
2 What / number?
3 Could / give / email?
4 Do / company web address?

7 Work with a partner and practise two similar phone conversations. **Student A**, turn to **page 137**. **Student B**, turn to **page 142**.

Key expressions

Asking for contact details
Could you give me her details?
Can I have his number?
What's your web address?
Do you have his/her email?

Saying phone numbers and emails
00 = double zero / zero zero / double oh
Say phone numbers in groups: 095...745...6745
@ = at   . = dot   / = slash
_ = underscore   – = dash
lower case = a, b, c, etc.
UPPER CASE = A, B, C, etc.

Checking numbers and spelling
So that's ...
Do you spell that with one N or double N?
A for apple. / A as in apple.
A not E.

Asking for repetition and clarification
Can you say that again?
Can you repeat that?
Is that E-R or A-R?
Sorry, was that E-R or A-R?

TALKING POINT

Corridor conversations

Work in small groups. Each player places a counter on 'Start'. Take turns to roll a dice and move to another square.

GREEN SQUARES Ask all the players a question using the phrase.
BLUE SQUARES Move to the nearest square another player is on and speak to that player.
PINK SQUARES A player talks to one other player.
PURPLE SQUARES Follow the instructions.

The player who lands on 'End' first is the winner.

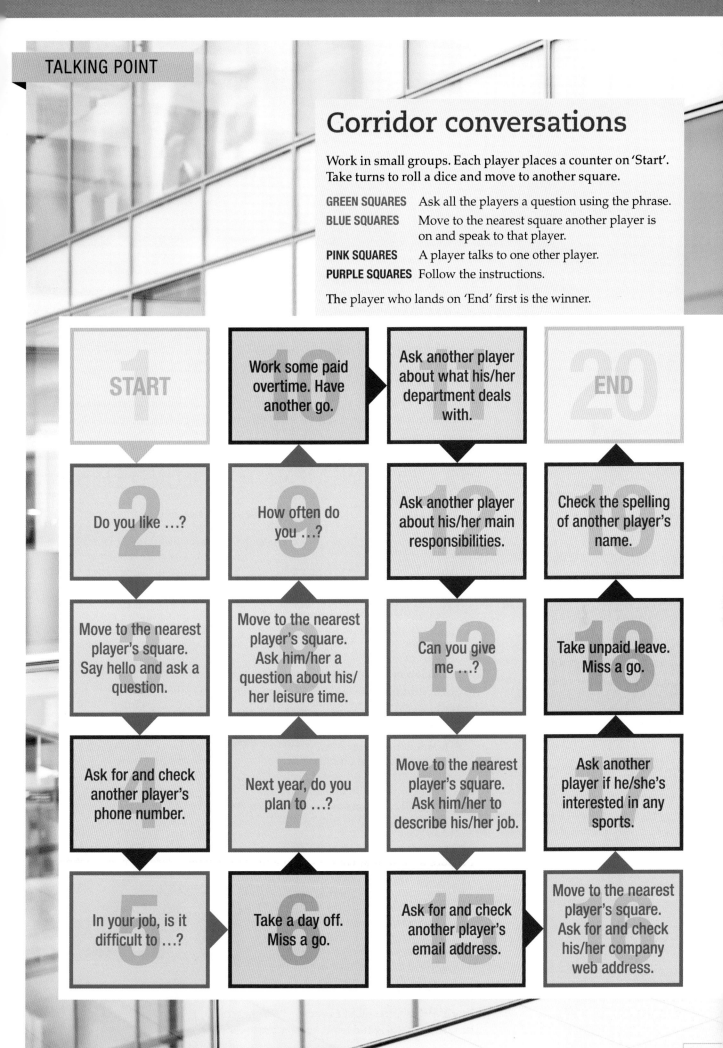

1 START

10 Work some paid overtime. Have another go.

11 Ask another player about what his/her department deals with.

20 END

2 Do you like …?

9 How often do you …?

12 Ask another player about his/her main responsibilities.

19 Check the spelling of another player's name.

3 Move to the nearest player's square. Say hello and ask a question.

8 Move to the nearest player's square. Ask him/her a question about his/her leisure time.

13 Can you give me …?

18 Take unpaid leave. Miss a go.

4 Ask for and check another player's phone number.

7 Next year, do you plan to …?

14 Move to the nearest player's square. Ask him/her to describe his/her job.

17 Ask another player if he/she's interested in any sports.

5 In your job, is it difficult to …?

6 Take a day off. Miss a go.

15 Ask for and check another player's email address.

16 Move to the nearest player's square. Ask for and check his/her company web address.

3 Projects

Starting point

1 What makes a project successful?

2 Do you prefer to lead a project or be part of the team? Why?

3 Do you like being involved in long-term projects? Why/Why not?

Working with words | Projects

1 How can a business help a charity? What are the benefits for the company and its employees?

2 Read the article and decide if sentences 1–4 are true (*T*) or false (*F*).
   1 The idea of volunteerism is increasingly popular in business.
   2 Employees at Timberland have to do some voluntary work.
   3 Companies like Timberland and Credit Suisse also benefit from the projects.
   4 Samira uses the same skills in the volunteer project as in her usual job.

A COMMITMENT TO VOLUNTEERISM

For many employees, work rarely involves helping local communities in the rainforests of the Amazon or teaching children in schools with little or no access to modern technology. However, these examples of volunteer projects are becoming more and more common in the business world, and many companies now offer their employees the opportunity to take part in volunteer programmes.

Timberland is one such company with a commitment to volunteerism. The global clothing manufacturer encourages staff to spend up to 40 paid hours a year on community and social projects. The community benefits from the company's **resources**, and staff gain new skills and **teamwork** improves.

Another example is the financial services firm Credit Suisse. It sends employees overseas to help educational and microfinance projects in developing countries. These projects can last for up to three months. The two **objectives** are to offer expertise to regions of the world that lack access to highly-qualified professionals and for the employees to develop new transferable skills.

Samira Khan is one employee who took advantage of her company's volunteer scheme. Samira normally spends her days behind a desk as a software engineer but currently she's also managing a volunteer project to redecorate a community centre for the elderly in Chicago. Managing a project like this means that Samira is learning new skills such as organizing the **schedule** so that they complete each **milestone** by its **deadline**. She also has to control a limited **budget**, and every few days she gets **updates** from her project team to check on their progress. She finds working on this project very rewarding and is pleased to be learning new skills.

3 Does your company or its staff ever take part in volunteer projects?
- If you answer 'yes', describe one of the projects.
- If you answer 'no', what kind of volunteer project do you think it could offer?

4 Replace the words in *italics* with a word in **bold** from the text in **2**.
1 Can you email the *plan of all the work you have to do and the key dates*? _schedule_
2 We only have a limited *amount of money available for the project*. _____
3 The main problem is that no one knows what anyone else is doing. We need *a situation where everyone works together* for this project to succeed. _____
4 Could you send me regular *reports with the most recent information* about our progress? _____
5 We have to finish the project by a *certain point in time*. _____
6 This project has three main *things we are trying to achieve*. _____
7 I really feel we are making progress now because today we completed a *very important stage* in the project. _____
8 The reason we're behind schedule is because I don't have all the *supplies and human expertise* that I requested at the beginning. _____

5 ▶ 3.1 Samira is telling someone about the volunteer project that she is working on. Listen to these extracts from the conversation and answer the questions.
1 Which items in **4** does she talk about?
2 What does she say about each one?

6 ▶ 3.1 Listen again and complete the phrases that Samira uses in column A.

A		B
1 _____ the deadline	=	finish on time
2 fall _____ schedule	=	make slow progress
3 catch _____	=	make up lost time
4 be back _____ track	=	return to the original schedule
5 finish _____ schedule	=	finish before the planned date
6 _____ resources	=	make use of people, money and time
7 stay _____ budget	=	spend the right amount of money
8 _____ tasks	=	give people different responsibilities
9 get _____ with a task	=	do a job
10 _____ updates	=	receive reports on progress

7 Work with a partner. Take turns to cover the phrases in column A while your partner tests you using the definitions in column B.
> *Example:* **A** *How can you say 'finish on time'?*
> **B** *'Meet the deadline'?*
> **A** *Yes.*

≫ For more exercises, go to **Practice file 3** on page 110.

8 Work with a partner. Read the comments describing a problem in four current projects. Say what the problem is and what the project manager needs to do, using phrases from **6**.
> *Example:* *The project is falling behind schedule, so the project manager needs to make sure we catch up again so we can meet the deadlines.*
1 'We didn't expect so many delays.'
2 'We're currently spending 50% more than we planned.'
3 'I'm working late every night. I can't do everything on this project.'
4 'No one knows what each other is doing. There's no communication!'

9 Think of a project you, your department or company are currently working on. Make notes on the following and then tell your partner about the project.
- The objectives of the project
- The project team and the resources needed
- The budget
- The deadlines and milestones in the schedule
- Any problems and possible solutions

Tip | *in time / on time*

In time means having enough time to be able to do something:
*If we leave now, we'll be there **in time** for the meeting.*
On time means at the correct time:
*I have to be at work at 9 a.m. and I always arrive **on time**. I'm never late, but I don't like to be early either.*

Language at work | Present perfect and past simple

1 Look at this chart for a project. What kind of information does it give about the project? Does your company use similar charts for managing projects?

Office relocation

STAGE	DATE								
	WEEK 1	WEEK 2	WEEK 3	WEEK 4	WEEK 5	WEEK 6	WEEK 7	WEEK 8	WEEK 9
	11–17	18–24	25–31	1–7	8–14	15–21	22–28	29–5	6–12
1 Confirm equipment requirements									
2 Equipment costings		✓	✓						
3 Place order with office supplier				✗					
4 Send plans to depts for review		✓							
5 Collate feedback and finalize plans				✓					
6 Packing and delivery									
7 Unpacking									
8 New equipment arrives									
9 Install									

2 ▶ 3.2 A company is relocating its office from an old building to some modern premises. Listen to a meeting between Judith (the project manager) and somebody on the team (Dawud). Use the chart in **1** to help you answer questions 1–3.
1 What is the purpose of the meeting?
2 Which stages on the chart are completed?
3 Which week is it on the chart?

3 ▶ 3.2 Listen again. <u>Underline</u> the verbs in *italics* that you hear.
1 I *agreed / 've agreed* the approximate equipment costings with finance.
2 *Did you place / Have you placed* the order for the equipment yesterday?
3 *Did anyone give / Has anyone given* their feedback?
4 Everyone *replied / has replied* before the deadline.

4 Answer the questions in the *Language point*.

LANGUAGE POINT

Do your answers in **3** use the past simple or present perfect? Match each sentence in **3** with explanations a or b.
a We use the present perfect to talk or ask about an action in the past where the time is not specified: _____, _____
b We use the past simple to talk or ask about an action in the past where the time is specified: ___2___, _____

Look at three more sentences from the meeting with the present perfect tense. Complete explanations 1–3 with the adverbs in **bold**.
*Some departments haven't sent their requirements **yet**.*
*I've **already** received everyone's feedback.*
*I've **just** emailed them another reminder.*
1 We use __just__ to show the action happened in the very recent past.
2 We use __yet__ in negative sentences and questions to talk about something that hasn't happened but you expect it will happen.
3 We use __already__ to emphasize the action happened sooner than expected.

Tip | The present perfect and past simple
In conversation, we often ask a question using the present perfect and then answer with extra information using the past simple:
Has everyone **sent** their feedback?
Yes, they **have**. And overall they **were** very positive.

» For more information, go to **Grammar reference** on page 111.

5 ▶ 3.3 Look at the chart in **1** again and read a later phone conversation between Judith and Dawud. Write the verbs in brackets in the past simple or present perfect and choose the correct adverb in *italics*. Then listen and check your answers.

Dawud Hello?

Judith Hi, Dawud. Just calling to see how things are going. ¹_____ the new equipment _____ (arrive) ²*just / yet*?

Dawud No, it hasn't, but I've ³*just / yet* called the supplier and the truck ⁴_____ (leave) the warehouse this morning. It'll be here around four o'clock.

Judith ⁵_____ they _____ (deliver) everything else on schedule?

Dawud Yes, they did. We ⁶_____ (unpack) most of the boxes ⁷*already / just*.

» For more exercises, go to **Practice file 3** on page 111.

6 Work with a partner. Ask and answer questions about this schedule for an office relocation project. Use the past simple, present perfect and adverbs (*already, just, yet*) in your questions and answers.

> *Example:* **A** *Have you ordered the headed stationery?*
> **B** *Yes, I have. I sent it yesterday. (OR) Yes, I've already sent it.*

Task	Done?	Additional information
Order headed stationery	✓	Sent order yesterday
Order new furniture	✓	Furniture has arrived
Send new address cards to clients	✓	Sent this morning
Issue staff with new badges	✗	To do

7 Work with a partner. Talk about a project or task you are working on and say what you have or haven't done.

Practically speaking | How to give short answers

1 Match the questions to the short answers.

1 Are you back on track again?
2 Did you email me the schedule?
3 Have you returned your feedback?
4 Can we meet for an update?

a Yes, I did.
b Yes, OK.
c No, not yet.
d Yes, I am.

2 ▶ 3.4 Add these sentences after the short answers in **1**. Then listen to the four conversations and check your answers.

1 In fact, the whole project is ahead of schedule now.
2 Sorry, but I've been really busy this week.
3 I'll come to your office right now.
4 I sent it two minutes ago.

3 Match each sentence in **2** to its purpose a–d.

a To promise action. ___
b To describe the action you took. ___
c To give an update. ___
d To give a reason. ___

4 Write three questions for your partner which require 'yes' or 'no' answers. Then take turns to ask and answer your questions. Use short answers with more information (to promise action, give a reason, etc.).

> *Example:* **A** *Have you done your Business English homework?*
> **B** *No, not yet. I'll do it tonight.*

Tip | Short answers to *yes/no* questions

We don't normally just answer a question with 'yes' or 'no'. We normally make short answers by using auxiliary verbs or expressions:

Have you placed the order yet?
Yes, I have. / No, I haven't yet. / Not yet.

Did they deliver the order?
Yes, they did. / No, they didn't.

In addition, we often add further information:

No, I haven't yet. I've been really busy.

Yes, they did. The order came last week.

Business communication | Updating and delegating tasks

1 How often do you have meetings with people in your department or team? How important is it to receive regular updates on everyone else's work?

2 ▶ 3.5 Ramon is leading his department meeting. Listen to part of the meeting and complete his notes on the discussion.

Recruitment
- Update: [1] *They have recruited frontline staff but they need to interview for the post of manager.*
- When: [2] _____
- Problem: Sue needs [3] _____
- Action: Eloise will [4] _____

Induction training
- Update: [5] *Xavier scheduled induction training for new frontline staff.*
- When: [6] _____
- Problem: [7] _____
- Action: [8] _____

---

3 ▶ 3.5 Look at these expressions from the meeting. Listen again and number the expressions 1–12 in the order you hear them.

- _1_ Can you update me on that?
- ___ Sorry, but I've never run induction training before.
- ___ Eloise is going to interview with Sue.
- ___ Is that something you can help with?
- ___ Let's check we all know what we're doing.
- ___ What's happening with that?
- ___ Can anyone else help you?
- _12_ Let's meet again in three weeks' time.
- ___ I'd like you to help if possible.
- ___ Would you like to help with that?
- ___ Yes, no problem.
- ___ I'd do it, but I'm away as well that week.

>> For more exercises, go to **Practice file 3** on page 110.

4 Work in groups of three. Ten business students are visiting your company on the 23rd. You need to book a room for the talk (task 1), get name badges (task 2), organize refreshments (task 3). Have a short meeting using the flow chart.

A Ask B for an update on the students' visit (How many? When?).

B Give an update.

A Ask C to do task 1.

C Agree to do task 1.

A Ask B to do task 2.

B Agree to do task 2.

A Ask C to do task 3.

C Say you can't do task 3 and give a reason.

A Ask B to do task 3.

B Agree to do task 3.

A Sum up the action plan.

5 Work with a partner. Ask for and give updates about two projects. **Student A, turn to page 137. Student B, turn to page 142.**

Key expressions

Asking for an update
Can you update me on ...?
What's the progress on ...?
How's everything going?
What's happening with ...?
Where are we with ...?

Giving an update
We've done/finished/completed ...
So far, so good.
Everything's on track.
We're currently (verb + -ing ...)

Delegating
Is that something you can help with?
Can anyone else help you?
Would you like to help with that?
I'd like you to help ...
Yes, no problem. / I'll do it.
Sorry, but ... / I'd do it, but ... / I'm afraid I can't do it.

Summing up the action plan
So, let's check we all know what we're doing ...
You're going to ... and I'm going to ...
Let's meet again in two weeks to review the situation/progress.

Scenario planning

The oil multinational Royal Dutch Shell is famous for its use of scenario planning. After the company makes its initial plans, it then asks questions about those plans using 'What if …?' For example, 'What if the price of oil falls?', 'What if technology changes?', 'What if the world population rises to nine billion by 2050?' In other words, the company can have a Plan A, but scenario planning means they also have a Plan B.

Developing a Plan B

Scenario planning isn't only for multinationals like Shell. Having a Plan B is important for planning any kind of project and it's easy to use:

1 List all the key stages of your project with deadlines, resources needed, the people involved and their responsibilities. Prepare a schedule or chart for your project with each of the stages. This is your Plan A.

2 Now try scenario planning for your project. For each stage of your plan, ask yourself a 'What if …?' question. For example, 'What if this doesn't arrive on time?', 'What if this supplier doesn't have it in stock?', or 'What if there is a change in government?' Try to answer each of these 'What if …?' questions.

3 Use all your answers in 2 to prepare a Plan B.

Discussion

1 How important do you think scenario planning is for a company? Give a reason for your answer.

2 What kind of things can go wrong in a plan? Think about both strategic (long-term) and operational (short-term) planning.

3 Describe the kind of planning you or your company are involved in. Do you think scenario planning could be helpful for you and your company? Why/Why not?

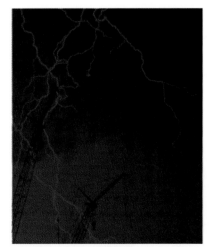

Task

1 Work in groups. You are going to prepare Plan A and Plan B for a project. Imagine your company wants to celebrate an important anniversary in its history with a special day of events. Discuss different ways that the company could do this and choose the best ideas.

2 Discuss and prepare Plan A. You have eight weeks to organize the event starting from today. Discuss what resources you will need and who is responsible for each stage. Take notes during the discussion and make a basic schedule or chart showing the stages of the plan.

3 Now do scenario planning with Plan A to make Plan B for your project. Ask and answer 'What if …?' questions about each stage.

4 Give a short presentation of your Plan A and Plan B to the class.

Focus

1 Look at the list of workplace things. Which of these things do you share with other people? Tell your partner.
- Transportation to and from work
- Your office
- Your desk
- Meeting rooms
- Computer equipment
- Photocopiers and stationery
- Your job
- Anything else?

2 ▶01 Watch three people talking about sharing at work. Make notes about their answers in the table.

	What do they share?	Are there any advantages or disadvantages?
Speaker 1		
Speaker 2		
Speaker 3		

3 Work with a partner and compare your answers in **2**. Then discuss questions 1–2.
1 How similar were the speakers' answers to your answers in **1**?
2 Can you think of any more advantages or disadvantages with sharing things at work?

The HUB

4 You are going to watch a video about a shared workspace called the HUB. Before you watch, match words and phrases 1–7 from the video to definitions a–g.
1 diverse background ___
2 sectors ___
3 campaigners ___
4 go crazy with loneliness ___
5 perspective ___
6 resources ___
7 a global network ___

a become very unhappy because you are on your own most of the time
b point of view
c different experience
d connections around the world
e people who want to change a political or social situation
f something useful for your work (e.g. a person or object)
g areas of economic activity (e.g. financial, health, educational)

5 ▶02 Watch the video about the HUB and the interview with Anna Levy who works there. As you watch, number the parts of the video A–E in the correct order 1–5.
A The location of the HUB ____
B The HUB as a global network ____
C Sharing equipment at the HUB ____
D Comparing the HUB with working from home ____
E The people who use the HUB ____

6 Work with a partner. Decide if these sentences are true (*T*) or false (*F*).
1 Most of the people at the HUB are employed by the HUB. ____
2 Anna Levy has worked for the HUB for about three years. ____
3 She says the people who use the Hub come from similar backgrounds with similar businesses. ____
4 People like the HUB because they can socialize with others. ____
5 Users don't need to spend money on expensive equipment at the HUB. ____
6 At the moment, there is only one HUB in the world. ____
7 The HUB network has around 5,000 members. ____

7 ▶02 Watch the video again and check your answers in **6**. As you watch, write down any important words or phrases from the video to support your answers.

8 Would you like to work in the HUB? Why/Why not?

Sharing a workspace

9 Work with a partner. Imagine you are Anna Levy at the HUB and a person with a small business who is interested in using the space. You are going to have a conversation.
Student A: You are Anna.
- Prepare a list of the reasons for sharing a workspace at the HUB. (e.g. socializing, better than home-working, etc.)
- Think of questions you want to ask the other person about their business. (e.g. How much space will you need?)

Student B: You are the person with a business.
- Think about what type of business you have and other details. (e.g. what you sell/provide, number of employees, the equipment you need, etc.)
- Prepare a list of questions about the HUB. (e.g. How does it work? Why do people like working there?)

10 When you are both ready, start the conversation. Is the HUB a good place for Student B to work?

11 Change partners and swap roles. Practise the conversation again.

4 Services & systems

Starting point

1 What types of online services do you use?
- Online banking
- Cloud storage
- Newsfeeds
- Others?

2 What are the benefits of these services?

3 Does your company offer any online services? Tell the class about them.

Working with words | Services and systems

1 How often do you use apps? Which app do you find most useful? How does it help you?

2 Read reviews of three apps and answer these questions for each one.
a What are the main benefits of the app?
b What type of person would use this kind of app?

Was this review helpful?

Yes 1,469

No 27

'A HANDY APP'

This **handy** app lets you book a taxi and reduce your waiting time. It uses the GPS on your phone to find the nearest driver. You can even see all the taxis within a mile of you. The system sends you a text with an **accurate** waiting time. Once your taxi arrives, you receive another text to check the driver's identity, so it's all very safe and **secure**. And the really nice part is that you don't need to hand over any local currency to the driver because your credit card is automatically charged.

Was this review helpful?

Yes 1,672

No 15

'SIMPLE AND USER-FRIENDLY'

Many people say meetings are the worst part of their job but, for me, arranging the meetings is worse! Emailing everyone, waiting for their replies and then working out when everyone is available can take longer than the meeting itself. For an **efficient** way to organize a meeting, this simple, **user-friendly** app makes it easier for you to schedule a meeting by offering everyone a choice of time slots. You tick the time slots that are possible and the app decides which time slot suits the majority. Automatic reminders mean there's no excuse for being late.

Was this review helpful?

Yes 1,803

No 9

'HIGHLY RECOMMENDED'

This app allows you to keep track of all your investments in one place. **Up-to-date** newsfeeds allow you to log into any stock market in the world and follow the daily ups and downs, and **high-quality** infographics illustrate the latest trends. I highly recommended it for any investors on the move.

3 Would you be interested in these apps? Do you already use something similar? Why/Why not?

4 Match the positive adjectives in **bold** in the text in **2** to adjectives 1–7 with the opposite meaning.
1 difficult-to-use _____
2 incorrect _____
3 unsafe _____
4 poor-quality _____
5 useless _____
6 old _____
7 time-consuming _____

5 Complete these sentences with a positive or negative adjective from **4**.
1 Online ordering is more _____ than going to a shop. It saves you lots of time and these days orders arrive within hours.
2 Our automatic downloads help to keep your computer software _____ .
3 My online banking is very _____ because it always asks for your username, PIN code and password.
4 Cloud storage is a _____ way to store your files and access them easily from anywhere.
5 Travelling to meetings takes so long. I think video-conferencing would be much less _____ .
6 Why is this photocopier so _____? I never know how to print on both sides of the paper!
7 Our new track and trace app lets you know the progress of your delivery with a precise location and an _____ estimate for the time of delivery.

6 Which of the adjectives in **4** could you use to describe the following services and systems?
- Online banking
- Passport control at an airport
- System for booking a meeting room at work
- A childcare service for working parents

7 ▶ 4.1 Listen to three people talking about a service or system in **6**. Make notes about each question in the table.

1 Which service or system is each person talking about?
Speaker 1:
Speaker 2:
Speaker 3:
2 Does the speaker think it makes life easier? Give reasons for your answers.
Speaker 1:
Speaker 2:
Speaker 3:

8 These sentences are from the reviews of the apps in **2** and the listening in **7**. Underline the correct verb in *italics*. In two sentences, both verbs are possible.
1 This simple, user-friendly app *helps / makes it easier* for you to schedule a meeting.
2 This handy app *lets / enables* you book a taxi.
3 This app *allows / makes* you to keep track of all your investments in one place.
4 The system of colour coding *lets / helps* you see if a room is free.
5 They've even introduced a new self-service system which *enables / allows* you to put your passport on a screen and walk through.

≫ For more exercises, go to **Practice file 4** on page 112.

9 Think of three more services and systems which make your life easier. Tell your partner about the benefits of these services and systems.
Example: Online video-conferencing is an efficient way to communicate and lets us talk to our overseas staff.

Tip | *let*
Verbs such as *help, allow* and *enable* are usually followed by an object + infinitive with *to*. However, the verb *let* is followed by an object + infinitive without *to*:
This app **lets you** to **download** your boarding card.

Language at work | Comparative forms and modifiers

1 What types of software and online systems does your company use? How do they help your work?

2 Ercho Management Systems has received user feedback on its new warehouse management systems software. Complete the comments with the correct form of the adjectives in brackets.

Please leave your comments below:

1 'So far, there have been fewer mistakes. The new system seems *far* _____ (accurate).'

2 'It takes *a little* _____ (long) to learn how to use it.'

3 'When existing customers place an order, it's *slightly* _____ (easy) to find their information.'

4 'It's much faster and *a lot* _____ (time-consuming) than the old system was.'

5 'The old system was *almost* as _____ (user-friendly) as this upgrade, but I think the new customer-profile option on this version makes life easier.'

---

3 Look at the modifiers in *italics* before each comparative adjective in **2**. Complete the explanations in the *Language point*.

LANGUAGE POINT

1 We use *much*, _____ and _____ to talk about big differences.
2 We use *a bit*, _____ and _____ to talk about small differences.
3 Before *as* + adjective + *as*, we use *nearly* and _____ to talk about small differences.

» For more information, go to **Grammar reference** on page 113.

4 ▶4.2 Listen to part of a phone conversation between an after-sales representative from Ercho and a user of their software. Complete the representative's notes about the new version.

User feedback on ...	Better?	Big difference?	Comments?
the new version of the software	Y / N		
using the customer-profile system	Y / N		
filling in the order forms	Y / N		

5 ▶4.2 Listen again and write the missing words.
1 Do you think it's _____?
2 Overall, it works a lot _____ than the old version.
3 You could find a profile almost as _____.
4 The options are a lot more _____.
5 Staff are filling it in a little _____.

6 Which comparative forms in **5** are adjectives and which are adverbs?

» For more exercises, go to **Practice file 4** on page 113.

Tip | Comparative adverbs

Most comparative adverbs use *more* + *-ly*:
*We need to work **more** quickly.*
Note that some adverbs are irregular:
*We did **well/badly**.*
→ *We did **better/worse**.*

7 Work with a partner. Make sentences to compare two financial software products on the market. Use the information in the table and the modifiers + adjective or adverb below in the comparative form.

Example: Financepro is a lot cheaper than Accounter 3.1.

a lot / cheap   almost / secure   far / up-to-date   a little / easily   much / quickly

	Financepro	Accounter 3.1
1 Price?	$499	$710
2 Easy-to-use?	Staff can learn to use it easily.	Staff can learn to use it very easily.
3 Security features?	Secure	Very secure
4 Technical support?	They can help within 24 hours.	They can help within one hour.
5 Most recent version?	Two years old	Last month

8 Make a similar table of notes about one of your company's products or services in comparison to your main competitor. Then work with a partner and tell each other about your product or service.

Example: We're a bit more expensive than our competitor, but …

Practically speaking | How to be approximate

1 Ercho Management Systems recently surveyed businesses about their management software needs. The graph below shows the results for one of the questions. How many people responded to the question? How do most companies install new software?

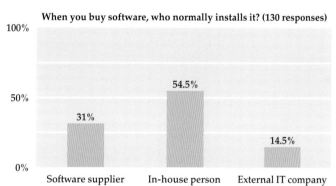

When you buy software, who normally installs it? (130 responses)

2 ▶ 4.3 Listen to someone describing the results in the table. Write the missing words for approximating numbers.

130: _____ _____ one hundred   31%: _____ a third
54.5%: _____ half   14.5%: ___ _____ _____ 15%

3 Match the language for approximating in 1–4 to the synonyms in a–d.

1 well over   a almost
2 nearly   b just below
3 a little under   c around
4 about   d well above

4 Work with a partner. Take turns to describe these numbers in different ways.

Example: Nearly a quarter / Just below a quarter.

24%   1,002   37%   240   49%   67%

5 Tell your partner approximate numbers or percentages for your company and country. Talk about:
- annual turnover
- number of part-time employees
- number of customers
- population
- inflation
- unemployment

Example: My company's annual turnover is just over three million a year, I think.

Tip | Fractions

We often use fractions for approximate numbers:
a fifth = 20%
a quarter = 25%
a third = 33%
(a) half = 50%
two-thirds = 66%
three-quarters = 75%

Business communication | Explaining features and benefits

1 A company wants to use a new type of software. Read about its key features and discuss questions 1–2 with a partner.

1 What concerns do you think some employees might have about this software?

2 How could the company explain the benefits of the software to the employees?

> ### Key features
>
> - The software tracks when an employee starts and ends work from when they log on and off or when they switch their computer on and off.
> - It monitors the number of hours worked and sends this information to payroll.
> - The mobile app enables employees to log on from home or when travelling.

2 ▶ 4.4 Listen to an IT trainer explaining the features of the new software to a group of employees. Make notes about:

1 the main benefits of the software

2 the employees' questions and concerns

3 ▶ 4.4 Match 1–10 to a–j to make sentences and questions from the discussion. Then listen again and check.

1 The main benefit is ___
2 It's a lot more accurate because ___
3 One of the problems is that ___
4 What happens if I ___
5 That's a good ___
6 But wouldn't that require us to ___
7 It might seem that you'd need to adjust your settings, ___
8 Will it let me ___
9 I'm not convinced that ___
10 I'm sure you'll find it much ___

a log on from a hotel?
b it automatically knows how many hours you've worked each month.
c the payroll feature.
d have to adjust the settings on our computers?
e it's possible to do that every time you're abroad.
f your manager has to fill in a form for each of you.
g but in fact the software can do this automatically.
h question.
i forget to log on in the morning when I start work?
j easier to use than the current system.

》 For more exercises, go to **Practice file 4** on page 112.

4 Work with a partner. Read about a new company system below and make two lists:

1 A list of the benefits of this system. How can it make things better?

2 The problems of this system. What objections might employees have?

Afterwards, present your list to the class and share your ideas.

> A company wants to introduce a new system to improve employee performance. The key features of the system are:
> - Managers measure the performance of employees in their departments.
> - Each employee has a meeting with their manager at the end of every month to discuss their performance.
> - Managers can give bonuses for an excellent performance.
> - The company will introduce an 'employee of the month' award.

5 Work with the same partner. You are going to discuss the features and benefits of the new system. **Student A, turn to page 138. Student B, turn to page 142.**

Student A, turn to page 138. Student B, turn to page 142.

Key expressions

Explaining the features and benefits
The main benefit is ...
It'll let you / It'll make it easier to / It'll help you to / It'll enable you to ...
Another useful feature is ...

Comparing services and systems
It's a lot more accurate / It's a lot less time-consuming because ...
The new system will be much ...
One of the problems is that ...

Asking questions and expressing concerns
Will it let me / allow me to ...?
What happens if ...?
But wouldn't that ...?
I'm not convinced that ...
I have a question, too.

Handling questions and concerns
That's a good question.
That's true, but ...
It might seem ..., but in fact ...
I'm sure you'll find it much ...

TALKING POINT

Stack ranking

Many companies have systems to rate their employee's performance, but one of the more controversial systems is called 'stack ranking'. It's based on the idea that in any company, you have about 20% of the employees whose work is excellent and they are the future managers. Then you have the majority of employees (around 70%) who are average and, finally, 10% of employees are ranked as 'poor'. One argument for the system of 'stack ranking' is that it increases employee motivation: the idea is that by ranking a group of employees according to these percentages the system encourages healthy competition between employees and allows managers to identify (and eventually get rid of) the bottom 10%. Many companies have tried this or similar systems of ranking employee performance. However, in recent years many companies, including Microsoft, have abandoned the system because, overall, employees hated it and it had a negative effect on performance.

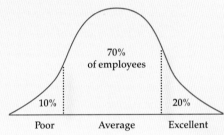

Discussion

1 Why do you think the article describes the system of stack ranking as controversial?

2 What are the arguments for and against the system of stack ranking? Can you think of any more arguments for and against this system?

3 Overall, do you think it is a good or bad system? Why?

Task

1 Imagine you work for a company with a system of 'stack ranking'. You are going to role-play a meeting between managers and employees at the company. Work in groups of four. Decide which two are managers and which two are employees.

2 Work with your partner and prepare your positions before the meeting.

- Managers: Before you meet the employees, make a list of arguments for stack ranking in your company but also be prepared to make some changes to the current system in order to improve employee performance.

- Employees: Before you meet the managers, make a list of arguments against stack ranking in your company and prepare a list of changes to the current system in order to improve employee performance.

3 When both sides are ready, start the meeting. Allow time for managers and employees to present their arguments and then discuss possible changes. Try to reach an agreement.

4 After the meeting, each group presents their changes to the rest of the class.

5 Customers

Starting point

1 Who are your main customers?

2 How does your company keep its customers happy?

3 What percentage of your company's business is online?

Working with words | Customer service

1 Read this quote. How true is it for your type of business?

'If you make customers unhappy in the physical world, they might each tell six friends. If you make customers unhappy on the Internet, they can each tell 6,000.'
Jeff Bezos, founder of Amazon

2 Read about the company, Zappos. What is the best title for this article?

a Training staff to care

b Delivering happiness

c The customer is always right

ZAPPOS:

For many companies, having a call centre means two things: firstly, that you have unhappy customers and secondly, that you have the costs of paying staff to deal with customer complaints.

However, Zappos, the online shoes and clothing retailer, has a positive view of its call centre and uses it to build customer loyalty. Its team answer around 5,000 calls per day and 1,200 emails per week about its products. New staff receive four weeks' training in how to make customers happy and Zappos staff will do anything to go beyond basic customer expectations.

- One customer was staying at a hotel in Las Vegas. She wanted a pair of shoes but they weren't in stock. So, a Zappos customer service rep found the required shoes in a local shop and hand-delivered them to the woman's hotel room.

- The best man at a wedding arrived with no shoes. The company delivered in time for the wedding – for free.

- One member of the customer service team has the world record for the longest customer care phone call ever: it lasted ten hours and 29 minutes.

Clearly, with 75% repeat orders, customer satisfaction at Zappos is very high.

3 Read the article again. What do these numbers refer to?

5,000   1,200   4   10'29"   75

4 What do you think of the Zappos call centre? <u>Underline</u> the correct words in *italics* and complete the sentences. Then read out and compare your answers.

I *think / don't think* it's a good idea because …

It *could / couldn't* work in my company because …

5 Complete this table with the word forms in the article in **2**.

Verb	Adjective	Noun
1 to care	caring	_care_
2	loyal	_____
3 to expect	expected	_____
4 to require	_____	requirements
5 to serve		_____
6 to satisfy	satisfied	_____
7 to produce	productive	_____
8 _____		delivery

6 Complete this text with the correct form of the words from the table in **5**. More than one word is correct for some answers.

Customers always ¹_____ an online company to ²_____ their order on time and in good condition. They are ³_____ if their ⁴_____ are met. However, if there is a problem, it is the role of the customer ⁵_____ department to solve it quickly and efficiently. As a result, if the customer feels that the company really ⁶_____ about them, they become ⁷_____ to the brand.

7 Look at the Zappos text in **2** again. Find different word combinations with the word 'customer' and add them to the mind map below.

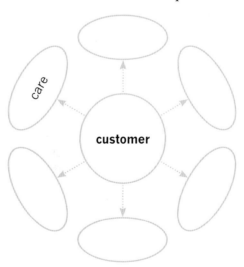

Tip | Customer, client or consumer?

A *customer* is someone who buys a standard product or service.

A *client* is someone who buys an individually designed product or service (e.g. financial advice).

Consumer is a general term to talk about any person who buys things, not a specific product or service.

8 Complete these questions with an appropriate 'customer' collocation from **7**.

1 How important is customer _____ in your company?

2 How does your company build customer _____?

3 How does your company deal with customer _____?

4 Do you think it's ever possible to guarantee customer _____?

9 Work with a partner. Ask and answer the questions in **8**.

>> For more exercises, go to **Practice file 5** on page 114.

10 Make five rules and guidelines for successful customer service in your company using words from the table in **5**.

Example: Rule 1: Don't meet your customer's expectations. Go beyond them.

33

Language at work | Present tenses for future reference

1 How busy is your schedule this week, next week and next month? Which are the busiest periods for you/your department/your company?

2 Anita and Hakan are planning a series of customer visits in Turkey. Read the schedule and then Anita's email. What changes and additions need to be made to the schedule?

---

6 Monday

5.45–11.45
Flight TK 1988 London – Istanbul.

14.30
Meeting at Aksa.

22.00 – 23.05
Flight to Ankara. Meet Giray.

7 Tuesday

10.00
Leave hotel for meetings from 11.00.

19.00
Flight TK 1983 Istanbul – London.

Subject: Next week

Hi Hakan,

I'm really sorry but there are changes to the original schedule. We still **leave** early on Monday and **come back** on Tuesday, but the bad news is that on Monday we**'re not meeting** the people at Aksa until five – I'm afraid they**'re** busy until then. Anyway, I **hope** to arrange another visit so we **aren't waiting** around all afternoon. Other than that, everything **is** fine for the rest of the trip. By the way, our new agent in Ankara **is joining** us at 10.00 for the customer visits on Tuesday. His name is Giray Demir.

Anita

3 Do the verbs in **bold** in the email refer to the present or the future? Match the verbs in the email to the explanations in the *Language point*.

> **LANGUAGE POINT**
>
> 1 We use verbs in the present simple such as *arrive, go, start* to talk about a scheduled or timetabled event in the future: _____ , _____
> 2 We use verbs in the present continuous to talk about an arrangement for the future: _____ , _____ , _____
> 3 We use the present tense of verbs such as *plan, intend, expect* + *to* + infinitive to talk about future plans, hopes and expectations: _____
> 4 We use the present tense of *be* + adjectives such as *free, available* to talk about future availability: _____ , _____

>> For more information, go to **Grammar reference** on page 115.

4 5.1 Listen to a message from Giray in Anita's voicemail. What additional changes need to be made to the schedule?

5 Read Giray's voicemail message. Underline the correct words in *italics* 1–9. Then listen again and check.

Hi, Anita. This is Giray. I'm sorry but I ¹*be* / *'m* busy next Monday evening, so I can't meet you personally at the airport. When your flight ²*arrives* / *is arriving*, a driver will meet you. Let's plan ³*to meet* / *meeting* in your hotel reception on Tuesday morning at around eight thirty because we ⁴*meet* / *are meeting* the first client at nine thirty instead of eleven. By the way, do you intend ⁵*checking* / *to check* out in the morning or ⁶*do you stay* / *are you staying* another night in Ankara? I'm afraid I ⁷*'m not* / *don't* free in the evening, but I can book you an excellent restaurant near the hotel for dinner if you ⁸*stay* / *are staying*. It ⁹*opens* / *is opening* around eight, I think. Anyway, let me know your plans.

Tip | State verbs

Verbs used to talk about states (e.g. *understand, know, like, mean, need*) are not usually used in the present continuous.

6 Look at the schedule below and make sentences using prompts 1–9.

Example: *I'm going to a conference next week.*
The conference starts on Tuesday.

1 go / conference / next week
2 conference / start
3 not /go / first session. / busy
4 give / my presentation
5 hope / go / buffet reception

6 free / Thursday morning
7 plan / have lunch
8 fly / Paris
9 flight / leave

May

		a.m.	p.m.
7	Tuesday	CONFERENCE 9.30 ~~First session~~ / Meet clients	
8	Wednesday	CONFERENCE	14.00–15.00 My presentation 18.00 End-of-conference buffet reception
9	Thursday	CONFERENCE Free morning	12.30 Lunch with Sally and Remi
10	Friday		To Paris 14.20 Flight from LHR

》 For more exercises, go to **Practice file 5** on page 115.

7 Tell your partner about your schedule for next week. Talk about when:
• scheduled events start and end
• you are available or busy
• you plan or hope to do something
• you are meeting people or have an arrangement

Practically speaking | How to say 'sorry'

1 Think of a situation when you had to say 'sorry' at work. Who was it to? Why?

2 ▶ 5.2 Listen to sentences 1–5 and match them to reasons a–e.

1 I'm sorry, but I'm busy next Monday evening. _b_
2 I'm sorry, but can you repeat that? ___
3 I'm sorry to keep you waiting. ___
4 I'm sorry, but the traffic was terrible this morning. ___
5 I'm sorry, but can I say something at this point? ___

a You did something wrong.
b You can't do something.
c You give a reason.
d You interrupt someone.
e You ask for repetition.

3 ▶ 5.3 Match responses a–e to sentences 1–5 in **2**. Then listen and check.

a **Sure**. It's A as in Alpha. ___
b **Of course**. Go ahead. ___
c **Not to worry**. We haven't started yet. ___
d **That's OK**. There was a problem with my train as well. ___
e **No problem**. How about Tuesday instead? ___

4 Work with a partner. Practise each situation by saying sorry to your partner and responding.
• You can't get to work because of a train strike. Call your partner from the train station and explain.
• You can't attend your partner's presentation next week. Give a reason.
• Your partner is a visitor waiting for you in reception. After 15 minutes, you arrive.
• Your partner is explaining something but you didn't hear all the information.

Business communication | Making and changing arrangements

1 Who are your company's main suppliers? What do they supply you with?

2 ▶ 5.4 Elena Schenker works for a chain of hotels in Switzerland. She calls Sergio Boccherini, a supplier of gym equipment. Listen to their conversation and write *E* (Elena), *S* (Sergio) or *B* (Both) next to each sentence.

1 _B_ was at a trade show in Geneva last month.
4 0 s 2 _E_ is based in Bern.
1 :10 3 _S_ has clients in Geneva.
1 : 2 0 4 _E_ is always busy on Mondays.
1 : 28 5 _S_ can meet on Tuesday 1st at 3 p.m.

3 ▶ 5.4 Read expressions 1–8 for making arrangements. Try to say each expression in a different way, using the words given in brackets. Then listen again and check.

1 Can we fix a date to meet? (arrange) _____ *Can we arrange a date to meet?* _____
2 I'm sorry but I can't on Mondays. (afraid I'm busy) _____
3 I'm not free on that day. (can't make it) _____
4 What about Tuesday? (How) _____
5 That's good for me. (suits) _____
6 Is two o'clock OK? (convenient) _____
7 Can we meet later? (make it) _____
8 We've confirmed Tuesday the first at three. (So that's) _____

>> For more exercises, go to **Practice file 5** on page 114.

4 ▶ 5.5 Listen to these short expressions from the conversation for suggesting and checking days, dates and times. Note if the intonation is rising or falling. Then listen again and repeat.
On Monday?   The 1st?   At three?

5 Work with a partner. Take turns to answer the phone and make arrangements for the situations below. Use the flow chart and your own diaries if you want.
- meeting a new customer
- playing golf or tennis
- visiting the new company headquarters
- meeting a colleague to plan a product launch

A Answer phone.

B Give reason for calling. Suggest date/time to meet.

A Say you can't.

B Suggest another date/time.

A Agree.

B Confirm and say goodbye.

6 ▶ 5.6 Sergio calls Elena again. Listen to their conversation.
1 What is the main reason for his call?
2 What can't Sergio make?
3 Do they bring the meeting forward or move it back a day?

7 Repeat your calls in **5** but now you can't make the appointments. Change the arrangements to a new time. Use your own diaries if you want.

Key expressions

Calling to make an arrangement
The reason I'm calling is ...
I'm calling to arrange ...
It's about our meeting next ...

Suggesting times/dates
Can we arrange a meeting?
Can we fix a date to meet?
What/How about ...?
Is ... convenient/OK?
Is ... any good?
Does ... suit you?

Accepting/Declining
Yes, of course.
That suits me.
That's good/convenient for me.
I'm afraid I can't come on ...
I'm sorry but I can't make it.
I'm not free on ...

Changing arrangements
Can we make it later?
Can we move it back to Friday?
Can we bring it forward to Wednesday?
The afternoon is free/convenient.

Confirming
So that's Tuesday at three.
We've confirmed Monday at 10 a.m.

Upside down management

Timpson is a family business with a turnover of more than 150 million pounds. Timpson shops offer a variety of services including shoe repair and key cutting. The secret of the company's success, according to company chairman John Timpson, is to make sure you have 'happy customers' and offer 'great jobs'. To achieve this, the company uses an organizational system called 'upside down management'.

'Upside down management' means that the customers are always at the top and senior management are at the bottom. The role of the managers is to support the frontline staff in the middle, who can then serve the customers. This organogram shows how Timpson works with some of its key principles at each level.

Customers

- They come first.
- Make them smile.
- Happy customers will advertise your company, so don't spend money on marketing.

Frontline Staff

- Charge customers whatever you like. The price list is only a guide.
- Try new ideas. If they work, tell management. If they don't work, just stop.
- Staff can use one of the company's five holiday homes.
- High-performing staff can receive a weekly 15% bonus.
- You always get an extra day off on your birthday!

Management

- Serve your frontline staff. Don't give them orders.
- Praise frontline staff ten times more than you criticize.
- Avoid meetings. They waste time.
- Get rid of poor-performing staff quickly.

Discussion

1 Why do you think 'upside down management' has been successful at Timpson?

2 Discuss each of the key principles in each level. Which principles does your company have? Which other principles do you agree or disagree with?

3 Overall, how well do you think 'upside down management' could work in your company?

Task

1 Work in groups of four. Imagine your company is thinking of introducing 'upside down management'. Divide your group into two pairs.

Pair A: Write a list of arguments *for* introducing 'upside down management' and why you think it *will* work in your company.

Pair B: Write a list of arguments *against* introducing 'upside down management' and why you think it *won't* work in your company.

2 When you are ready, work with the other pair again. Take turns to present your arguments for and against and discuss both sides of the arguments. Try to reach a final agreement and choose one of the decisions:

A The company should introduce 'upside down management'.

B The company should use some (but not all) of the ideas from 'upside down management'.

C The company should not change the current system of management.

3 Present your final decision to the rest of the class and give your reasons.

Starting point

1 How often does your company have business guests and visitors?

2 Why do they visit the company?

3 Does the company entertain them in the evenings? If so, how?

4 How often do you visit other companies?

5 Do you prefer being the visitor or the host?

Working with words | Business travel

1 How important are trade fairs and conferences in your area of business? Do you ever attend such events?

2 ▶ 6.1 Two people are planning a conference. Listen to their phone conversation and complete the missing information in the notes.

• Dr Miles Doyle

Arrival time: Tuesday evening at ¹_____

Requirements: Wants to see the main **auditorium** and check the **facilities** before his talk on ²_____.

Action: Driver to take him from the ³_____ to the **exhibition centre**.

Joel is helping **delegates** with their **stands** so will show Dr Doyle around.

• Alexis Cruz

Arrival time: Tuesday ⁴_____

Requirements: Would like to look around the ⁵_____ and do some **sightseeing**.

Action: Call ⁶_____ to arrange an early check-in.

Action: Joel will book an afternoon **excursion** with the hotel ⁷_____ service, including eating out and trying some local **specialities**.

3 Match the words in **bold** in the notes to definitions 1–8.
1 the venue where a conference or trade fair is held *exhibition centre*
2 equipment and services provided (e.g. by a hotel or conference centre) _____
3 the largest room in a conference centre for lectures and presentations _____
4 types of food or products that a restaurant or place is famous for _____
5 visiting interesting buildings and places as a tourist _____
6 a short organized trip made for interest or pleasure _____
7 the people registered at a conference or trade fair _____
8 an area at an exhibition where you can display and advertise your products or services _____

Tip | *travel/trip/journey*

Travel is mainly used as a verb:
*I like to **travel** by train.*
There are some exceptions such as *business travel, travel arrangements* and *travel agents.*
Don't say: ~~*Did you have a good travel?*~~
Do say: *Did you have a good* **journey/trip/flight**?
Journey is the period spent travelling to your destination.
Trip is a short visit with a specific purpose
(e.g. *a business trip*).

4 Work with a partner. Cover up your answers in **3** and take turns to test each other with the definitions.

5 ▶ **6.1** Listen to the conversation again. Match the words in A and B to make a new phrase. Then match each new phrase to pictures A–H.

A	B
freshen	out
pick	around
look	(someone) off
check	up
meet	(someone) up
show	in
drop	up with (somebody)
eat	(someone) around

>> For more exercises, go to **Practice file 6** on page 116.

6 When you travel (either for work or on holiday), which of the activities in **5** do you normally do and in what order? Explain your choice to your partner.
   Example: First of all, I check in at the hotel, so that I can freshen up. Then I …

7 Work with a partner. Two important speakers are coming to give talks at a conference in your nearest city. You have to look after them. Look at each speaker's information and requirements and organize their schedules (the people involved, transportation, places, times, etc.).

	Dr Rhona Emanuel	Marek Sobolewski
Arrival	Wednesday 11.15	Wednesday 11.30
Day / Time of talk	Wednesday 17.00 in main auditorium	Wednesday 14.00 in main auditorium
Departure	Thursday 08.35	Thursday 19.05
Requirements	• Six-hour flight, so she needs to go to hotel before her talk • Needs to set up equipment in advance of talk • First time in city, so wants to see places of interest if time • Likes eating out and trying local food	• Wants to know number of people attending his talk • Plans to meet up with an old friend on Wednesday evening • Likes historic places and would like to visit the craft market

Language at work | Articles

1 If you are going to a conference, what type of information can you normally find on the conference website?

2 Work with a partner. Read four sections of a conference website and write an appropriate heading for sections 2–4.

HOME   TICKETS   NEWS   WHAT'S ON   PARTNERS   CONTACT US

GW Conference

1 About the conference

The Gaming World Expo attracts over 4,000 delegates from all over the world and is one of **the biggest** annual gaming events in **Europe**.

2 _____

The venue offers over 200 stands to show new products, make contacts and recruit new talent. Reserve **a stand** by 1st March to guarantee your place.

3 _____

Delegates are advised to travel **by public transport**, as parking is limited. An airport shuttle bus runs every day with stops at all major hotels. **The bus** is free for all delegates.

4 _____

Delegates should go directly to the registration desk to collect a badge and for **information** on the day.

BOOK YOUR TICKETS HERE

3 Complete the examples in the *Language point*, using the words in **bold** in **2**.

LANGUAGE POINT

We use *a/an*
- to talk about singular countable nouns in a general way (the person or thing could be one of many): *an airport bus, a badge,* [1]_____
We use *the*
- to talk about specific nouns (it's clear to the listener which person or thing): *the registration desk,* [2]_____
- to refer back to the same noun for a second time: [3]_____
- with superlatives: *the best,* [4]_____
We use **no article**
- with plural nouns and uncountable nouns in a general way: *hotels,* [5]_____, *coffee,* [6]_____
- with proper nouns (names, countries, continents, cities, languages, etc.) *New York,* [7]_____
- with transportation: *by taxi,* [8]_____

≫ For more information, go to **Grammar reference** on page 117.

4 Work with a partner. Think of two more nouns to add to each category in **3**. Try to choose nouns that are important for your work.

Tip | *the* + country
Some countries need *the* before their name because they are groups of:
- countries (e.g. *the United Kingdom*)
- states (e.g. *the United States*)
- islands (e.g. *the Philippines*)

5 Study these delegates' questions at the conference. Correct the mistakes with articles. Two questions contain no mistakes.

1 Which day is Doctor Doyle giving ^{*a*}⌃talk?
2 Can you tell me the way to main auditorium?
3 There's a presentation about next-generation mobile games today. What time does presentation start?
4 Are there any sightseeing tours for delegates?
5 Is quickest way to the airport by bus or by taxi?
6 Do you have excursion with a guided tour of the old city?
7 Can I have an accommodation as close to exhibition hall as possible?
8 Is the conference in Asia next year?
9 Is it possible to get taxi to the city centre, please?

» For more exercises, go to **Practice file 6** on page 117.

6 Work with a partner. Read some information about a trade fair. **Student A, turn to page 137. Student B, turn to page 142.**

Practically speaking | How to address people

1 When you meet someone at work for the first time, do you like them to address you by your first name or your title and last name?

2 ▶ 6.2 Say these different titles with the names. Listen and check.

Dr Billah	Miss Pfaner	Madam Sargie
Ms Walker	Mr Cardoso	Mrs Ludwig
Sir James Logan	Prof. Halsdorff	

3 Look at this list of situations with different people. In your country, how would you normally address these people? Using their first name, last name, title and last name or something else?
• A visitor arriving at your company for the first time.
• Your work colleagues.
• Offering help to someone who looks lost.
• You start making conversation with someone at a conference.
• At a meeting with the managing director of your company.
• Meeting your mother-in-law for the first time.

4 ▶ 6.3 Listen to three conversations. Tick (✓) the expressions you hear.
Please, call me … ☐
You can call me … ☐
Please, call me by my first name. ☐
I'd prefer it if you call me … ☐
How would you like me to address you? ☐
Is it OK if I call you …? ☐
Can I call you …? ☐
Do you mind if I call you …? ☐

5 Imagine you are at a conference and you don't know anyone in the room. Stand up and introduce yourself to different people in the class. Start conversations using your full titles and last names, and then find out how the other person wants to be addressed.

Business communication | Welcoming visitors

1 When someone comes to visit your place of work, what do you show them? Are there any areas which are 'off-limits' (private or secret)?

2 ▶ 6.4 Jacinta Ross works for HYB Electronics. She meets Marvin Bernstein at reception. He is visiting the company for the day. Listen to their conversation and complete the agenda for Marvin's visit.

Agenda for Marvin Bernstein's visit to HYB Electronics

Monday 2 October

Morning:	
Lunchtime:	
Afternoon:	

3 ▶ 6.4 Listen again and match Jacinta's expressions to Marvin's responses.

Jacinta	Marvin
1 Welcome to our new facility.	a Oh, that's OK, I'll hang on to it for now.
2 So, how was your journey?	b Thanks.
3 And did you have any trouble finding us?	c No problem.
4 Here, let me take your coat.	d Thank you very much.
5 Can I get you a coffee?	e It was fine, thanks.
6 OK. Come this way and I'll run through today's programme.	f No, not at all.
7 Have a seat.	g That sounds nice.
8 So, first of all, I thought you could take a tour of the facility this morning.	h Great.
9 You'll need this ID card to get around the site. Make sure you keep it on you at all times.	i Sounds interesting.

4 Work with a partner. Have a conversation with a visitor to your place of work using this flow chart. **Student A** is the visitor and **Student B** is the host. When you have finished, change roles.

A Introduce yourself to B.

B Identify yourself and welcome A.

A Respond.

B Ask about A's journey.

A Respond.

B Offer tea, coffee, etc.

A Respond.

B Talk about today's programme and any other information.

A Respond.

>> For more exercises, go to **Practice file 6** on page 116.

5 Work with a partner. Imagine you are welcoming a new person to the class today. Have a short conversation about their journey to the office/classroom and go through the schedule for the lesson.

Key expressions

Welcoming
Welcome to ...
On behalf of ... welcome to ...
It's nice to meet you in person.
Good morning.
Good afternoon.

Asking about a journey
How was your journey?
Did you have any trouble finding us?

Being hospitable
Come this way.
Can I get you a coffee?
Let me take your coat.
Have a seat.

Explaining the programme
I'll run through today's programme.
First of all, I thought you could ...
We'll catch up again later.

Giving extra information
You'll need this ...
Make sure you ...
Don't worry about ...

TALKING POINT

Cultural expectations

Hotel facilities

Free wifi

FREE

Menu with
international dishes

menu

Ice machine

Staff speaking
different languages

Hallo Herr Braun

Hello Mr Brown

いらっしゃいませ

Vending machine

How to help international guests enjoy their stay

TV programmes from
different countries

International
adapter socket

Room facilities

Tea and coffee
making facilities

Slippers

Bowl of fruit

Hotel information
translated into
different languages

Discussion

1 Look at the information for hotel managers. Which things do you expect when you stay at a hotel? What makes you happier at a hotel?

2 ▶ 6.5 Listen to part of a radio programme about cultural differences. Which ideas in the infographic do they talk about? In which parts of the world should you expect them?

3 Do you think hotels in your country meet the cultural expectations of international visitors? What ideas might make these visitors happier when they stay?

Task

1 Work in groups. Imagine you have a group of foreign visitors coming to your company for a week. Each day they will have some free time after work and they would like to learn more about your country and its culture. Discuss and plan a schedule for the week from Monday to Friday. Your schedule should include some or all of the following aspects:

- eating out and trying different dishes
- visiting places of cultural importance
- watching traditional theatre or festivals
- going shopping in local markets
- other?

2 Present and compare your final schedules with the other groups.

Preview

In this video lesson, you will watch an interview with Michael Dickmann, an expert in cultural awareness in business. He describes how cultural differences in communication can affect business between people of different nationalities and also within different company cultures.

Focus

1 When you travel abroad, what is one of the first differences you tend to notice? What differences do you notice when you are in a new country for a long time? Talk about any of the items below or choose a new one.

- language
- attitudes to time
- gestures and body language
- food and meals
- clothes
- attitude to management
- social behaviour
- relationships between colleagues and clients

2 ▶01 Watch four people talking about differences they have noticed in countries they have lived and worked in. Make notes about their answers in the table.

	Country	Differences	Changes over time
Speaker 1			
Speaker 2			
Speaker 3			
Speaker 4			

3 Work with a partner and compare your answers in **2**. Did the people in the video describe any similar differences to you?

Culture in business

4 You are going to watch an interview with Michael Dickmann, an expert in cultural differences in business. Before you watch, match words and phrases 1–8 to definitions a–h.

1 mediocre ___
2 ethics and values ___
3 disciplined ___
4 power distance ___
5 bribes ___
6 behaviour ___
7 norms ___
8 save face ___

a your actions in particular situations
b your beliefs about what is right or wrong which affect your behaviour
c average, not very good
d behaving in a very controlled way
e money you offer in a dishonest way to make someone do something for you
f the accepted way of doing things in a society or culture
g an expression meaning to avoid humiliation or not being told you are wrong in front of other people
h a term to refer to the relationship between people in power and the people who take orders, e.g. between management and workers

5 ▶02 Watch the interview with Michael Dickmann. He talks about four areas of cultural difference in business. As you watch, number the areas A–D in the correct order 1–4.

A The hamburger approach ___
B Language in business ___
C Power distance ___
D Ethics ___

Cultural awareness

6 ▶03 Watch Part 1 of the video again and answer questions 1–3.

   1 What might a British person mean if they say, 'It's not too bad'?
   2 What might a German person think it means?
   3 A Nigerian company might describe giving money to get something as Public Relations. What might a western company call it?

7 Discuss these questions as a class for your country or countries.

   1 If you heard someone say 'It's not too bad', what would you think it means?
   2 In your country, is giving money to win a business deal considered good public relations or is it a bribe? Is it acceptable or is it wrong?

8 ▶04 Watch Part 2 of the video again and complete sentences 1–4. Use words you hear in the video.

   1 How polite you are and how _____ you are can affect what people think about you.
   2 Some people might think that if you are not punctual then you are not _____.
   3 If you come from a _____ power distance culture, then you won't disagree with your boss.
   4 If you come from a _____ power distance culture like Denmark and you work in a country like Japan, or Nigeria and you speak up against your boss, that is a big problem.

9 <u>Underline</u> the correct words in *italics* to make the sentences true for your company. Then, compare your choices with the rest of the class and give reasons for your answers.

   1 In my company, *it's OK / it isn't OK* to disagree with the views of your boss.
   2 Overall, I think I come from a country with *high / low* power distance.

10 ▶05 Watch Part 3 of the video again and answer questions 1–4.

   1 In what way is performance management similar to a hamburger bun?
   2 If you make a mistake in the USA, how will your manager comment on your work?
   3 Why does the Japanese manager miss out the 'meat'?
   4 What does Michael Dickmann suggest the approach of the German manager is?

11 If you made a mistake in your company, how would your manager discuss this with you? What kind of 'hamburger approach' would he or she take?

Identifying culture in the workplace

12 Work in groups. Read about three different business situations and discuss what problem is happening in each situation and why.

   1 An Italian business person and a Japanese business person are making small talk with each other. Afterwards, the Italian comments that, 'She seemed nice but she never really said anything'. The Japanese says, 'She was very friendly, but she never gave me a chance to speak.'
   2 A Belgian manager is working in Thailand. He is unhappy because his Thai assistant is often late for work (between 30 minutes to an hour sometimes). One day he tells her off in front of other employees. She resigns soon after.
   3 An American business person is in a meeting with a group of German colleagues. The discussion is very heated and the American feels uncomfortable. Afterwards, he's surprised that everyone decides to go and have a friendly drink together before they go home.

13 Now read the explanations on page 137 and compare them with your own.

Situations above adapted from Critical incidents in *Intercultural Business Communication* by Robert Gibson, 2000, Corenelson & OUP GmbH & Co.

7 Working online

Starting point

1 Which online mobile devices do you have with you all the time?

2 How important is it for you to be online 24/7?

3 How do you feel when you can't access the Internet and go online? Give reasons for your answer.

Working with words | Online security

1 Work with a partner and discuss these questions.
  1 How secure is your computer and data?
  2 How do you protect your documents and data?
  3 What makes a password weak or strong?

2 Read this article. What is the writer's main purpose?
  • To report examples of cybercrime in businesses.
  • To convince businesses to invest in online security.
  • To explain that online security is important for businesses.

How safe is your business?

Spamhaus is an international non-profit organization based in Switzerland. One day, without warning, the Spamhaus servers were compromised and the website was down for nearly a week. The organization had become another victim of a cyberattack.

For Spamhaus, the attack was especially bad because the organization manages databases of spammers and blacklisted users for business corporations, governments and Internet providers. In other words, Spamhaus had a special understanding of online security. But even it couldn't prevent the cybercriminals.

It's a warning to all organizations and businesses that they are vulnerable to such attacks. And yet, in a recent survey by Deloitte of almost 2,000 executives, 79% were not confident about their company's level of online protection

Hackers can spend an average of 243 days on the victim's network before the company realizes there's a problem.

but only 58% planned to increase spending on their cybersecurity. This is a surprisingly low figure considering the risks.

According to a recent study by Mandiant, a provider of corporate cybersecurity systems, there are three reasons for the lack of spending. Firstly, hackers can spend an average of 243 days on the victim's network before the company realizes there's a problem. Secondly, cybersecurity is cost-saving but not money-making, so investors are less interested in paying for it. And finally, many companies feel that if they follow basic procedures such as regularly changing passwords and encrypting files, then they are safe and don't need to invest in more security. They'd prefer to wait and see.

Unfortunately, as businesses become more and more reliant on the Internet, how can businesses afford not to spend more on cybersecurity?

3 The writer thinks we should spend more money on online security. Discuss these questions with a partner.

1 How does the writer support this view in the article?

2 Do you agree? Do you think this is true for your company? Why/Why not?

4 Match these words from the article in **2** to definitions 1–8.

compromised   was down   hacker   encrypt   prevent
vulnerable   network   victim

1 when a protected thing is no longer secure *compromised*

2 stopped working _____

3 person or organization who is attacked as a result of a crime _____

4 stop something from happening _____

5 weak or easily attacked _____

6 person who secretly looks at and changes information on a computer system

_____

7 connected computers and devices for sharing information _____

8 make computer data impossible to read unless the user has a password

_____

5 Have you or anyone you know ever been a victim of cybercrime? What happened? Why wasn't the data or identity secure?

6 ▶7.1 Listen to three people talking about online security. Match each person to the type of online security a–c.

Speaker 1: ___   a Regularly changing your log in details

Speaker 2: ___   b Making copies of documents and other data

Speaker 3: ___   c Checking for viruses

7 ▶7.1 Listen again. Match verbs 1–7 with nouns a–g.

1	upgrade	a	data
2	back up	b	files
3	encrypt	c	documents
4	create	d	scans
5	open	e	attachments
6	share	f	software
7	run	g	a new password

8 Work with a partner. Make and ask each other questions with 'How often do you ...?' and a verb and noun from **7**. Answer the questions and give reasons.

Example: A How often do you upgrade your software?
                 B About once every three years because new software is expensive.

≫ For more exercises, go to **Practice file 7** on page 118.

9 Work with a partner. Discuss and write a list of guidelines for people working online at your company.

Example: To prevent hackers, create a new password once every three months.

QUIET ZONE

Language at work | Obligation, prohibition and permission

1 Does your company provide its employees with rules about ...?
- use of Internet
- behaviour towards colleagues
- dress and appearance
- any other areas?
- punctuality and timing
- use of phones
- expenses

2 Read two rules for employees at a company. Do you have similar rules? Which parts of the rules are different?

> 1 Employees **must** keep passwords secure at all times and **have to** change passwords every 12 weeks. Employees **are allowed to** choose their own password; note that it **needs to** be a strong password consisting of at least eight characters including one number and one capital letter.
>
> 2 Employees **can** access the Internet but **are not allowed to** download or upgrade software without permission. Employees **mustn't** use personal thumb drives.

3 Complete the categories in the *Language point* with the verbs in **bold** from **2**.

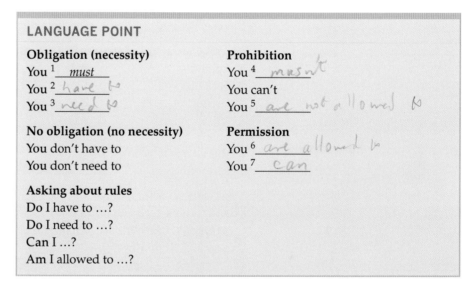

> **LANGUAGE POINT**
>
> **Obligation (necessity)**
> You ¹ _must_
> You ² _have to_
> You ³ _need to_
>
> **No obligation (no necessity)**
> You don't have to
> You don't need to
>
> **Asking about rules**
> Do I have to ...?
> Do I need to ...?
> Can I ...?
> Am I allowed to ...?
>
> **Prohibition**
> You ⁴ _mustn't_
> You can't
> You ⁵ _are not allowed to_
>
> **Permission**
> You ⁶ _are allowed to_
> You ⁷ _can_

» For more information, go to **Grammar reference** on page 119.

4 Read two more rules for employees. <u>Underline</u> the correct verb in *italics*.
1 Employees ¹*are allowed to / need to* make personal phone calls from company phones in the case of an emergency. For any other reason, employees ²*have to / can't* ask for their line managers' permission before calling.
2 Employees ³*don't have to / mustn't* access the Internet for personal use during working hours. However, employees ⁴*can / must* use the Internet as long as it is not excessive and during lunchtime or breaks only.

5 Work with a partner. Finish these sentences about rules and company policies so that they are true for you.
1 In my company, we have to ...
2 We don't have to ...
3 During working hours, we aren't allowed to ...
4 At lunchtime and breaks, we can ...
5 If you work here, you mustn't ...

» For more exercises, go to **Practice file 7** on page 119.

Tip | *must* or *have to*?

Both *must* and *have to* can express obligation or necessity. We use *must* when the speaker makes a personal decision to do something:
*I **must** remember to change my password.*

We use *have to* when the speaker is talking about a decision made by someone else:
*I **have to** change my password every 12 weeks because it's company policy.*

Ask a question about obligation with '*Do I have to ...?*' NOT '~~*Must I ...?*~~'

6 ▶ 7.2 Listen to a conversation with a new employee on their first day. Which rules do they discuss?

7 ▶ 7.2 Listen again. What three questions does the employee ask?

8 Work with a partner.
Student A: You are welcoming a new colleague to your place of work. Tell him/her about the rules you have to follow.
Student B: It is the first day of your new job. Ask questions about the rules. Talk and ask about some or all of these things:
- personal use of the Internet and phones
- Internet security (use of passwords, new software, etc.)
- security and identification entering and leaving the building
- punctuality and working hours
- health and safety rules
- dress code
- any other rules?

Practically speaking | How to sequence an explanation

1 Do you often register with websites? What sort of information do you provide? What kind of information won't you give?

2 ▶ 7.3 Listen to someone explaining how to register with a website. Number these stages in the correct order 1–6.
___ Click 'register' button   ___ Agree to terms and conditions
_1_ Fill in the personal details   ___ Receive temporary password
___ Start using the site   ___ Change temporary password

3 ▶ 7.3 Listen again and write in the missing sequence words.
1 OK, so _____ by filling in these details first.
2 … and _____ click 'register'.
3 _____, it'll email you a temporary password which you can change …
4 _____ you've done that …
5 So, _____ you've changed the password, you can log on.
6 You need to click this box _____ you finish.

4 Work with a partner. Choose one of these processes in your workplace and ask your partner to explain it.
- A security system to enter your workplace
- Logging into a conference call or teleconference
- Booking a room to hold meetings in your offices
- Any other process or system in your own workplace
  Example: **A** *Do you know how I …?*
  B *Sure, begin by …*

Tip | Sequence words
We often use sequencing words with verb + -ing or the perfect form:
*Begin/Start/Finish by fill**ing** in/click**ing** …*
*Once/Now/After/When you**'ve** done/changed that …*

Business communication | Teleconferencing

1 Look at the picture. What are the pros and cons of communicating this way compared to a face-to-face meeting? Give reasons for your answers.

2 ▶ 7.4 A pharmaceutical company is planning to introduce new security that reads employees' fingerprints. Listen to three parts of a teleconference and answer questions 1–6.

1 Who is in the same room as Vance?
2 Is Raymond too loud or too quiet?
1:30 3 Who interrupts Lauren?
4 How does Vance manage the interruption?
2:24 5 What does Vance ask everyone at the end?
6 What does he promise to send everyone?

3 ▶ 7.4 Listen again to Vance leading the teleconference. Number his expressions in the order he uses them.

Starting	___ We're just waiting for Raymond.
	1 Lauren is here with me.
	___ Your line isn't very good. Can you speak up?
Managing	___ Lauren, can you speak first, please?
	___ Would you like to comment now?
	___ OK, let's begin. Today, I want to discuss …
	___ Raymond, can you speak first? And then Helmi, you can speak next.
Ending	___ Well, I think that covers everything.
	___ Thank you everyone for coming.
	___ Are there any questions before we finish?
	___ I'll sum up the main points in an email.

》 For more exercises, go to **Practice file 7** on page 118.

4 You are going to attend a teleconference meeting. First read this email from your Managing Director. Then prepare for the teleconference on your own by noting down a few ideas for the meeting.

> ✉
>
> Following the recent media coverage of cyberattacks on businesses, I would like the heads of our different branches to schedule a teleconference asap to discuss ways of preventing such attacks on our own company's computer systems. By the end of your meeting, I would like to receive a plan of action for the company.
>
> Regards

5 Work in small groups. Choose one person to lead and manage the teleconference meeting. By the end of the teleconference, you should have an action plan to send to your Managing Director.

Key expressions

Starting
(name) is here with me.
(name), are you there?
We're just waiting for …

Dealing with technical problems
(name), can you hear me OK?
(name), are you there?
Your line isn't very good.
Can you speak up?

Managing the teleconference
OK, let's begin/start. Today, I want to discuss …
(name), can you speak first?
And then (name), you can speak next.
(name), would you like to comment?

Interrupting
This is (name). Can I ask a question?
Can I come in here?
Can I say something here?

Ending
I think that covers everything.
I'll sum up the main points in an email.
Thank you everyone for coming.
Are there any questions before we finish?

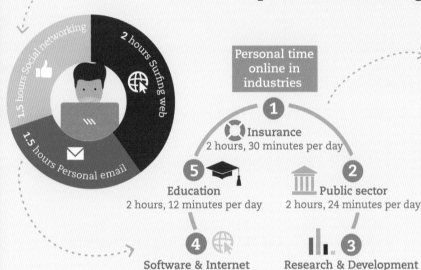

Online, but are you working?

25% of office workers' time online is **spent not working**.

1.5 hours Social networking
2 hours Surfing web
1.5 hours Personal email

Personal time online in industries

1 **Insurance** 2 hours, 30 minutes per day

5 **Education** 2 hours, 12 minutes per day

2 **Public sector** 2 hours, 24 minutes per day

4 **Software & Internet** 2 hours, 12 minutes per day

3 **Research & Development** 2 hours, 18 minutes per day

What's the evidence?

64% of employees say they use the Internet for personal reasons at work.

60% of online shopping happens between 9.00 am and 5.00 pm.

65% of YouTube videos are watched during work hours.

77% of workers access their social networking sites at work.

$? **What's the cost?**
18 hours a week online, but not working = $800 billion of employee salaries

Discussion

1 What do you think is the most/least surprising piece of data? Give reasons for your answers.

2 How much do you believe surveys and data like this? What can affect people's answers?

3 If you carried out a similar survey at your place of work, do you think the data would be very similar or very different? Why?

Task

1 Work in groups of four. Your company has asked management and office workers to agree upon a policy that outlines how much office workers can use computer equipment and the Internet for their own personal use during working hours. First of all, list four to five areas that need to be addressed in the policy.

   Example: The length of time you are allowed online for personal interest per day.

2 Divide your group into two pairs.
   Pair A: You are the management. Discuss each area in 1 and decide what the guidelines and rules for employees should be.
   Pair B: You are office workers at the company. Discuss each area in 1 and decide what the guidelines and rules for employees should be.

3 Work as a group again. Each pair presents their proposals for the policy. Find out where you have similar views and then discuss your differences. Try to reach an agreement and prepare a final list of points for the policy. Present these to the class.

8 Finance

Starting point

1 Who is in charge of dealing with financial matters in your …?
- company
- department
- home

2 Do you ever work with a budget at work or at home? How do you decide what to spend?

3 Do you think it's easier to manage your own money, or someone else's money (e.g. your company's money)? Why/Why not?

Working with words | Finance and money

1 Look at the list of ways of raising money to start a business. Discuss the pros and cons of each one.
- from a bank
- from a rich relative or friend
- from a business investor
- find a business partner
- use lots of credit cards
- save up the money

2 Read the article and answer the questions.
1 How did Lauren Peers and Mike Thompson raise money for their businesses?
2 What did Lauren and Mike have to give their investors in return?

Crowdfunding

Lauren Peers needed over £100,000 in **capital** to open her new business: a cat café in London, where customers would pay for a meal while playing with cats. Cat cafés exist in Japan but they are new to the UK, so a bank was unlikely to give Lauren a **loan**. Instead, she registered with the crowdfunding site Indiegogo.com.

Here, **budding entrepreneurs** look for **potential investors**. You explain your business and set a figure which you must reach within a time limit. If you fail to reach the target, then you pay back any money to any investors. But Lauren didn't need to. She received offers from all over the world and raised £110,000 within 60 days. Months later, she opened the cat café with 7,000 customer bookings on its first day.

Crowdfunding sites like Indiegogo are attractive for small, new businesses because you don't give away any **equity** and you don't pay out **dividends**. Instead, you give your investors a reward; for example, one woman paid £20,000 towards Lauren's business in return for owning one of the cats in the café.

For more serious investors, sites like Seedrs.com or Crowdcube.com expect their entrepreneurs to offer detailed business plans, **financial forecasts** and **shares** in their company. For example, Mike Thompson was able to launch his company, 'Mike's Fancy Cheese', because 98 investors on Seedrs.com paid £80,000 for a 40% share in Mike's business. From such deals, these crowdfunding sites take a **commission** of around 5% of the amount raised.

3 Do you think crowdfunding is a good way to raise money to start a new business? Why/Why not?

4 Match the words or phrases in **bold** in the text in **2** to definitions 1–9.
1 money the bank lends and someone borrows _____
2 large amount of money to start a business _____
3 people who would like to start their first business _____
4 people (or organizations) who might put money into a business to make more money _____
5 profits that a company pays to people who own shares in the business _____
6 predictions about how much money a company might make in the future _____
7 a payment to someone who sells the goods or service on your behalf _____
8 units which a company can be divided into and sold to raise money _____
9 shares in a company _____

5 Work with a partner. Cover up your answers in **4**. Take turns to read out the nine definitions and try to remember the word or phrase.

6 Find four examples of *pay* + preposition in the text and write the missing preposition in these questions. Then ask and answer the questions with a partner.
1 How much do customers pay _____ your company's best-selling service or product?
2 If a customer isn't satisfied with the service or product, do you always pay them their money _____?
3 If a close friend needed $20,000 to start a business, what percentage would you pay _____ his or her start-up costs?
4 Would you want a reward in return for your investment or would you want your friend to pay _____ a dividend every year?

7 Work with a partner. Find these numbers in the text and discuss what they refer to.

100,000	98
60	£80,000
7,000	40%
£20,000	5%

» For more exercises, go to **Practice file 8** on page 120.

8 Work in groups. You are entrepreneurs with a new business idea and you plan to raise money via a crowdfunding website. Discuss and make notes about these questions.
• What is your business idea?
• What kind of investors will you attract, e.g. new or established businesses or specialist businesses?
• How much capital will you need to raise?
• What will the investors receive in return, e.g. a gift or shares in the business?

9 Present your ideas in **8** to the rest of the class. Decide which group is offering the best investment opportunity.

Language at work | Talking about the future

1 Work in groups. List the expenses your departments have to budget for.
Example: wages, office equipment

2 Look at part of a department's budget for the first six months of its financial year. Where is the department over budget? Where can it still spend more?

EXPENSES

	Budget	Actual spend	Variance
Wages	550,000	545,000	5,000
Overtime	5,000	15,500	-10,500
Phones	500	500	0
Travel	1,300	1,830	-530
Training	3,500	1,200	2,300
Recruitment	750	400	350
Legal Fees	200	0	200

3 ▶8.1 Listen to three parts of a meeting about budgets. Write which budget expenses they discuss.

Part 1: _____

Part 2: _____

Part 3: _____

4 ▶8.1 Listen again and match 1–7 to a–g to make sentences.

1 We're going to   a increase the travel budget.

2 That might   b spend even more if we don't employ someone else.

3 It may not   c be OK, but let me check with HR first.

4 Next year, we'll probably d expand your department next year.

5 Everything could   e go up by about 5%.

6 You'll definitely   f need more for travel.

7 We'll possibly   g happen.

5 Answer the questions in the *Language point*.

> ### LANGUAGE POINT
>
> Use the sentence numbers 1–7 in **4** to complete a–c.
>
> a The speaker makes a strong prediction based on some evidence in sentence ___.
>
> b The speaker uses *'ll* + adverb to talk about the future. The speaker is very certain in sentence ___, fairly certain in sentence ___ and less certain in sentence ___.
>
> c The speaker uses a modal verb to make a prediction about something that is possible but not certain in sentences ___, ___ and ___.
>
> What form are the main verbs in all the sentences? _____

Tip | *might/may/could*

Use *might/may/could* to make positive predictions. Use *might not/may not* to make negative predictions.

We don't use *could not* to make negative predictions because it has a different meaning:

We might/may not increase the budget = it's possible we won't.

We couldn't increase the budget = we weren't able to.

>> For more information, go to **Grammar reference** on page 121.

6 <u>Underline</u> the correct verbs in *italics*. Both verbs are possible in one sentence.

1 We're *going to / might* increase our sales budget next year in order to take on more staff in other regions. Finance have already agreed to my request.

2 We'll *probably / may* go over budget again this year depending on what happens in the last quarter.

3 It *may / 'll definitely* be cheaper to take on more staff than to give out more overtime. I'm sure of it.

4 There *could not / might not* be enough money to pay for any training next month.

5 He's *going to / 'll probably* call us back with the figures. In fact, I'm expecting his call right now.

6 The government *could / might* increase the rate of tax next year, so let's keep a bit extra in the bank.

7 It *probably won't / definitely won't* happen this year. I have no doubt about that.

8 Although the European markets are slow, the possible growth in the Asian economy *could / is going to* mean that we avoid another global recession.

>> For more exercises, go to **Practice file 8** on page 121.

7 Make your own predictions about the future. Talk about these topics and give reasons for your answers.
- Departmental budgets in your company next year
- Rates of tax in your country over the next five years
- The retirement age and pensions in your country
- The cost of borrowing and interest rates
- The global economy in the next decade

8 Your company is setting up a new office in another country. Work in groups of four and divide into two pairs. **Pair A**, turn to **page 137**. **Pair B**, turn to **page 142**.

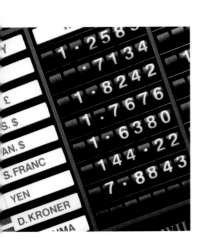

Practically speaking | How to use *will*

1 Read sentences 1–4 from different situations. What do you think each situation might be?

1 I'd keep them. I'm sure they'll go up again.

2 If you pay before the end of the month, I'll give you a 10% discount.

3 Yes, I think I'll have soup for starters and steak for my main course.

4 No, sorry. I'll get it to you tomorrow at the latest.

2 ▶ 8.2 Listen to the four conversations and check your answers from **1**.

3 Match the four sentences from **1** to the different uses of *will* (a–d) below.

a To promise action ___

b To make a prediction ___

c To make a decision ___

d To give a condition ___

4 Work with a partner. Make four short conversations with these sentences. Then work with another partner and perform your conversations.

1 Don't worry, I'll do it before the end of today.

2 It'll probably arrive today.

3 I think I'll have the same thing.

4 I'll do it on one condition.

Business communication | Presenting visual information

1 Look at the four slides (A–D). What do you think the presentation is going to be about? Why might investors be interested?

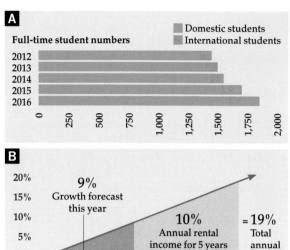

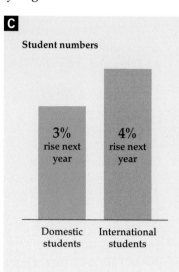

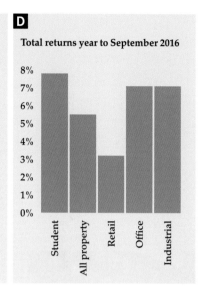

2 ▶ 8.3 Listen to the presentation by a speaker for a property firm. Check your predictions in **1** and number slides A–D in the correct order 1–4.

A ___ B ___ C ___ D ___

3 ▶ 8.3 Listen again. Tick (✓) the expressions the presenter uses with each slide.

	Slide 1	Slide 2	Slide 3	Slide 4
Take a look at this chart.				
As you can see on this chart, …				
This slide shows a forecasted annual return of 19%.				
This chart shows you the returns …				
It's based on data from one of the country's leading estate agents.				
Each line is split into two …				
Also notice in particular this grey line.				
I'd like to draw your attention to the first line …				
This upward trend will definitely continue.				
The demand for student accommodation is going to increase.				
We think your investment will rise annually by 9%.				

4 Work with a partner. Take turns to present slides A–D in **1**. Remember to:
- refer to the visuals
- refer to any sources of data
- explain the chart
- focus on important information
- forecast any future trends or changes

5 Do you think student accommodation is a good investment? Why/Why not?

» For more exercises, go to **Practice file 8** on page 120.

6 Work with a partner. Prepare a short presentation with a slide and present it to each other. **Student A**, turn to **page 138**. **Student B**, turn to **page 143**.

Key expressions

Referring to visuals
Take a look at this table/graph/chart.
As you can see from this …
This chart shows/illustrates/represents …

Referring to sources
It's based on figures/data from …
They're from a survey of …

Explaining
It's divided/broken/split into …
The green line indicates/represents
This upward/downward trend shows …

Focusing
I'd like to draw your attention to …
Notice in particular …
This figure represents …

Forecasting trends and changes
This increase will definitely continue over the next few years.
This is going to fall in the future.
It will rise/fall/increase/decrease …

Investment opportunities

Crowdfunding has become a very popular way to raise money. Here are four real examples of organizations and businesses who tried to attract investors on crowdfunding websites.

Fish on wheels

A Dutch company called Studio Diip created a device which lets a fish drive round your living room. A sensor turns the vehicle in the direction that the fish swims. They wanted people to invest €40,000.

MiRing

Two undergraduate brothers, Zach and Max Zitney, invented the MiRing. You put the ring on your finger and it would light up and vibrate when you received a call or message on your mobile. They needed to get $150,000 in 30 days.

New York City Opera

In 1943, New York City Opera started producing operas which ordinary people could afford. By 2013, it didn't have enough money to put on operas for another year, so it used crowdfunding. Its aim was to raise $1 million from the public in return for gifts such as shopping bags, posters and tickets to events.

Form1

A group of researchers at Massachusetts Institute of Technology (MIT) developed a 3-D printer which was both professional and affordable. The idea was that the general public would be able to buy a 3-D printer for their home. The project needed crowdfunding of $100,000 to take it to the market.

Discussion

1 What are the pros and cons of each crowdfunding idea as an investment?

2 What do you think makes a successful investment?

3 Why do you think some ideas fail in getting any crowdfunding?

Task

1 Work in groups of four. Each person chooses one of the crowdfunding ideas above.

2 Prepare a two-minute presentation to convince investors to invest in your idea. You will need to explain what you want the money for and what kind of return the investors will receive.

3 Take turns to give your presentations. Afterwards, the group must decide which idea is the most attractive investment opportunity.

4 Turn to page 138 and find out what happened to each of the crowdfunding ideas. Did you choose the most successful one?

9 Logistics

Starting point

1 What does the term 'logistics' mean?

2 Have you ever experienced problems with the delivery of goods at home or at work? What happened?

Working with words | Logistics and supply chains

1 When businesses import products from different countries around the world, what do they have to consider?

2 Read the interview with Emad Razavi and answer the questions.
1 What are the main stages of importing his goods?
2 What does he have to consider about each stage?

Business-owner Emad Razavi imports and sells **handmade** rugs. In this interview, he talks about the challenges of managing a **supply chain** that begins in some of the remotest regions of Asia and ends in one of Europe's busiest capitals.

Who exactly are your suppliers?
Each rug is individual, so we buy them from different nomadic tribes in countries and regions such as Turkey, Afghanistan, the Caucuses and Armenia. I've collected rugs from a very young age, so I have solid contacts with many of these tribes. I also work with **middlemen** who I've known for a very long time and I can trust.

So when you have a large shipment of new stock, what transportation do you use?
It depends on where they come from. They can arrive by road from Turkey in about five days. For countries further away, I could ship them but that can take three to five weeks, and they might get damaged. Personally, I prefer to pay extra and transport them by air. It costs a little extra but they arrive in about three days and in excellent condition.

*How do you **keep track of** stock at the warehouse?*
Well, we aren't the same as other companies. Normally, if you **run low on** an item, you reorder it. But each of our rugs is unique, so we keep an **inventory** with information about the **origin**, size and colour. And, of course, we can email a photo when a client contacts us. They can also visit us at our **showroom** and talk about what they are looking for – it's a very personal service.

Glossary
nomadic tribe (n) group of people (often related families) with the same language and culture who move from place to place

3 Match the words in **bold** from the text in **2** to definitions 1–9.

1 a series of processes and people or companies involved in the production and distribution of a product _____

2 made by a person, not a machine _____

3 a list of items in stock _____

4 where a product came from (e.g. country or region) _____

5 a retail outlet where customers can look at goods before buying _____

6 people who buy product from a supplier and sell it on to seller (e.g. a distributor) _____

7 a large amount of goods sent together _____

8 to not have many in stock _____

9 to have information about where something is _____

4 In the interview, Emad says the following are important to his business. Are they also important for your type of business? Why/Why not?

- Solid contacts with suppliers
- Working with middlemen you can trust
- Costs of transportation
- Keeping track of stock
- Providing a personal or unique service

5 ▶ 9.1 Listen to an interview with another business owner and answer the questions.

1 In what way is Steve's company similar to Emad Razavi's? _personal_

2 How does he manage his stock? _barcode, computer warns him_

3 How does he keep track of his orders? _tracking numbers_

6 ▶ 9.1 Listen again. Complete the phrases in *italics*.

_2 0S_ 1 That means you have to *keep* a lot of components __in__ *stock*.

2 How do you make sure that you don't *run* __out__?

3 It tells us what we have left, if it's __on__ *order* ...

4 Will it order automatically if you're *running* __low__ on something?

_4 2_ 5 You don't want to *stock* __up__ *on* components which are not going to sell.

7 Which phrase in **6** means ...?

- to have a product available for sale _____
- to not have many _____
- to not have any _____
- to buy a lot of something _____
- to be waiting for a delivery _____

» For more exercises, go to **Practice file 9** on page 122.

8 Work with a partner. Think of a product you often order or buy, or use one of the ideas in the list below. Describe what happens in each stage of the supply chain, from production to delivery to the customer.

- Ink cartridge for a printer
- Replacement light bulb
- Groceries in a shop
- New item of clothing
- Cup of tea or coffee
- Meal in a restaurant

Language at work | Direct and indirect questions

1 Look at the pictures and compare these three ways of transporting goods. What do you think are the advantages and disadvantages of each one?

 **A**
 **B**
 **C**

2 ▶ 9.2 Listen to a customer enquiry.
   1 What do they want to deliver?
   2 What type of transportation are they going to use?

3 ▶ 9.2 Read the five pairs of questions. Listen again and tick (✓) the questions you hear (a or b).
   1 ✓a I was wondering if I could get a quote. ___
     b Could I get a quote? ___
   2 ✓a I'd like to know how much it costs to send a package. ___
     b How much does it cost to send a package? ___
   3 ✓a Could you tell me how big the package is? ___
     b How big is the package? ___
   4 a Do you have any idea how long that takes? ___
     ✓b How long does that take? ___
   5 a Would you mind telling me what the price is? ___
     ✓b What's the price? ___

4 Which questions in 3 are direct? Which are indirect? Underline the phrases which introduce the indirect questions.
   Example: I was wondering if I could get a quote.

5 Compare the pairs of questions in 3. Choose the correct option to complete the explanations in the *Language point*.

> **LANGUAGE POINT**
>
> 1 We often use indirect questions to sound *more / less* polite.
> 2 We often ask *indirect / direct* questions at the beginning of an enquiry.
> 3 For indirect questions with a 'yes' or 'no' answer, we use *if / what*.
> 4 With indirect *wh-* or *how-* questions, the subject comes *before / after* the verb.

» For more information, go to **Grammar reference** on page 123.

6 Work with a partner. Think of one direct and one indirect question to ask for each of these situations.
   Example: You want to speak to the manager of a shop.
   When will the manager be back? Do you know when the manager will be back?
   1 You are arranging a delivery for an important client. You want to know whether morning, afternoon or evening would be the most convenient time.
   2 You are importing some items by ship but they still haven't arrived. Call the shipping company to find out about the shipment.
   3 A customer has called with an enquiry but it's a bad line. It's difficult to understand what she is saying.
   4 A customer is calling again with a complaint. You need to know which of your colleagues the customer spoke to last time.

» For more exercises, go to **Practice file 9** on page 123.

7 Work with a partner. You are going to make two phone calls. **Student A**, turn to page 139. **Student B**, use the information below. Think about what questions you might need to ask to get the information you need. (Use a mix of indirect and direct questions.)

Student B

Call 1: You want to ship a container of handmade goods from Singapore to New York. Call the shipping firm for a quote. Find out about:
- the size of the containers
- the price per container
- the approximate time for a shipment
- warehouse storage in New York for two weeks
- insurance

Call 2: You work for a road transport company. Use this information to answer your partner's questions about a delivery from Istanbul to London.

Prices	Delivery times	Additional costs
Minimum: £150 Up to 1,000 kilos: £270	10–14 days	Customs clearance: £50 per order
		Warehouse storage: We can only store the items for up to 48 hours.
		Price includes insurance for goods. Full details emailed on request.

Practically speaking | How to use *say* and *tell*

1 ▶ 9.3 Listen to part of a meeting between a sales manager and a member of staff. What does the employee report on? What does the manager decide?

2 ▶ 9.3 Write *say* or *tell* in these sentences from the meeting. Then listen and check.
1 Can you _____ me how the meeting went?
2 He _____ that he's looking for a long-term agreement.
3 I couldn't _____ .
4 Did he _____ when?
5 Let's _____ the week after.
6 I'll _____ you what.

3 Match the meaning of *say* and *tell* in the sentences in **2** to definitions a–f.
a Ask for information   _1_
b Ask what someone said   ___
c Report what someone said   ___
d Make a suggestion   ___
e Make a decision   ___
f Unable to judge or know correctly   ___

4 Work with a partner. Have a conversation using the information below. Use *say* and *tell* in your conversation.
Student A runs a logistics company. **Student B**, who works for the company, had a good meeting with a potential new client. The client wants worldwide shipments and a long-term agreement with discounts.

Tip | *say* or *tell*?
When you report information, you can use *say* or *tell*.
tell + person: He **told me** that he's looking for a long-term agreement.
say + no person: He **said** that he's looking for a long-term agreement.

A Ask Student B for information on the meeting and the client.	
	B Report what the client said.
A Ask how much discount the client wants.	
	B Say you don't know at this stage. Suggest they both meet the client again.
A Make a decision to meet the client and agree a time and date.	

Business communication | Placing and handling orders

1 Gisele Kern works for a computer assembler in Hamburg. Read her email to Composource, a Singapore-based supplier and answer questions 1–4.

1 What does she want to order?

2 Is she a regular customer?

3 When does she want delivery?

4 How will she pay?

From: giselekern@abracomp.com
Subject: Order – motherboards

Dear Sir/Madam,

I would like to place an order for 2,000 motherboards. This is a repeat order. We need these urgently, so please send them asap. Please charge it to our account as usual.

Kind regards,

Gisele Kern

Abracomp

---

2 Underline the expressions for placing an order in the email in **1**.

3 ▶ 9.4 Two weeks later, Gisele is still waiting for the components. She calls her supplier, Composource, to find out what is happening. Listen and complete the supplier's information.

Account: **Abracomp**   Account reference: _____

Date of order: _____

Product description: _____

Quantity: _____

Dispatched: Yes ☐   No ☐

Date and time dispatched: _____

---

4 ▶ 9.4 Listen again. Match 1–8 to a–h to make sentences.

1 I'm calling about   a it was dispatched that afternoon.

2 I'd like to find out   b quick as I can.

3 Can you tell me   c when you placed the order?

4 Do you have any idea   d problem for me.

5 It says here that   e what's happened to it.

6 This is a real   f an order I placed two weeks ago.

7 I'll look into it   g your account number?

8 I'll be as   h immediately.

» For more exercises, go to **Practice file 9** on page 122.

5 Work with a partner. Take turns to role-play two situations on the phone. In one situation you will be a customer, and in the other situation a call handler. In each situation you will have two conversations. **Student A**, turn to **page 139**. **Student B**, turn to **page 143**.

Key expressions

Placing an order
I'd like to place an order.
This is a repeat order.
Please send them asap.

Asking for details
Do you have an account with us?
Can you tell me your account number?
When did you place the order?

Checking on an order
I'd like to find out about an order.
I'm chasing/following up an order.
Could you check it out for me?
I really want to know what's happened to it.

Explaining what happened
We put it (straight) through to …
It says here that …
It was dispatched on …

Complaining
I'm not happy about this.
This is a real problem for me.
This is unacceptable.

Promising action
I'll look into it immediately.
I'll find out.
I'll be as quick as I can.

Shadow work

Do you feel like you have less and less free time? If so, what's happening to your free time?

In the book *Shadow Work*, the author Craig Lambert believes that businesses are using modern technology to fill our day with unpaid, unseen jobs. Take booking a flight, for example. The airline industry makes us buy a ticket online, print out a boarding pass and scan our own passports – all in our own free time. And even when we arrive at our destination, more and more hotels provide a screen in reception for checking in. Instead of self-service, we have 'no-service'!

In fact, everywhere you look, Lambert says that customers are doing shadow work: At petrol stations, drivers fill their own tanks, and in supermarkets they scan and bag their own shopping. Tech companies have 'user forums' where customers solve each other's technical problems. Banks are closing branches because their customers manage transactions online. We transport flat-packed furniture home and build it ourselves. And in the future, household appliance companies won't need to keep any spare parts in stock, because their customers will just print them out on 3-D printers.

In other words, 'free time' is no longer free; it's when we do shadow work.

Discussion

1 Which shadow work in the article do you often do? How do you feel about doing it? How much do you think it reduces your free time?

2 What are the advantages of this shadow work for businesses? Are there any disadvantages?

3 Although the article is critical of shadow work for customers, can you think of any advantages? Why do some people enjoy shadow work?

Task

1 Think about your own business and make a list of some of the different jobs involved in producing your goods or offering your services.

2 Look at your list in 1. How can you make some of these jobs into shadow work? How would this benefit your business and its customers?

3 Work with a partner. Take turns to present your ideas in 1 and 2.

Focus

1 Here are six common computer problems. Which have you experienced? How did you solve the problem?

1 A virus on your computer
2 Unable to log in with a username or password
3 Accidentally deleting important files
4 Losing data because you forgot to back up your files
5 The computer won't recognize your USB device
6 You can't connect to the Internet or you keep losing the connection

2 ▶01 Watch six people talking about their computer problems. Make notes about their answers in the table.

	What was the problem?	How did they solve the problem?
Speaker 1		
Speaker 2		
Speaker 3		
Speaker 4		
Speaker 5		
Speaker 6		

3 Work with a partner and compare your answers in **2**. Did the people in the video have the same problems as you in **1**?

An Internet security firm

4 You are going to watch an interview about cybercrime with Fraser Howard, from the Internet security firm Sophos. Before you watch, replace the words in **bold** in sentences 1–8 with the words from the list.

installs   tricks   browses   secure   steals   redirects   adapts   gets into

1 We need to **protect** our home networks, mobile phones and tablets. _____
2 The hacker **fools** you into paying them money. _____
3 Malware **infects** your computer. _____
4 It happens when a user **looks at** the Web. _____
5 Without you knowing, the website **sends** your browser to another server. _____
6 To respond to the changes in cybercrime, Internet security continually **changes** its approach. _____
7 The site **loads** the malware onto your computer. _____
8 The hacker **illegally takes** the data in order to profit financially. _____

5 ▶02 Watch the interview with Fraser Howard. As you watch, number the scenes from the video A–E in the correct order 1–5.

A An application called 'Security Shield' ___
B A man on a bench using his mobile phone ___
C Maps showing where a computer virus came from ___
D Finger scrolling up and down on a tablet _1_
E Outside the company headquarters of Sophos ___

What is cybercrime?

6 ▶03 Watch Part 1 of the video again. Match 1–3 to a–c to make sentences.
1 Cybercrime ___
2 Internet security ___
3 Criminals ___

a are targeting users, targeting businesses, looking to steal data in order to profit financially from Internet attacks.
b is basically the steps taken to protect yourself from online attacks.
c is fundamentally crime but specifically using computers or the Internet to deliver the attack.

7 ▶04 Watch Part 2 of the video again. In this part Fraser gives an example of Cybercrime. Number the stages A–F in the correct order 1–6.
A They pay money for problems which don't exist. ___
B A person is browsing the Web. _1_
C They come across a page which has been hacked. ___
D 'Security Shield' is installed. ___
E It says they have lots of problems. ___
F They are redirected somewhere 'bad' and 'bad stuff' happens. ___

8 ▶05 Watch Part 3 of the video again. Write the four locations.
1 Where is the person browsing?
_____
2 Where is the server for the first site?
_____
3 Where do the hackers redirect the browser to?
_____
4 Which server does the browser go to in the end?
_____

9 ▶06 Watch Part 4 of the video again. Which sentence summarizes Fraser's answer?
A The criminals are more interested in your mobile phone.
B The criminals are trying to hack your network of devices.
C The criminals are trying to hack the Internet security companies.

Summarizing information

10 Work with a partner. Try to summarize the interview using these words and phrases from the video.
Example: Cybercrime is when hackers try to steal data by …

infected bad stuff happens
targeting users and businesses
cybercrime
steal data secure
browsing the Web information,
hackers devices and
trick into paying networks

11 Write your summary of the video using between 100–120 words only.

10 Facilities

Starting point

1 Work with a partner. List as many places of work as you can in two minutes.

2 Which ones would you most like to work in? Which ones would you least like to work in? Give reasons for your answers.

Working with words | Describing a place of work

1 What do you know about Google's offices? What kinds of facilities do you think they have?

2 Read the article and answer the questions.

1 How did the company change its workplace?
2 What facilities does it provide?
3 What are the advantages of this kind of workspace?

GOOGLE OFFICES

When Google decided to remodel its London Headquarters, it began by knocking down the walls and getting rid of any **old-fashioned** office furniture. Into the empty space, they mixed **hi-tech** video-conferencing facilities alongside **spacious** breakout areas, including one which has grass, deckchairs and even a rowing boat – good for one-to-one meetings.

'You won't find private offices. We prefer **open-plan** spaces,' explains Nelson Mattos, Vice President for Product and Engineering. 'Our experience is that a **comfortable**, open and **fun** environment encourages creativity and openness. Open spaces make chance interactions more likely, and chance interactions often lead to the greatest ideas.'

Many of these chance interactions probably take place in the **futuristic** corridor that links the different spaces. Along its walls are whiteboards with the notes and scribbles left by employees. At one end, there's a **state-of-the-art** presentation suite which looks like a small cinema – it even has film posters on the walls.

And for employees who need a break from this **stress-free** environment, there's a gym, and a games room with pool table and video games console. If you like music, there's even a **fully-equipped** music room where colleagues can jam together. The company believes it all goes towards generating new ideas and keeping employees at the top of their game.

Glossary
to jam *(v)* to play music with other people
at the top of your game *(idiom)* to be the very best at what you do

3 Which of the facilities at Google does your workplace have? Which facilities would you like to have? Why?

4 Match the adjectives in **bold** from the text in 2 to definitions 1–9. One answer matches two adjectives.
   1 out-of-date _____
   2 the most modern and up-to-date _____
   3 few or no walls separating workspaces _____
   4 lots of room, not cramped _____
   5 relaxing _____
   6 pleasant (to be in) _____
   7 in the style of science fiction _____
   8 not boring _____
   9 has everything _____

5 Work with a partner. Take turns to describe your place of work. Use some of the facilities below and adjectives in 4.

breakout
area
factory stores showroom offices
presentation suite warehouse
coffee area canteen video-conferencing
meeting rooms

6 ▶ 10.1 Listen to two people talking about workspaces and facilities. What adjectives do they use to describe them?
   Speaker 1: _____ _____ _____
   Speaker 2: _____ _____ _____ _____

7 The speakers use these adverbs to intensify the adjectives. Write them in the correct position on the scale, from weak to strong.
   very   really   fairly   not very   extremely   pretty   not exactly

weak ←————————————————————————→ **strong**

8 ▶ 10.1 Listen again and match the adverbs in 7 to the adjectives in 6.

>> For more exercises, go to **Practice file 10** on page 124.

9 Work with a partner. Take turns to describe the following, using adverb + adjective combinations.
   • Your ideal place of work
   • Your favourite building in the world
   • Part of the building you work in which you don't like so much
   • A place where you often relax

10 Work with a partner. You are going to talk about some different types of places of work. **Students A and B, turn to page 140.**

Tip | *like*
We use *like* in different ways to describe something.
What you enjoy:
*I **like** listening to music while I work.*
Appearance:
*It looks **like** a cinema.*
Asking for general description:
*What are your offices **like**?*
A bit old-fashioned.

Language at work | Quantifiers

1 What kind of health and safety rules do you have at work? How do they protect employees?

2 Read part of an information leaflet about workplace health and safety facilities. Write the following headings in 1–3:

Health   Safety   Welfare

Employers must provide the right workplace facilities for everyone in your workplace. These include:

1 _____   **2** _____   **3** _____

- Drinking water
- A place to store clothing
- Somewhere to take breaks

- Suitable lighting
- A clean workspace
- Comfortable seating

- Clearly marked fire exits
- Windows that can be opened in all rooms

---

3 ▶ 10.2 Listen to two conversations between a health and safety inspector and an employer. Tick (✓) the items in the leaflet they discuss.

4 ▶ 10.2 Complete the sentences with the quantifiers from the list. Then listen again and check.

much   some   a little   a lot of   not many   any   a few   any   many

1 _____ *employees* cycle to work and get changed in here.
2 How _____ *people* use this facility?
3 There isn't _____ *space* for 20.
4 We also have _____ *lockers* along the wall outside.
5 Are there _____ *places* for staff to go during their breaks?
6 This room has a table and _____ *chairs*.
7 To be honest, _____ *staff* use it.
8 It doesn't have _____ *windows*.
9 Perhaps _____ *paint* on the walls might improve it.

5 Put the nouns in *italics* from **4** into these categories.
1 Countable nouns _____
2 Uncountable nouns _____

6 Complete the information in the *Language point* with the quantifiers from **4**. Use the quantifiers more than once.

LANGUAGE POINT

1 quantifiers used with countable nouns *some, many,* _____
2 quantifiers used with uncountable nouns _____
3 talk about small quantities/amounts _____
4 talk about large quantities/amounts _____
5 ask questions about quantities/amounts _____
6 make negative statements about quantities and amounts _____

>> For more information, go to **Grammar reference** on page 125.

7 <u>Underline</u> the correct words in *italics*. In one sentence, both words are correct.
1 How *much / many* free time do employees have at lunchtime?
2 There's *many / a lot of* extra space in my office. Most of the cupboards are empty.
3 Do you have *much / any* facilities for people with children?
4 *A few / A little* people were interested in your suggestion for starting a choir but most didn't reply.
5 Since the café closed, we don't have *some / any* good places to go for lunch.
6 There's *some / a few* space over there for chairs and a table.
7 There's only *a few / a little* coffee left in the jar. Can we order some more?
8 Not *many / a lot of* companies have facilities for musical instruments.

» For more exercises, go to **Practice file 10** on page 125.

8 Work with a partner. Take turns to ask and answer questions about these facilities for staff in your workplace.
• Lockers and storage facilities
• Water coolers
• Areas to relax
• Exercise facilities (e.g. a gym)
• Places to eat and make drinks
• Parking spaces
• Meeting rooms
• Other?
   Example: **A** *Do you have any lockers for employees?*
   B *No, there aren't any lockers for employees but there is a lot of space next to everyone's desk.*

Practically speaking | How to use *too* and *enough*

1 ▶ 10.3 Listen to a conversation with a health and safety inspector in a factory. What facility are they discussing? Write *too* or *enough* in the sentences.
1 This room isn't big _____.
2 We don't have _____ lockers.
3 The room is _____ dark.
4 There are _____ few chairs.

2 Look at the sentences in **1**. Do we use *too* or *enough* ...?
a before an adjective _____
b after an adjective _____
c before *much/many/few/little* + noun _____
d before a noun to say whether there is / isn't the correct quantity _____

3 Work with a partner. Describe each situation with *too* or *enough*.
• Fifty people work in this building. It was designed for 35.
• These files need about 100 GB. My laptop has 50 GB of spare memory.
• The sun is very bright today. I can't see my computer screen.
• I'm freezing. Why is the air conditioning on?
• The staff are all chatting. We need to find them some more work to do.
• There are three empty shelves in the storeroom. Three boxes of stationery have just arrived.
   Example: *This building is too small. / This building isn't big enough.*

4 Make three more sentences about your company facilities with *too* and *enough*. Tell your partner.

Business communication | Making suggestions and recommendations

1 How do you make suggestions in your company? By email or comment forms? Do you use a suggestion box?

2 Complete the comments from a suggestion box with expressions from the list.

why don't   have you thought about   we could always   couldn't we do

---

COMMENT FORM

Because so many parents work here now, ¹_____ we have a crèche for young children? Then we wouldn't have so many problems with childcare. And ²_____ see our children at lunchtimes, which would also be good for motivation.

COMMENT FORM

I don't want to complain about the new relaxation room – it's extremely comfortable and spacious! But ³_____ having some entertainment in there? I read about employees at one company where they have a special room called an Anarchy Zone. They can play computer games, table football, or watch TV. ⁴_____ something like that?

---

3 ▶ 10.4 The facilities manager is discussing the suggestions in **2** with an architect. Listen and answer the questions.
1 Why can they only choose one of the ideas?
2 Which one do they choose and why?

4 Choose the correct words in *italics*.
1 Well, it might prove *difficult / difficulties* to have both.
2 I think we should consider *have / having* …
3 Besides, I have a few *reserves / reservations* about …
4 You might be *better / the best* off without it …
5 I'd rather not *have / having* it.
6 I'd recommend *to put / putting* it here.

5 ▶ 10.4 Listen again and tick (✓) the responses you hear in the meeting.
I really like it. ☐
Good idea. ☐
Sorry, but I don't think that would work. ☐
I'm not sure. ☐
Great! ☐
Exactly. ☐

>> For more exercises, go to **Practice file 10** on page 124.

6 Work with a partner. An architect is redesigning your office space. Turn to **page 140**.

7 Work in small groups. After redesigning your offices, imagine that your company lets you have an Anarchy Zone – an area to relax and forget about work for a few minutes – with four items in it.
1 Make suggestions for what you would put in your Anarchy Zone. For example, a TV, computer games, books, etc. Give reasons for these suggestions. Respond to others' ideas. Decide on the four items you will have in the zone.
2 Present your final recommendation to the rest of the class.
3 Comment on the other groups' recommendations.

Key expressions

Suggesting
What/How about (+ verb + -*ing*)?
Why don't we (+ verb)?
Maybe we should (+ verb)
Perhaps we could (+ verb)
Couldn't we (+ verb)?
Have you thought about (+ verb + -*ing*)?
We could always (+ verb)

Recommending / Expressing doubt
I think we should consider (+ noun / + verb + -*ing*)
We might be better off (+ verb + -*ing*)
It's probably worth (+ verb + -*ing*)
I'd recommend (+ that / + -*ing*)
It would be better to (+ verb)
It might prove (+ adjective)
I have a few reservations about (noun / + verb + -*ing*)
I'd rather not (+ verb)

Responding
I really like it.
It's/That's a good idea.
Sorry, but I don't think that would work.
I'm not sure.
Great.
Exactly.

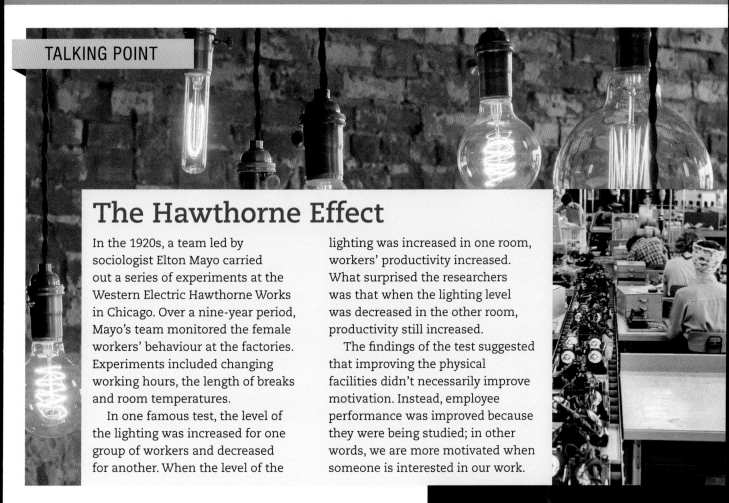

The Hawthorne Effect

In the 1920s, a team led by sociologist Elton Mayo carried out a series of experiments at the Western Electric Hawthorne Works in Chicago. Over a nine-year period, Mayo's team monitored the female workers' behaviour at the factories. Experiments included changing working hours, the length of breaks and room temperatures.

In one famous test, the level of the lighting was increased for one group of workers and decreased for another. When the level of the lighting was increased in one room, workers' productivity increased. What surprised the researchers was that when the lighting level was decreased in the other room, productivity still increased.

The findings of the test suggested that improving the physical facilities didn't necessarily improve motivation. Instead, employee performance was improved because they were being studied; in other words, we are more motivated when someone is interested in our work.

Discussion

1 Do you think the conclusion in the final paragraph is relevant to 21st century businesses? Why/Why not?

2 What do you think are the top five factors that motivate people at work (e.g. *pay, hours, good facilities*, etc.)?

3 What are some of the main ways your company motivates its staff to improve their performance?

Task

1 Work in small groups and take part in an experiment looking at how factors such as facilities and benefits affect motivation. Look at the list of factors below which motivate people. You have 30 points to share between the items. Discuss each item and give it points according to how important it is for staff motivation. For example, if you think a company car is an important motivator, then you might give it 5 or 6 points. Give an item 0 or 1 point if you do not think it is very important.

- A company car
- New company policies
- Relationship with boss
- Salary
- Recognition of good performance
- Advancement

- Job security
- Achievement
- The nature of the work
- Relationship with colleagues
- Your personal life
- Level of responsibility

2 Join another group. Compare your results and explain your scores.

3 This simple experiment is based on the work of Frederick Herzberg. Turn to **page 141** to read about his conclusions. How similar were your findings? What do you think the experiment tells you?

11 Decisions

1 Read how four people make decisions. Who are you most like?

1 'I trust my instincts. If I think too much about something I often get it wrong.'

2 'Sometimes I rush into decisions too quickly and I often regret what I have done.'

3 'I make a list of advantages and disadvantages of each option before I decide.'

4 'I ask people I trust what they think before I make up my mind. I find it hard to make decisions on my own.'

2 What was the best decision you ever made? What was the worst? (Either at work or in your personal life.)

Working with words | Decision-making

1 When you have a long list of individual tasks at work (or at home), how do you decide which to do first? Tell your partner.

2 ▶ 11.1 Look at 'The Priority Matrix' below and listen to a trainer explaining the four parts of the matrix. Number each part (1–4) in the order you hear them talked about.

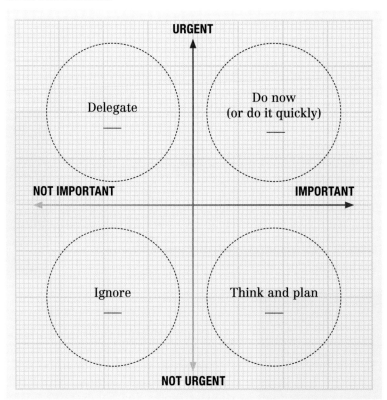

3 Work with a partner. Look at four tasks a–d. Where would you put them in the Priority Matrix? Give reasons for your answers.

a The launch of a major new product in 12 months' time.

b Arranging a leaving party for an employee who has been with the company for over 20 years.

c Your key customer has left a voicemail with a complaint about a large order. He sounds very angry.

d You receive an invitation to visit the new showrooms of an office furniture company.

4 Make a list of four or five jobs that you currently have to do. Decide where to put them on the Priority Matrix.

5 Tell your partner about your decisions in **4**. How helpful was the Priority Matrix in your decision-making?

6 ▶11.1 Replace the words in **bold** in sentences 1–8 with the verbs from the list. Then listen again and check.

*make up your mind   invite   avoid   evaluate   ignore   prioritize
reach   delegate*

1 The hardest part is to **decide** which job to do first. *make up your mind*
2 **Immediately deal with** any job which is urgent and important. Do it straightaway. _____
3 Spend some time thinking before you **arrive at** a final decision. _____
4 It might be useful to **ask for** suggestions from colleagues. _____
5 **Compare and consider** their opinions before making a final plan. _____
6 These are the types of jobs you can often **give** to others. _____
7 **Stay away from** dealing with those kinds of jobs for a while. _____
8 If you **don't think about** them, they might disappear altogether. _____

7 Read about decision-making at a company called Suma. Complete the article with six of the answers from **6**. Change the form of the verb if necessary.

Suma

Suma is a healthfood wholesaler with a truly **democratic** system of management. At its regular General Meetings, the company [1]_____ any major decisions through a system of **consultation** and **consensus** in which every employee is [2]_____ to speak out and no one's view or opinion is ever [3]_____.

While Suma has a management committee to implement the decisions made at the General Meetings, the company is able to [4]_____ the traditional **confrontation** between managers and workers in **hierarchical** structures. This is partly because all the employees are paid the same wage and have an equal stake in the success of the company.

At a day-to-day level, self-managing teams of employees make a list of tasks and then [5]_____ them in order of importance. Suma also uses a system of multi-skilling so employees learn more than one role within the **cooperative**. This means that different jobs can be [6]_____ more widely and every **member** has the chance to learn more about the company.

8 Match the words in **bold** in the article about Suma to definitions 1–7.

1 a discussion where different opinions are heard _____
2 an argument or open conflict _____
3 a system where decision-making always starts at the top _____
4 when everyone has an equal vote _____
5 an employee in a cooperative _____
6 general agreement between a group of people _____
7 a company which is owned by all the employees and profits are shared

   _____

≫ For more exercises, got to **Practice file 11** on page 126.

9 Work in two groups.
Group A: Make a list of the advantages of decision-making with a cooperative like Suma and the disadvantages in more hierarchical company structures.
Group B: Make a list of the disadvantages of decision-making with a cooperative like Suma and the advantages in more hierarchical company structures.

10 Now each group presents its lists of advantages and disadvantages. Then the whole class can discuss the different views. Try to reach a consensus about the best approach to decision-making.

Language at work | First and second conditionals

1 If you need to make an important decision at work or in your personal life, do you talk to other people first? Which people usually give you good advice?

2 Read this email from Ilse, a business owner, to Jeff, a consultant, and answer the questions.
   - What decision does Ilse have to make?
   - What are her options?
   - What advice do you think Jeff will give her?

Dear Jeff,

I'm writing to you to ask for your expert advice. We've got the opportunity to relocate our computer games shop to a new out-of-town shopping centre. If we move, we'll probably have a larger base of potential (and wealthy) customers.

However, there is a downside. If we don't keep our shop in town, we may lose our current customers who are local students without cars. I don't think they'll travel all the way to the new premises. Obviously, if we had more money, we'd keep the shop in town and open up at the shopping centre too, but that's not a realistic option.

We'd greatly appreciate it if you could advise us on this matter.

Many thanks and best wishes,

Ilse

3 Match sentences a–c from the email to the two types of conditionals in the *Language point*. Use the words in **bold** to help you.

> **LANGUAGE POINT**
>
> a If we **move**, we**'ll** probably **have** a larger base of potential customers.
> b If we **don't keep** our shop in town, we **may lose** our current customers.
> c If we **had** more money, we**'d keep** the shop in town.
>
> 1 First conditional: *if* + present simple, *will/may/might/can* + infinitive
>   We use the first conditional to talk about possible future situations.
>
> 2 Second conditional: *if* + past simple, *would/could* + infinitive
>   We use the second conditional to talk about an imaginary or unreal situation that is improbable or impossible.

» For more information, go to **Grammar reference** on page 127.

Tip | *if not* and *unless*

if + not = unless:

If we **don't keep** this shop, we'll lose most of our current customers.

Unless we **keep** this shop, we'll lose most of our current customers.

4 Underline the correct words in *italics*.

1 If you asked the bank for a loan to keep both shops, they probably *won't / wouldn't* give you it.

2 I might be able to put you in touch with an investor if you*'re / were* interested.

3 If you *want / wanted* to meet me tonight, I can give you some detailed feedback on your idea.

4 I'd even lend you the extra money if I *have / had* it.

5 *If / Unless* your customers have cars, they won't be able to travel to your shop.

6 *Will / Would* you need to move if your online business takes off?

7 What *will / would* you do if there wasn't a new shopping centre?

>> For more exercises, go to **Practice file 11** on page 127.

5 Complete sentences 1–8 with your own words and ideas.
Example: If you ignore unimportant jobs which aren't urgent, they normally disappear.

1 If you ignore unimportant jobs which aren't urgent, they …

2 If you don't trust your instincts sometimes, then …

3 One day, I might start my own business if …

4 Unless a business consults its employees from time to time, it …

5 If managers didn't delegate, they …

6 If managers can't make quick decisions, then they …

7 No group of workers can achieve a consensus if …

8 If my company offered me early retirement, I …

6 Work with a partner. Take turns to read your full sentences in **5**. As you listen, compare your ideas and check your partner used the correct verb form.

7 Work with a partner or in small groups. What will/would you do if …?
• your company is/was relocated to another part of the country or abroad
• your company is/was taken over by its main competitor
• your partner gets/got a new job a long way from home/abroad
• your boss's job becomes/became vacant

Practically speaking | How to use *if*

1 ▶ 11.2 Listen to the four conversations. Answer the questions.
Conversation 1: What is difficult? Does the other person agree?
Conversation 2: What is their deadline to pay? What don't they have?
Conversation 3: What is starting? Where is Walter's appointment?
Conversation 4: How much is the increase in the cost?

2 ▶ 11.2 Match sentences a–d to the conversations in **1**. Then listen again and check.
a **What if** we gave them after-sales support for free? _____
b **If I were you**, I'd take it. _____
c **If you don't mind**, I'd like to leave a bit early today. _____
d **If only** we had more time. _____

3 Look at the words in **bold** in **2**. Which *if*-expression is for …?
giving advice   suggesting   wishing   making a request

4 Work with a partner. Take turns to:
• give your partner advice about his/her job
• suggest a place for the whole class to go to this evening
• wish for something to improve in your working life
• request an extra day off this week

Business communication | Negotiating

1 Have you ever been in any of these situations? Did you have to negotiate with the other people? What happened?
- Agreeing the price of a product or service with a supplier
- Deciding who will pay for a meal out
- Asking your boss for additional time off
- Discussing with family and/or friends which film to see at the cinema

2 ▶ 11.3 Patricia works for a UK manufacturing company which is trying to sell its products in Hungary. She is negotiating with Laszlo, who is a distributor in Hungary. Listen to part of the negotiation and answer the questions.
1 How long does the draft contract last?
2 Why does Laszlo want exclusivity in the region?
3 Why does Patricia want to review the contract every 12 months?
4 Why don't they reach an agreement?

3 ▶ 11.4 Listen to a different version of Patricia and Laszlo's negotiation. Which of these negotiation stages do you hear?
- Introducing the issue
- Explaining your position
- Asking about the other person's position
- Making an offer
- Compromising
- Rejecting an offer
- Accepting an offer

4 ▶ 11.4 Listen again and number the expressions in the correct order 1–8.
___ The concern we have is that …
___ How about if we review the sales targets every 12 months …?
_1_ There's something we need to discuss …
___ If I offer a review after 18 months, will you agree?
___ Yes, I think that would be fair.
___ I'll meet you halfway on this.
___ It's a deal.
___ I'm sorry, but I can't agree to that.

» For more exercises, go to **Practice file 11** on page 126.

5 Work with a partner and practise a negotiation. **Student A** wants to buy Student B's ten-year-old car. **Student B** wants about $2,000 for the car. Afterwards, swap roles and repeat the negotiation.
A Introduce the issue. Explain your position. Ask about B's position.
B Explain your position.
A Make your first offer.
B Reject the offer.
A Make a second offer and ask for something in return.
B Accept the offer.

6 Work with a partner. You are going to negotiate an agreement. **Student A**, turn to **page 141**. **Student B**, turn to **page 139**.

7 After the negotiation, make notes on these questions. Then report back to the class on your answers.
1 Did you reach a final agreement?
2 Was the negotiation successful for both sides?
3 What did you offer each other?
4 What key expressions did you use to help the negotiation?

Key expressions

Introducing the issue
I'd like to discuss an issue with you.
There's something we need to discuss.
We have an issue/problem with ...

Explaining and asking about each other's position
My position is that ...
The problem/concern I have is that ...
What's your position?
Do you have any views/concerns about ...?

Making an offer
Let me make you an offer.
What/How about if I offered you ...?
Imagine/Supposing we ...

Compromising
In return, would you consider ...
If I offer X, will you do Y?
I'll meet you halfway.
I can't accept that, but I can offer you ...
No, but how about if ...

Reject an offer
I'm sorry, but I can't agree to that.
I'm afraid that isn't possible.
I'm not in a position to accept that.

Accept an offer
I think that would be fair.
I can agree to that.
It's a deal.

The Decision Game

Work in small groups. You work at the Central Bank, a British bank with branches in most towns and cities. All of your call centres are based in the UK, in areas of high unemployment. You must make a series of decisions which will affect the future of these call centres. Work together and make your first decision by choosing option **a** or **b**. Start at **1**. Follow the instructions.

1
Senior management want you to cut costs and improve profitability. In India, call centre workers are paid five times less than in the UK. You decide to
a keep the call centres in UK and accept higher costs. **Go to 6.**
b investigate more fully the cost and benefits of moving the call centres. **Go to 2.**

6
Shareholders complain that you are less profitable than rival banks. They are still putting pressure on you to cut costs. You decide to
a please shareholders by closing some less profitable branches. **Go to 9.**
b organize a newspaper campaign explaining to the public why you want to keep the call centre jobs in the UK. **Go to 4.**

11
Your negotiations with the union have reached a crossroads. The union wants to reduce UK job losses to a minimum. You decide to
a keep just 150 UK call centre jobs and risk a strike. **Go to 14.**
b keep 400 UK jobs which will satisfy the union. **Go to 5.**

2
If you close the UK call centres, 1,000 jobs will be lost. You do not want to cause an unnecessary panic because you are still at the investigation stage. You decide to
a be open about your plans. **Go to 8.**
b keep your plans confidential for the moment. **Go to 15.**

7
Customers are even angrier when they receive your letter. They don't care what your motives are. You decide to
a ignore the complaints. **Go to 13.**
b invest more money in staff training. **Go to 3.**

12
Union negotiations have been successful. Both sides have compromised. You have agreed to keep 250 UK jobs. The bank offers you a tough new mission which involves closing other unprofitable branches. You decide to
a accept their tough new mission. **Go to 10.**
b stay where you are, happy that you have survived a difficult moment. **Return to 1 or end here.**

3
The India call centre is now a success and complaints have dropped. However, an Indian worker now costs a third as much as a UK worker and soon will cost half as much. You will now have to look for a cheaper alternative or think of other places where costs might be cheaper. **Return to 1 or end here.**

8
UK call centre employees have heard about your possible plans to go to India. They want full consultation with the union. You decide to
a involve the union and discuss the plans with them. **Go to 11.**
b ignore the union and go ahead with your plans. **Go to 14.**

13
Angry customers contact Head Office and name you as personally responsible for the problems. Senior managers are happy to use you as a scapegoat. You are moved to manage a small branch in the countryside. It is the end of your ambitions. **Return to 1 or end here.**

4
A newspaper has run a campaign praising you as the patriotic bank. This is good for your image, but means that your hands could be tied in the future. **Return to 1 or end here.**

9
Your plan to close smaller branches will cost 500 jobs. This causes protest from the union and from customers who live near the small branches. You decide to
a carry on with the closures. **Go to 10.**
b reconsider other ways of cutting costs, including the call centre option. **Go to 2.**

14
There have been three one-day strikes in selected branches. You decide to
a face up to the union and refuse to change your position. **Go to 13.**
b re-open negotiations with the union. **Go to 12.**

5
Now you have solved the union problems, the call centre is going ahead. However, UK customers say there are often communication problems with the Indian-based call handlers. You decide to
a ask senior management to invest more money in staff training. **Go to 3.**
b send a letter to customers explaining the need to set up in India. **Go to 7.**

10
Going ahead with the branch closures loses the bank several thousand customers and gets a lot of negative publicity. You lose your job! **Return to 1 or end here.**

15
Someone has leaked the story about the India plans to the union. You are attacked in the tabloid press as an exporter of British jobs. You decide to
a deny everything and go ahead with the plans in secret. **Go to 14.**
b open up negotiations with the union. **Go to 11.**

12 Innovation

Starting point

1 When and where do you get your best ideas?

- At work
- After lunch
- In the middle of the night

2 During your lifetime, what have been the most important innovations in ...?

- business
- technology
- transport and travel

Working with words | Innovation

1 Why is it important for businesses to be innovative? How can older companies stay innovative?

2 Read the article and match sub-headings a–c to paragraphs 1–3.
 a The secret of survival ___
 b The early days ___
 c The ongoing challenges ___

The innovations of Cirque du Soleil

1 The internationally famous Cirque du Soleil is famous for its **innovative** performances, which amaze audiences all over the world. It was originally the **brainchild** of a street performer, Guy Laliberté, in 1983. His **concept** was to bring together a group of entertainers and acrobats who would **revolutionize** our traditional view of the 'circus'.

2 Thirty years later, Guy Laliberté is the Chief Executive of a worldwide brand which employs over 4,000 employees working on 20 different shows at any one time. Around 90 million people have seen at least one Cirque du Soleil show,

so nowadays Guy's biggest **obstacle** to maintaining this success is to **come up with** new and **original** ideas which keep audiences coming back.

3 As a result, Cirque du Soleil is always creating new shows in new ways. For example, the music of the Beatles was the **catalyst** for the show *Love*, which has run for over ten years in Las Vegas. And the concept behind *Kà*, another success story, was to use movement from the martial arts. So the real secret of Cirque du Soleil's survival is constant **reinvention** and never standing still.

3 What is the main challenge for Cirque du Soleil? What is its solution? What do you think other types of businesses can learn from its approach?

4 Match the **bold** highlighted words in the article in **2** to definitions 1–9.
1 an idea for something new _____
2 someone's new idea or invention _____
3 new and imaginative way of doing something _____
4 a new idea that is based on something that exists _____
5 to change something completely _____
6 something which causes change _____
7 to think of a new idea or plan _____
8 something which stops you _____
9 unique or the first example of something _____

5 ▶ 12.1 Listen to three conversations. Match conversations 1–3 to topics a–c.
a innovative technology ___
b new business ___
c changing jobs ___

6 ▶ 12.1 Listen again and match these adjectives to conversations 1–3.
traditional _1_   simple ___   revolutionary ___   dynamic ___
reliable ___   original ___   up-to-date ___   sophisticated ___

>> For more exercises, go to **Practice file 12** on page 128.

7 Work with a partner. Discuss these questions and give reasons for your answers.
1 Which of the adjectives in **6** describe your company or job?
2 How would you describe the technology you use in your job or at home?

8 Read these quotes from people talking about ideas and obstacles in their lives. Work in small groups. Think of different ways to help these three people. Then tell the class.

'I have this really simple idea for setting up a cleaning company where we clean local companies and people's houses. The only problem is I have two small children who aren't at school yet. How can I do both?'

'My brainchild is a motorbike that runs on hydrogen, not petrol. I've already built one in my garage, but how can I get the money to manufacture and market it?'

'I've retired with a pension but I'm bored. I have some money but I don't know what to do with it. I don't want to work too hard. What could I do?'

9 Work with a partner. Think of your discussion in **8** and answer these questions.
1 Did you hear any ideas which were …?
• innovative
• original
• simple
• revolutionary
• other
2 Which was the best 'brainchild' you heard?
3 Who was the most useful catalyst in your group?
4 What obstacles did you meet?

Tip | *innovation* and *invention*

An *innovation* is a new idea or way of doing something. An *invention* is a design of something new.

Language at work | Superlative forms

1 The article below is from a press release about an awards ceremony. Does your industry give similar types of awards? How important do you think these kinds of events are?

THE WORLD INVENTION AWARDS

The British Inventors Society is pleased to host one of the most important annual events of the year in the world of invention. Since the earliest award ceremony in 2001, the event recognizes and celebrates the work of the best new innovators we've seen each year. A panel of 25 judges will announce the winners. Platinum and silver awards are given to third and second highest achievers, with gold awards given to the winners in different categories, including the 'Young inventor award'.

2 Read the press release again and answer questions 1–4.
1 Is this the only annual event for invention in the world?
2 When was the first World Invention Award ceremony?
3 Which inventors and innovators are awarded at the event?
4 Who receives a platinum or silver award from the judges?

3 <u>Underline</u> the superlative adjectives in the press release. Which are regular forms? Which one is irregular?

4 Match extracts a–d from the press release to explanations 1–4 of superlative forms in the *Language point*. Use the words in **bold** to help you.

> **LANGUAGE POINT**
>
> a … **one of the most important** annual events of the year.
> b … silver awards are given to **third and second highest** achievers.
> c … **the best** new innovators **we've seen** each year.
> d Since **the earliest** award ceremony in 2001 …
>
> 1 to describe an extreme value (maximum or minimum) in a range ___
> 2 to place something in a position after first place ___
> 3 to say something is important but not the only important one ___
> 4 before the present perfect to describe our experience of something ___

» For more information, go to **Grammar reference** on page 129.

5 Work with a partner. Say these sentences in a different way, using a superlative form.
1 There are many important conferences this month. This is one of them.
   This is one …
2 I've never seen profits as high as this.
   These are the …
3 The XP50 is our bestselling product, but the new XP55 now sells nearly as well.
   The XP55 is now our …
4 In the last century, I don't think any other invention has had as much impact as the microchip.
   In the last century, I think the microchip …

» For more exercises, go to **Practice file 12** on page 129.

6 Make sentences about your business with these phrases. Tell your partner and explain your answers.

1 ... is one of our bestselling products/services.
2 ... is the most popular we've ever sold.
3 ... was the year with our highest turnover.
4 ... was our second most-profitable year.
5 ... was the company's least successful innovation.

7 Work with a partner. Using the words in the table below, take turns to ask and answer questions. You will need to use the superlative form of the adjectives.

> *Example: A What's **the worst** decision you've ever made?*
> *B Leaving my first company.*
> *A So what's **the second worst** decision you've ever made?*
> *B Joining this one!*

What's/Who's the (second/third)	bad	country/place		met?
	good	film		made?
	big	decision		had?
	nice	person	you've ever	seen?
	beautiful	hotel		stayed at?
	friendly	idea		visited?
	exciting	experience		heard?

Practically speaking | How to praise and thank people

1 How important is it to tell someone they're doing a good job and to thank them for their hard work? How often should we praise and thank them?

2 ▶ 12.2 Listen to three people praising and thanking other people. Match each conversation 1–3 to situations a–c.

a At the end of a long project ___
b A leaving event for a member of staff ___
c A manager working with a new employee ___

3 ▶ 12.2 Listen again to these expressions from the conversations. Decide if you would normally use them formally (*F*) or informally (*I*).

1 You've done an excellent job. _F_
2 Good job! _I_
3 On behalf of everyone here, I'd like to thank you for all your hard work. ___
4 Thanks for all your hard work on this. ___
5 Well done. ___
6 Everyone appreciates you both as a colleague and also as a friend. ___
7 I'm very impressed by the results. ___
8 You're doing really well. ___
9 Your work is always of the highest quality. ___
10 Keep at it! ___

4 Write down three jobs you have completed recently. Work with a partner. Take turns to tell each other about what you've done, and then praise and thank your partner. Decide how formal or informal the situation is.

> *Example: A I've just come to the end of managing a huge project.*
> *B Well, on behalf of everyone, I'd like to thank you ...*
> *OR*
> *B Good job! Well done.*

81

Business communication | Presenting new ideas

1 Read this company mission statement. Do you have something similar for your company? Do you think company mission statements are useful? Why/Why not?

> **Bertran RL** aims to create innovative and state-of-the-art conferencing technology products of the highest value, with the greatest reliability and simplicity we can offer. We achieve this with employees who deserve the very best in professional support and development.

2 ▶12.3 A team of people at Bertran RL are meeting to discuss the company's mission statement. Listen to the team leader presenting the idea behind the meeting. What are the presenter's two aims?
A To present a new mission statement to the team.
B To explain the background to the meeting.
C To encourage the team to come up with new ideas.

3 ▶12.3 Number the expressions from the team leader's introduction in the correct order 1–8. Then listen again and check.
___ First, I'm going to talk …
_1_ Good morning, everyone, and thanks for coming.
___ We have a lot to do, so let's start.
_8_ Feel free to ask questions …
___ I'd like to begin by explaining …
___ The main reason for this meeting is to …
___ so finally we'll …
___ Then, we'll try to …

4 ▶12.4 Listen to the next part of the presentation and look at the slide. What do the coloured words on the slide represent?

> ## sophisticated, up-to-date, innovative
>
> ### simple, traditional, reliable

5 ▶12.4 Listen again and complete expressions 1–3 for referring to visuals.
1 First of all, let's _____ this slide.
2 As you _____, it has a number of words that describe our company.
3 _____ some words are in blue and some are in red.

6 ▶12.5 Listen to the final part of the team leader's presentation. What expressions does the presenter use to signal the end of the presentation? How does the presenter check if everyone has understood?

>> For more exercises, go to **Practice file 12** on page 128.

7 You are going to give a two-minute presentation about how your customers view your company, service or product. First of all, design a slide with adjectives that you think your customers use, similar to the slide in **4**.

8 Work in small groups. Take turns to present your slide. Remember to:
- introduce your presentation
- present the slide and explain the reasons for each adjective
- end your presentation and invite questions

Key expressions

Starting
Good morning and thanks for coming.
I'm here today to …
Let's start.
My name's … and I'm going to tell you about …
I'd like to begin by (+ verb + -ing)

Previewing
First, I'll …
Then, we'll …
And finally …
Feel free to ask questions.
I'll take questions at the end.

Adding emphasis
The main reason for this is …
The best thing about this is …
We think it's a good idea because …

Referring to visuals
Let's look at this …
As you can see, …
You'll notice that …

Closing
That's everything I want to say.
That brings me to the end of my presentation.
Thanks for listening.
Are there any (more) questions?

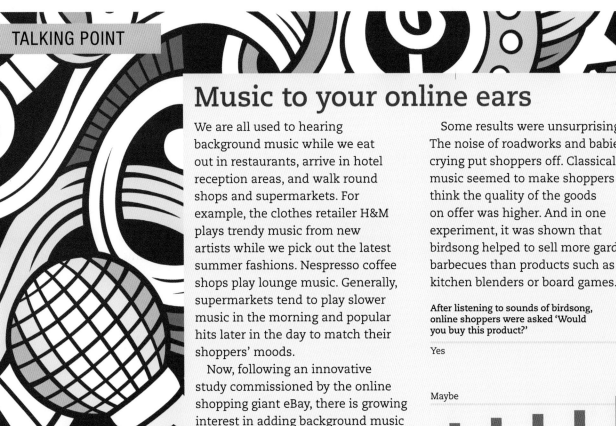

TALKING POINT

Music to your online ears

We are all used to hearing background music while we eat out in restaurants, arrive in hotel reception areas, and walk round shops and supermarkets. For example, the clothes retailer H&M plays trendy music from new artists while we pick out the latest summer fashions. Nespresso coffee shops play lounge music. Generally, supermarkets tend to play slower music in the morning and popular hits later in the day to match their shoppers' moods.

Now, following an innovative study commissioned by the online shopping giant eBay, there is growing interest in adding background music to retail websites. In the study, around 1,900 participants were asked to simulate online shopping while listening to different types of sounds.

Some results were unsurprising. The noise of roadworks and babies crying put shoppers off. Classical music seemed to make shoppers think the quality of the goods on offer was higher. And in one experiment, it was shown that birdsong helped to sell more garden barbecues than products such as kitchen blenders or board games.

After listening to sounds of birdsong, online shoppers were asked 'Would you buy this product?'

Yes

Maybe

No

Board game   Wine   Blender   Trainer   Barbecue

Discussion

1 Are you surprised by any of the results in the study?

2 When you go out, how much do you notice background music or sounds in places like restaurants or shops? Does it affect how you feel?

3 Do you think adding background sounds or music to websites is a good idea? If you answer 'yes', what types of music would you like to hear?

Task

1  12.6 Listen to six different types of music and match them to the words below.
   Bollywood   classical   jazz   opera   pop   rock

2 ▶ 12.6 Work in groups. Listen again and decide what kind of product or service you would associate it with.

3 Work in groups. Discuss each situation below and decide what type of music or sound you would recommend.

   • An insurance company wants music for customers to listen to on the phone when they are on hold.

   • A hotel restaurant specializing in different international dishes needs background music throughout the day and night.

   • A motorway service station would like to play background music or sounds.

   • Your own companies would like to add music or sounds to their websites.

4 Afterwards, present your ideas to the rest of the class and compare.

Focus

1 ▶01 Watch five people talking about transport problems in their city. Make notes about their answers in the table.

	What kind of transport problems does their city have?	Do they have a solution?
Speaker 1		
Speaker 2		
Speaker 3		
Speaker 4		
Speaker 5		

2 Work with a partner. Take turns to ask and answer the two questions in **1**.

A transport innovation

3 Look at the picture of a canal. Do you have any canals in your country? What other types of water transportation are used in your country?

4 You are going to watch two videos about transport and innovation. Before you watch, match words and phrases 1–7 from the video to definitions a–g.
1 internal combustion ___
2 Industrial Revolution ___
3 network ___
4 restore ___
5 lock ___
6 loch ___
7 waterway ___

a period in history when machines changed the way people lived, worked and travelled
b return something to its earlier good condition
c when energy is produced by burning fuel (inside an engine)
d large system connected together which allows movement or communication
e an area of water that boats can travel along, e.g. river or canal
f Scottish word meaning 'lake'
g two gates on a canal which allow boats to move between different heights of water

5 ▶02 Watch a short video about the history of the canals in the UK. As you watch, number the scenes from the video A–G in the order you first see them 1–7.

A A series of locks on a canal ___
B Tourists on a canal ___
C Motorway traffic ___
D Old canals and buildings ___
E A high-speed train ___
F A steam train ___
G Shipping containers ___

6 ▶02 Watch the video again and answer questions 1–6.

   1 Why were a lot of canals built in Britain in the eighteenth and nineteenth century? _____

   2 How many kilometres of waterways linked the industrial cities of the UK? _____

   3 What does the narrator describe as one of the greatest innovations of the Industrial Revolution? _____

   4 What was the main obstacle for the engineers when they were building the canals? _____

   5 What other type of transport caused canals to stop being used? _____

   6 What type of industry is using the canals again? _____

7 What other examples can you think of where something from the past is reused in the present for a different reason? (e.g. old buildings in your city) Has your business ever taken an old product or service and reused it in a new and different way?

The Falkirk Wheel

8 ▶03 Watch a video about an engineering innovation called the Falkirk Wheel. Choose the correct ending to these sentences.

   1 There used to be a series of 11 locks ___
     a in the city of Edinburgh.
     b in the city of Glasgow.
     c near the town of Falkirk.

   2 The Falkirk Wheel is designed to ___
     a lift boats up and down the canal.
     b turn the boats around in the water.
     c make water go through the canal.

   3 The narrator thinks the Falkirk Wheel is a good example of how ___
     a to use alternative energy in the future.
     b to take an old idea and improve it.
     c to attract tourists to a region.

9 ▶03 Watch the video again and make notes about these numbers and years. What do they refer to?

   1 eleven   *There used to be a series of eleven locks on the canal.*
   2 1933   _____
   3 1994   _____
   4 35 metres   _____
   5 1,200 tonnes   _____
   6 £17 million   _____
   7 2002   _____
   8 two   _____
   9 four   _____

A tour of the Falkirk Wheel

10 Work with a partner. Your teacher is going to play the Falkirk Wheel video again with the sound off. As you watch, practise a conversation between a tour guide and a tourist.

  Student A: You are a tour guide at the Falkirk Wheel. As you watch, explain to the tourist what the wheel is for, how it was built, and how it works.

  Student B: You are a tourist at the Falkirk Wheel. As you watch, ask your tour guide some questions about what the wheel is for, how it was built, and how it works.

11 Swap roles and repeat **10**.

13 Breakdowns

Starting point

1 How do you feel about companies that sell goods and services that are not 100% perfect?

2 What types of products would you buy at a discounted price if they had a defect? Why?

Working with words | Breakdowns and faults

1 What kinds of breakdowns can you think of? Have you had any breakdowns or faults at work recently?

2 Read parts of four news stories about different kinds of breakdowns and faults. Make notes in the table.

	What type of breakdown or fault?	Who did it affect?	Have they solved the problem?
1	Software / IT		
2		Car owners	
3			No, not yet
4			

1

A software problem at the local hospital caused all the computers to go down for 24 hours yesterday. As a result of the system failure, doctors and nurses couldn't access patients' medical records. A spokesperson said late last night that the problem had now been resolved and there was no danger to patients' health.

2

Because of a defect in the gearbox in the car, the manufacturer has asked thousands of owners to take their car in for free safety checks. The fault with the oil in the gearbox can lead to a loss of power, but this doesn't cause any long-term damage to the vehicle itself.

3

Complaints from eight shoppers has resulted in a recall of about 6.5 million packs of macaroni and cheese. Customers found metal bits in some boxes. The manufacturer has been unable to find the cause, but there have been no reported injuries and shops will refund the cost of the packs.

4

One Australian company has stopped staff writing emails in the workplace due to misunderstandings in internal communications. The CEO only allows emails with clients. Instead, staff only use instant messaging with each other because it's faster, more personal and avoids mistakes.

3 Find these pairs of words in the news stories and match them to the correct definition, a or b.

1 go down / failure
   a when something stops working
   b when a computer system stops working

2 fault / defect
   a a problem which stops something working
   b a problem which stops something working as well as it should

3 damage / injury
   a harm to something or somebody
   b physical harm to somebody

4 complaint / resolve
   a when a problem is dealt with and fixed
   b when someone says there is a problem with something

5 refund / recall
   a when a company gives customers their money back
   b when a company asks customers to bring a product back

6 misunderstanding / mistake
   a when you understand something in a different way from what is meant
   b when you do something the wrong way

4 Work in small groups. Use different forms of the words from **3** to discuss the various problems you might have with these things:
- buying electrical or electronic products abroad
- two teams from different countries working together
- working with new machinery in a factory
- buying a second-hand tablet
- buying things online

   Example: If you buy a product abroad and it is defective, it is very difficult to get it fixed or refunded.

5 Read two sentences from the first news story and answer questions 1–4.
A software problem at the local hospital <u>caused</u> all the computers to go down for 24 hours yesterday. <u>As a result of</u> the system failure, doctors and nurses couldn't access patients' medical records.

1 Look at the <u>underlined</u> words. Which is a verb and which is a connector?
2 In the first sentence, what is the cause and what is the result?
3 In the second sentence, what is the cause and what is the result?
4 Now read the three other articles again. <u>Underline</u> any verbs or connectors for talking about causes and results.

6 Work with a partner. Match causes 1–4 to results a–d. Then make different sentences using verbs or connectors.
   Example: A broken metal part caused damage to the engine. / As a result of a broken metal part, there was damage to the engine.

1 A broken metal part ___
2 No training with the new cutting equipment ___
3 New software ___
4 Poor language skills ___

a An injury to an employee's hand
b Misunderstandings between office branches
c Damage to the engine
d Systems failure with the database

» For more exercises, go to **Practice file 13** on page 130.

7 List three recent breakdowns, faults or problems at your place of work. What was the cause? What was the result? Tell your partner about them.

Language at work | Relative pronouns

1 What can you see in the four pictures? What do you think might be the connection between them?

 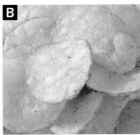  

2 ▶ 13.1 Listen to part of a radio programme about the topic of making mistakes in business. Which two things in the pictures does the presenter talk about?

3 ▶ 13.1 Listen again and complete sentences 1–6 with the relative pronouns from the list.

which   when   that   whose   where   who

1 These are the colourful notes _____ are stuck to office desks and walls all over the world.
2 He was a researcher _____ worked for 3M …
3 One day, he made an adhesive _____ wouldn't stick properly.
4 He's the scientist _____ discovery has saved millions of lives.
5 It was a September morning in 1928 _____ Fleming accidentally discovered penicillin.
6 He had just returned from holiday to the hospital _____ he worked.

4 Complete the *Language point* explanations with the relative pronouns from **3**.

> ### LANGUAGE POINT
>
> We use a relative pronoun at the beginning of a defining relative clause.
> We use _____ or *that* for things.*
> We use _____ or *that* for people.*
> We use _____ for people's possessions.
> We use _____ for time.
> We use _____ for place.
>
> *We can use *that* instead of *which* or *who* before a defining relative clause with no change in meaning: *He was a researcher who worked for 3M. = He was a researcher that worked for 3M.*

⟩⟩ For more information, go to **Grammar reference** on page 131.

5 Work with a partner. Complete the history of two more products created by accident. Join each of the sentences using one of the relative pronouns from the list.

~~which~~   where   who   when   whose   that

1 • It was an accident. It helped to create the first inkjet printer.
   It was an accident **which** *helped to create the first inkjet printer.*
 • It was accidentally discovered by an engineer. He worked for Canon.
 • One day, his pen fired ink out. He rested a hot iron on it by accident.

2 • The Carey Moon Lake House was a restaurant. George Crum worked as a chef.
 • One day, Crum had a complaining customer. His potatoes were 'too soft and thick'.
 • In the end, Crum made extremely thin, hard potatoes. They eventually became famous as 'crisps'.

Tip | Defining relative clause

A <u>defining relative clause</u> gives essential information about the person, object, place, time or possession in the main clause: *He's the man <u>who invented Post-it notes</u>.*

6 Complete these sentences so they are true for you and your work.
1 A successful product is something … *which* *is easy to use.*_____
2 A good manager is someone … _____
3 One of the busiest times of my day is … _____
4 We're a company whose customers are … _____
5 Our main office is a place … _____

» For more exercises, go to **Practice file 13** on page 131.

7 Work with a partner and play this guessing game. Take turns to think of an object, person, place or time. Without saying the word, define it for your partner using these phrases:
It's something which …   It's someone who …
It's a place where …   It's a time when …

Your partner must guess the word.
> **Example:** **A** *It's something which you can stick on the wall and write on.*
> **B** *Can you buy it in different colours?*
> **A** *Yes.*
> **B** *Is it a Post-it note?*
> **A** *Yes. Correct!*

Practically speaking | How to check someone understands

1 ▶ 13.2 Listen to four conversations. Which conversation (1–4) is about a problem or difficulty with …?
A software ___3___
B team members ___1___
C a colleague ___4___
D holiday request ___2___

2 ▶ 13.2 Listen again and match 1–4 to a–d.
1 Do you know   a make sense?
2 Does that   b clear?
3 Is that   c see?
4 Do you   d what I mean?

3 ▶ 13.2 Listen again. Does the listener understand what the first person is saying?

4 Which responses show the person understands (*U*), doesn't understand (*DU*) or partly understands (*PU*)?
1 Absolutely. ___
2 Kind of, but … ___
3 I don't get … ___
4 I see what you mean … ___

5 Work with a partner. Take turns to explain the following to your partner and check that they understand.
1 Why it is important to get on with your colleagues.
2 What you want to change about your working conditions and why.
3 How to make an important piece of office equipment work.
4 How to book time off from work.

Business communication | Discussing and solving problems

1 What kinds of problems do you have with office equipment or computers? How good are you at fixing them yourself?

2 ▶ 13.3 Listen to two conversations and complete the table.

Problem	Diagnosis	Solution
1		
2		

3 ▶ 13.3 Listen again and number the sentences in each conversation in the order you hear them 1–8.

Conversation 1

_1_ What's the matter?
___ Have you tried talking to her?
___ What do you mean by 'extra work'?
___ That should sort it out temporarily.
___ My boss keeps on giving me extra work.
___ I'd ask to speak to her if I were you.
___ I think you should ask for an extension.
___ It looks like you've got a communication problem to me.

Conversation 2

_1_ How can I help?
___ That should fix it.
___ It keeps on going wrong all the time.
___ It's always crashing and it won't remember the time or date.
___ What's wrong with it exactly?
___ It sounds as though it could be a battery problem.
___ The best thing would be to buy a new battery.
___ When you say 'it's always crashing', do you mean it stops working or it switches off?

>> For more exercises, go to **Practice file 13** on page 130.

4 Work with a partner. Discuss the two problems below using the flow chart.
  1 Your team members often have meetings without you, so you don't know what is happening with the project.
  2 You have received 15 complaints in the last week about one of your products not working. It is a piece of software that doesn't work on some systems.

| **A** Ask about the problem. |
| **B** Explain the problem. |
| **A** Ask for more details. |
| **B** Respond. |
| **A** Make a diagnosis. |
| **B** Respond. |
| **A** Suggest action. |
| **B** Respond and thank A. |

5 Work in groups and try to speak for at least a minute on these subjects. Then listen to the others in your group. Ask for more details and offer a solution.
  • A problem with a piece of office equipment
  • A communication breakdown at work
  • An unreliable or untrustworthy colleague

Key expressions

Asking what the problem is
What's the matter?
How can I help?
So what appears to be the trouble?

Explaining the problem
It keeps on (+ verb + -ing)
It's always (+ verb + -ing)
It won't (+ verb)
It means that ...

Asking for details
What's wrong with it exactly?
What do you mean by ...?
What sort of noise/smell is it?
When you say ..., do you mean ...?

Diagnosing the problem
It looks/sounds like ...
It looks/sounds as though ...
It could be ...
It might be ...

Advising
The best thing would be to ...
I'd advise you to ...
I think you should/could
If I were you, I'd ...
Have you tried (+ noun / + verb + -ing)?

Confirming a solution
There we are – that should fix it.
That should sort it out.
That should solve the problem.

A breakdown in public relations

On 20 April, 2010, a fault on the Deepwater Horizon oil rig resulted in the largest oil spill in history. For 87 days, oil poured out into the Gulf of Mexico. It caused terrible damage to the coastlines of five US states and to the lives of the people who lived there. As well as being one of the world's worst environmental disasters which led to the deaths of thousands of sea birds, BP was also criticized for its poor public relations. Famously, Tony Hayward, BP's CEO at the time, went on US TV and said, 'It wasn't our accident'. In the end, BP paid $18.7 billion in compensation and Tony Hayward was forced to resign.

So what can other companies learn from BP's mistakes?

- Admit the fault as quickly as possible: You don't want journalists to speculate about what happened, so explain the situation as quickly as possible.

- Be open and honest: Don't try to hide anything or lie. Tell the whole story before someone else tells it for you.

- Action speaks louder than words: Pay people back if they have lost money because of your mistakes and sack anyone responsible if necessary.

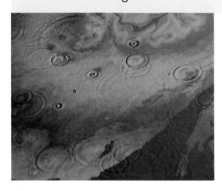

Discussion

1 Do you remember the Deepwater Horizon disaster or any similar disasters? How was it reported in your country?

2 People in business sometimes say that 'There's no such thing as bad publicity'. How true do you think this is?

3 Has your company ever had negative publicity? Did you need to follow the three pieces of PR advice in the article?

Task

1 Work in groups and read three different public relations situations. For each one, discuss how you would deal with the situation.

- Ex-employees of a well-known large multinational have started complaining about the company's working conditions via social media. They have said there is a company culture of long hours with no breaks and low pay. Now, a national newspaper is reporting the ex-employees' views and wants the company to respond. What should the company do?

- A well-known politician is on the board of a large company. Today, a newspaper has reported that the company owes over a million dollars in tax. The politician's picture is printed with the article, even though he is not directly responsible. The politician's party is worried about the connection. What should the party do?

- Accidentally, an online business has just emailed a list of over 500 customer names and credit card details to all its clients. Within minutes, customers have been calling to complain. The news has not reached journalists yet. What should the company do?

2 Present your group's PR advice for each situation to the rest of the class. Compare your ideas with the other groups.

14 Processes

Starting point

1 Work with a partner. Brainstorm the stages for the following processes.
- Applying for a job
- Moving your office
- Buying a house

2 Compare your stages with another group. Who has the most stages? Are they all necessary?

Working with words | Processes

1 How much waste does your company recycle? Does it have any systems for recycling waste?

   Example: paper recycling bins in your offices

2 ▶ 14.1 Listen to a description of a recycling business called TerraCycle®. Write the missing information in the company profile.

TERRACYCLE®

select your waste ➡ collect and send ➡ solve and benefit

Chief Executive: Tom Szaky

Year founded: [1]_____

Number of countries: [2]_____

Turnover: [3]_____

TerraCycle collects and processes [4]_____. Then it sells the materials to manufacturers or it makes its own new [5]_____. It has contracts with large companies such as [6]_____ and it also receives rubbish from individual consumers via drop-off points. In return for the rubbish, TerraCycle will [7]_____.

3 Are there similar companies in your country which collect waste for recycling? How do they collect the waste? Where is it recycled?

4 ▶ 14.1 Replace the words in **bold** with the multi-word verbs from the list. Change the form of the verb if necessary. Then listen and check.

drop off   pick out   pick up   set up   make out of   sign up   cut down on   turn into   take away   throw away

1 Tom Szaky is always looking for ways to **reduce** waste and help the planet. _____

2 TerraCycle specializes in finding waste and **transforming** it **into** something useful. _____

3 Tom **started** the company in 2002 in a basement. _____

4 TerraCylce will **collect** waste from special collection points. _____

5 The waste can include anything that people **discard** such as cigarette stubs, coffee capsules or biscuit wrappers. _____

6 It will **select** a type of rubbish and try to **create** something new **from** it. _____, _____

7 Large businesses such as Kenco pay TerraCyle to **remove** its waste. _____

8 Individual consumers can **deliver and leave** rubbish at collection points. _____

9 Any local business can **register** to become a drop-off point. _____

5 Individual people can also recycle their items with TerraCycle. Work with a partner and describe the process below using the multi-word verbs in **4**.

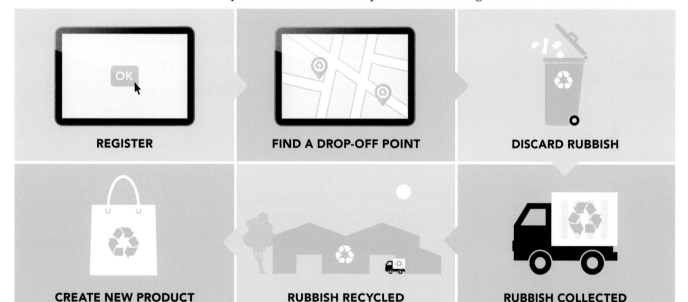

REGISTER   **FIND A DROP-OFF POINT**   **DISCARD RUBBISH**

CREATE NEW PRODUCT   **RUBBISH RECYCLED**   **RUBBISH COLLECTED**

>> For more exercises, go to **Practice file 14** on page 132.

6 Discuss these questions with your partner.
1 What types of objects are thrown away every day at your place of work?
2 What type of rubbish is picked up and taken away for recycling?
3 Do you think your company could cut down even more on unrecycled rubbish?
4 Is it possible to set up drop-off points around the company for certain types of rubbish? Do you think people would use them? Why/Why not?

7 Work with another pair of students. Imagine your team has to improve recycling around your company. Discuss some different ways to do this and list the actions you need to take.

> ***Example:*** *We could set up a system of paper recycling in the office with special bins.*

8 Present your action plan in **7** to the rest of the class.

Language at work | Passive forms

1 Work with a partner.
- Brainstorm different types of fuel and energy and write them down.
- Try to categorize them in different ways; for example, liquids, for cars, renewables, under the ground, etc.
- How many different categories did you come up with?

2 Read the article below. What uses of cooking oil and fat does it describe? How common is the use of biodiesel in your country?

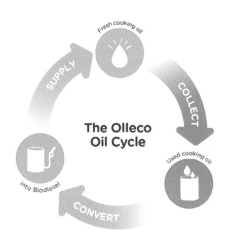

The Olleco Oil Cycle

SUPPLY · COLLECT · CONVERT · into Biodiesel

Fresh cooking oil · Used cooking oil

Food making us go faster

The basic idea of reusing cooking oil and fat is nothing new. It was turned into heating and candles by the ancient Chinese and Egyptians. Soap and cosmetics were made by Britain's Victorians, using the by-products of oil and fat. And nowadays, the oil and fat which is used to fry your food can be turned into biodiesel.

Olleco is a UK-based company which specializes in recycling used oil from a network of food businesses. The process works like this:

The client, such as a restaurant owner, is given a container to store any used oil after cooking. Later, after the oil has been collected by Olleco, it is taken to be reprocessed into biodiesel; in other words, some of the trucks you see on the road are being driven with the oil your French fries were cooked in.

3 Read these sentences with the verb in the active form. Find the same information in the text and the passive form of the verbs in **bold**.
1 The ancient Chinese and Egyptians turned oil and fat into heating and candles.
   _____*was turned*_____
2 Chefs **use** oil and fat to fry your food. _____
3 Companies **can turn** oil and fat **into** biodiesel. _____
4 After Olleco **has collected** the oil … _____
5 Olleco takes the oil **to reprocess** it into biodiesel. _____
6 Drivers **are driving** some of the trucks you see on the road with the oil …
   _____

4 Match the passive form of the verbs in **3** to these tenses and forms.

Present simple ___   Past simple _1_   Present continuous ___
Present perfect ___   Infinitive ___   Modal ___

Now, find more passive verbs in the text and match them to the tenses and forms above.

5 Compare the two sentences in the *Language point*. Then write *passive* or *active* in the explanations.

LANGUAGE POINT

Active: *Olleco turns the oil into biodiesel.*
Passive: *The oil is turned into biodiesel.*
We form the [1] _passive_ with be + past participle.
We use the [2] _____ to focus on the person or company responsible for the action.
We use the [3] _____ to focus on the result of the action.
We often use the [4] _____ to talk about a process or how something is done.

≫ For more information, go to **Grammar reference** on page 133.

6 Read about a type of biofuel. <u>Underline</u> the correct verb forms in *italics*.

Biofuels ¹*produce* / *are produced* from different types of plants such as corn. Over recent years, many companies ²*have tried* / *have been tried* to manufacture biofuel as a profitable alternative to non-renewable fuels. However, lots of land and water ³*need* / *is needed* to grow a plant like corn, making it expensive and potentially bad for the environment.

Unlike corn, the South American jatropha plant ⁴*can grow* / *can be grown* by farmers on poor land with much less water. The seeds of the jatropha ⁵*contain* / *are contained* high levels of non-edible oil and it ⁶*originally used* / *was originally used* in medicines and also oil lamps. Nowadays, the jatropha seeds are grown ⁷*to process* / *to be processed* into biofuel.

So far, jatropha biofuel hasn't had much commercial success but more and more research into using the plant as biofuels ⁸*is carrying out* / *is being carried out* by companies like SG Biofuels. The results are positive and it's highly likely that oil from the jatropha plant ⁹*will use* / *will be used* in the diesel engines of the future.

» For more exercises, go to **Practice file 14** on page 133.

7 Complete these sentences about your company's product or services, using the information in brackets. Tell your partner.
1 My company was set up in … (year)
2 Our product/service is used for … (purpose)
3 Our products/services have been sold to … (types of customers)
4 It's important to be known in different markets including … (markets)
5 Currently, a new product/service is being developed in order to … (reason)
6 In the future, we hope our products/services will be used by/for …

Practically speaking | How to explain a process

1 Work with a partner. Look at the set of pictures A–F on the left showing the process of turning jatropha plants into biofuel. Discuss which part of the process each picture shows.

2 ▶ 14.2 Listen to an explanation of the process and check your ideas in **1**.

3 ▶ 14.2 Listen again and number these expressions in the correct order 1–8.
<u>1</u> Let me explain how we …
___ First of all, …
___ Essentially, there are … main stages.
___ After the … have been …, they are …
___ Having taken …, you're …
___ The basic process is …
___ What you end up with is …
<u>8</u> It's also worth noting that …

4 Work with a partner. Take turns to explain the jatropha biofuel process using the pictures in **1** and the expressions in **3**.

5 Explain a process you are familiar with to your partner. For example:
• a production process in your factory
• procedures with all customer enquiries
• claiming expenses after a business trip

A
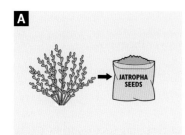

B

C
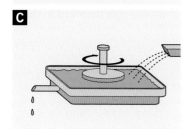

D
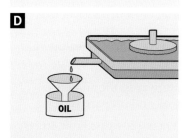

E
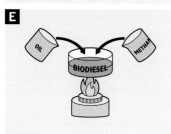

F

Business communication | Dealing with questions

1 If someone is injured in your workplace, is there a formal procedure that you must follow? Who do you report the injury to? Is any kind of report or form filled in?

2 ▶ 14.3 Listen to three parts of a presentation about a new procedure for reporting injuries at work. Answer the questions.
1 How quickly should the injury report form be filled in?
2 Who is responsible for dealing with workplace injuries?
3 Which types of injuries must be reported?

3 ▶ 14.3 Listen to the three parts again. Tick (✓) the expressions you hear.

Does anyone have any questions? ☐
If anyone has any questions, I'm happy to try and answer them now. ☐
That's a good question. ☐
That's an interesting point. ☐
I think there are two parts to that question. ☐
First of all … And for your second point … ☐
Sorry, I couldn't hear you. Can you repeat that? ☐
Sorry, I don't quite understand the question. ☐
Let me check I've understood you correctly. ☐
You're asking me if …? ☐
Have I answered your question? ☐
Does that answer your question? ☐

>> For more exercises, go to **Practice file 14** on page 132.

4 Work with a partner. Discuss these situations. How would you respond to the questions in each situation?
1 Someone on the phone asks you a question but it's a poor connection. You can't hear them properly.
2 In a job interview, the interviewer asks you a complicated question and you aren't sure if you understood it correctly.
3 In a meeting someone asks you a question which you can answer. You are very pleased they asked the question.
4 You have answered someone's question in a presentation but they still look confused.
5 At a press launch, a journalist asks a question about two different features of the new product.

5 You are going to give a 60-second presentation. Afterwards, the audience will ask you questions. Choose a topic you know well and prepare your presentation. It could be about:
• your company and its products
• a process you follow at work (or repeat the presentation in *Practically speaking exercise 5, page 95*)
• a hobby or interest you have outside of your work

6 Work in groups. Take turns to give your 60-second presentations. Afterwards, everyone in the group should ask at least one question about the topic. The presenter should:
• invite questions
• check understanding
• comment on the question
• structure the answer
• check he/she has answered the question satisfactorily

Key expressions

Inviting questions
Are there any questions?
Does anyone have any questions?
If anyone has any questions, I'm happy to try and answer them now.

Checking understanding
Sorry, I couldn't hear you. Can you repeat that?
Sorry, I don't quite understand the question.
Let me check I've understood you correctly.
You're asking me if …?

Commenting on the question
Thank you for that question.
That's a good / a great / an important question.
That's an interesting point.

Structuring your answer
I think there are two parts to your question.
I'll answer your first point and then deal with your second.
First of all, … and for your second point …

Checking you answered the question satisfactorily
Does that answer your question?
Have I answered your question?

TALKING POINT

Lean Coffee™

Lean Management is the approach of making small but regular changes to a business's processes to improve efficiency. The idea behind a *Lean Coffee* meeting is similar because the aim is to make meetings more efficient. The first *Lean Coffee* meeting took place in a coffee shop in Seattle in 2009, and nowadays there are *Lean Coffee* groups which meet in coffee shops in over 70 cities around the world (see www.leancoffee.org). But you don't need a coffee shop to run a *Lean Coffee* meeting. Try following the process below for your next meeting at work.

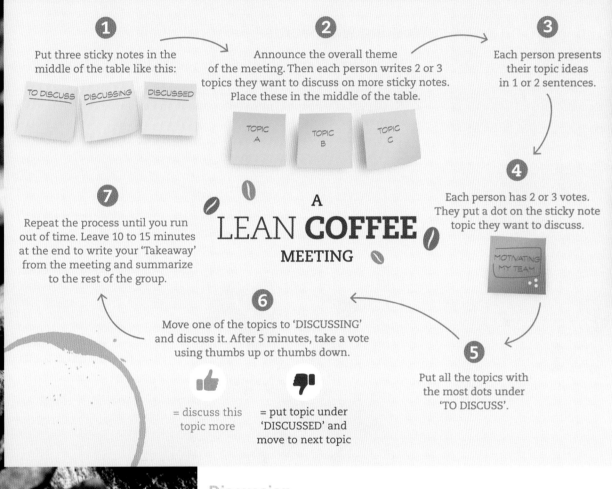

1 Put three sticky notes in the middle of the table like this:

TO DISCUSS — DISCUSSING — DISCUSSED

2 Announce the overall theme of the meeting. Then each person writes 2 or 3 topics they want to discuss on more sticky notes. Place these in the middle of the table.

TOPIC A — TOPIC B — TOPIC C

3 Each person presents their topic ideas in 1 or 2 sentences.

4 Each person has 2 or 3 votes. They put a dot on the sticky note topic they want to discuss.

MOTIVATING MY TEAM

5 Put all the topics with the most dots under 'TO DISCUSS'.

6 Move one of the topics to 'DISCUSSING' and discuss it. After 5 minutes, take a vote using thumbs up or thumbs down.

👍 = discuss this topic more

👎 = put topic under 'DISCUSSED' and move to next topic

7 Repeat the process until you run out of time. Leave 10 to 15 minutes at the end to write your 'Takeaway' from the meeting and summarize to the rest of the group.

A LEAN COFFEE MEETING

Discussion

1 How efficient do you think your discussions are at work? How could you improve them?

2 Why do you think Lean Coffee meetings have become so popular?

3 How effective do you think Lean Coffee meetings would be at your workplace? Which types of meetings would they work for? Why?

Task

1 Work in groups of around four or five and hold a Lean Coffee meeting. Sit together round a table and use sticky notes (or pieces of paper). The theme of the meeting is to discuss things you would like to improve in your workplace. Follow the instructions for a Lean Coffee meeting (above).

2 Afterwards, discuss the Lean Coffee meeting. Was the process easy to follow? Was it an effective way of running a meeting? Why/Why not?

15 Performance

Starting point

1 How do you assess your performance at work? What about activities outside of work such as sports, education, language classes, parenting?

2 How do you measure success in life? Which things on this list are important? What else would you add?
- money and wealth
- family
- good health
- job and career
- love and relationships
- qualifications
- busy social life

Working with words | Personal qualities

1 What kinds of personal qualities do you think people who work in hospitals need, such as doctors or nurses?

2 Read part of a hospital newsletter about an employee recognition scheme and answer questions 1–2.
1 How does Howard Lawrence feel about the success of the scheme?
2 Who recommends or nominates employees for the award?

EMPLOYEE OF THE MONTH
at Elmgrove Park Hospital

The employee of the month scheme, which recognizes the work of individual staff, has been very successful. Howard Lawrence, Associate Director of the hospital trust, is not surprised by this. 'At Elmgrove Park Hospital our staff is well known for its **dedication**. Everyone who works here is highly **motivated** to ensure that each patient is relaxed and comfortable during their stay,' he says.

Nominations can be submitted either by members of staff or by patients. Since the scheme was launched two years ago, the winners have included:

James Briggs, ward assistant: James was nominated for showing exceptional commitment to all aspects of his work. More experienced staff commented on his **confidence** with patients for someone so new to the profession. In addition, his **flexibility** in dealing with challenging situations received special praise.

Nathan Wells, porter: Nathan was chosen not only for being so **hard-working**, **dependable** and **efficient** but also, more importantly, for his sunny personality and **enthusiasm**.

Ana Suarez, clinical nurse specialist: Ana is well known for her **patience** on the job, so Ana's colleagues nominated her for being **caring** and understanding, not just to clients, their partners and families but also to the staff in the department.

3 Do you have a similar scheme to recognize success in your company? How else is good work rewarded (e.g. bonus or commission)? Do you think employee award schemes are a good idea? Why/Why not?

4 Look at the ten words in **bold** in the text which describe personal qualities. Which five are adjectives and which five are nouns?

5 Here are some nominations for employee of the month. Match an adjective in **bold** from the newsletter in **2** to descriptions 1–5.

'Paula really likes coming to work and she loves taking on new projects.'
2 _____

'You never see him relaxing. He's always busy doing something.'
1 _____

'I've never seen someone who can get so much done in so little time.'
3 _____

'He really looks after everyone – even with difficult customers, he'll listen for as long as it takes.'
4 _____

'Inga is always punctual and never off work.'
5 _____

6 Think of a colleague where you work and nominate them for employee of the month. Tell your partner about them using adjectives from **5**.

7 We often make noun forms of an adjective by adding these endings.
-ce   -ion   -iasm   -ity

Match the five nouns in **bold** in the newsletter to the endings.
> *Example:* patien<u>ce</u>

8 Complete this table of personal qualities with adjective forms and noun forms.

Tip | Adjective or noun?
We use the adjective form of personal qualities in everyday speech. We sometimes use the noun form in more formal situations such as at a job interview:
'I'm fairly **flexible**.'
'I think **flexibility** is one of my main strengths.'

Adjective	Noun	Adjective	Noun
patient	patience	5 _____	efficiency
dedicated	1 _____	enthusiastic	6 _____
2 _____	motivation	punctual	7 _____
flexible	3 _____	8 _____	creativity
confident	4 _____	ambitious	9 _____

9 Complete these sentences with the correct form of a word from **8**. Then work with a partner and say if the statements are true (*T*) or false (*F*) for you or your company, using a different form of the word.
> *Example:* It's not important for me to have flexible working hours.

1 It's important for me to have some _flexibility_ in my working hours.
2 I'm not a very _____ person – I always want everything to be done 'now'.
3 _____ is one of my strong points – I'm never late for anything.
4 I have a great deal of _____ in how my company is run and in its success.
5 My company offers good incentives to ensure ongoing enthusiasm and _____ amongst the staff.
6 My company is _____ to its employees and puts their needs before those of the customer.

>> For more exercises, go to **Practice file 15** on page 134.

10 Write down the job titles of three people you know. Write down qualities you think each person needs for their jobs. Then tell the class what you think. Does everyone agree with you?

11 Work with a partner. Talk about the qualities that are important for your job. How would you describe yourself? How do your qualities help in your job?
> *Example:* Patience is important because I work in after-sales, and customers sometimes call to complain about …

Language at work | Past continuous and past perfect

1 How often do you receive feedback on your performance from your line manager? Is the feedback informal or is it a formal performance review?

2 ▶15.1 Listen to Ahmed talking about his new job. Answer questions 1–3.
1 Why did Ahmed want to change his job?
2 Why were the first six months hard?
3 Why does he think he made the right decision?

3 ▶15.1 Listen again and <u>underline</u> the verb forms in *italics* that you hear.
1 I *'d had / was having* a few problems with my previous company so I started to look for a new job.
2 One of our competitors *had opened / were opening* a new office a few months earlier and they were recruiting more staff.
3 The first six months were hard because I *'d lived / was living* in a new city.

4 Match the verb forms in sentences 1–3 in **3** to the explanations in the *Language point*.

> **LANGUAGE POINT**
>
> We use the past perfect (*had* + past participle) to say that one event happened before another past event. ___
>
> We use the past continuous (*was/were* + *-ing*) to:
> • talk about something in progress at a particular time in the past ___
> • give background information in the past ___

>> For more information, go to **Grammar reference** on page 135.

5 ▶15.2 Listen to two more people, Helena and Matthias, describing some feedback they received. Listen and answer the questions.
1 What feedback did they receive?
2 What happened after their performance reviews?

6 ▶15.2 Complete these sentences from the listening with the past perfect or past continuous. Then listen and check your answers.
1 I _____ (work) for a large food company which didn't employ many women.
2 It was terrible to hear this, because I _____ (already / discuss) with him how difficult it was to be the only woman.
3 Six months after that, I _____ (run) the factory!
4 We _____ (talk) about the usual things, but during all of this, he answered the phone twice and even replied to an email.
5 This annoyed me because I _____ (prepare) very thoroughly.
6 Some weeks later I heard that he was fired, but I _____ (already / leave) by then.

>> For more exercises, go to **Practice file 15** on page 135.

7 Work with a partner. Look at this timeline for Helena. Make sentences about her, using the past perfect and past continuous.

> ***Examples:*** *She applied for the job while she was studying at university.*
> *She'd applied for the job by the time she graduated.*

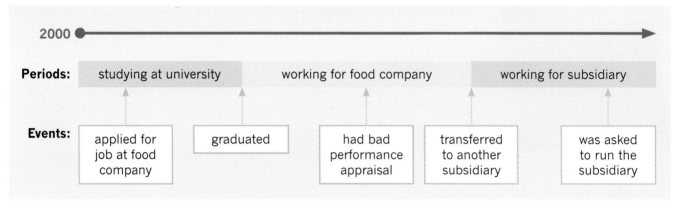

8 Make a timeline for yourself with periods of time and important events. It can be about your studies, career or life in general. Describe it to your partner.

Practically speaking | How to generalize or be specific

1 When was the last time you had a job interview? Do you remember any particular questions you were asked? In general, how did the interview go?

2 ▶ 15.3 Listen to part of a job interview and answer questions 1–3.
1 What question does the interviewer ask?
2 What particular details does the candidate remember about the team?
3 In general, how does the candidate feel the project went?

3 Compare the words in **bold** in these two sentences from the job interview. Which sentence is generalizing? Which sentence is specifying?
1 **In particular**, I remember that one of the team was very independent.
2 **Overall**, I found that worked fairly well.

4 Which of these words have a similar meaning to the words in **bold** in **3**?
> ***Example:*** *On the whole = Overall*

~~on the whole~~   *generally*   *particularly*   *all in all*   *especially*   *mainly*   *mostly*
in general   *specifically*   *generally speaking*

5 Work with a partner. Make sentences 1–5 general or specific.
> ***Example:*** *In general, I prefer to travel by train.*
> *I generally prefer to travel by train.*
1 I prefer to travel by train.
2 My company does more and more business online these days.
3 We communicate in English at work.
4 My last holiday was relaxing.
5 I'm happy with my job at the moment.

6 Now imagine you are both in a job interview situation. Take turns to ask and answer these questions. In your answer, say how you feel in general and also give a specific example from your personal experience.
• How do you feel about working on your own for long periods of time?
• What would you say is one of your main strengths as an employee?
• How confident are you about taking responsibility and being in charge of other people?

Tip | Position of *-ly* adverbs

Adverbs ending in *-ly* such as *generally, particularly, mainly, mostly, specifically* usually go after the subject and before the main verb:
*I **mainly** find I work better in teams.*

Business communication | Appraising performance and setting objectives

1 Chris Hately works in a factory producing shafts for cars. Chris is having his six-month performance review. Read what he has written on his form. Do you have similar forms at work?

Part A

Please answer the questions on this form and return it to your line manager before your performance review.

1 Have the last six months been good/bad/satisfactory? Why?

Good. I've really learnt a lot since I started here and everyone has been really helpful.

2 What do you consider are your most important achievements of the six months?

I completed my initial training in June and was given a permanent contract.

3 Which parts of the job interest you the most? And the least?

Solving problems with machinery.

4 How could your performance be improved in your current position?

Just continue what I'm doing – learning more.

2 ▶ 15.4 Listen to the first part of Chris's performance review and add any extra information to his answers in 1. Then compare the information with a partner.

3 ▶ 15.4 Match 1–7 to a–g. Then listen and check your answers.

1 In	a doing very well.
2 We're very pleased	b on.
3 You seem to be	c general …
4 One thing I wanted	d about working with other people?
5 Is it an area	e you'd like to develop?
6 How do you feel	f with your performance.
7 That's something I need to work	g to discuss was …

4 ▶ 15.5 Listen to the final part of Chris's performance review and answer questions 1–3.
   1 How does Chris's manager signal that it is the end of the meeting?
   2 What have they agreed to do?
   3 What two questions does Chris's manager ask to check agreement?

>> For more exercises, go to **Practice file 15** on page 134.

5 Imagine you have a performance review. Turn to **page 141** and fill in the form.

6 Take turns to appraise your partner using the form you have just completed. The person leading the meeting should:
   • make general comments at the beginning
   • give specific feedback
   • discuss and ask questions about performance
   • set and agree objectives at the end

7 Work with a partner. Take turns to talk about one of the areas below. Review your performance in the area you choose and say what improvements you could make. Decide with your partner on a plan of action.
   • A hobby
   • A sport you do
   • Your progress in English

Key expressions

Giving a formal appraisal
Overall … / In general …
I'm/We're very happy/pleased with your performance …
You seem to be doing very well.
One of your key strengths is …
Perhaps one thing to work on is …
One thing I wanted to discuss was …

Encouraging self-evaluation
How do you feel about …?
How are you getting on with …?
Have you thought about …?
What do you think would help you to …?
Is this an area you'd like to develop?

Evaluating your own performance
I'm really happy with …
Something I need to work on is …
I think … is an area for improvement.

Setting objectives
So let's summarize what we've agreed.
One thing you're going to …
You intend to …
You need to think about …

Agreeing objectives
How does that sound?
Is that OK with you?
Is there anything else you'd like to add?

Extroverts, introverts and ambiverts

1	2	3	4	5	6	7

Introverts ← → *Extroverts*

Ambiverts

Can we guess a person's personality by their job description? For example, is a sales representative always an extrovert? After all, their job consists of networking with large groups of people and giving presentations. And do introverts work as accountants with a private office where they mainly deal with money? According to one study*, the answer is 'No, not necessarily'.

In the study, 300 call centre sales reps took a personality test. It measured their personality on a scale from 1 to 7 (1 = most introverted, 7 = most extroverted). Next, the researcher studied their sales performance over three months and found that the 'introverts' earned less than the 'extroverts'. However, the 'extroverts' earned less than the group with scores on or between 3 and 5 on the personality test. This most successful group are called 'ambiverts'.

In fact, the good news is most people are ambiverts and most jobs need a combination of skills; from the social skills of the extrovert to the quiet hard work of the introvert.

*Study by Professor Adam Grant, University of Pennsylvania

Discussion

1 For your type of job, do you think it helps to be an extrovert, introvert or ambivert? Why?

2 Do you trust the types of tests and questionnaires that we use to measure people's personality and behaviour? Why/Why not?

3 Have you had to take a personality test for your job? Do you think it was accurate? Why/Why not?

Task

1 Here is a sentence from a similar test to the one described in the article. How would you score yourself for this sentence?
(1 = definitely not true for me, 7 = definitely true for me)

I always prefer working in teams and don't work so well on my own.

2 Work with a partner and design your own test. Discuss and write five more sentences (similar to the sentence in 1) to find out if someone is extrovert, introvert or ambivert.

3 Swap your five sentences with another group. Try taking each other's tests. Do you think the test scored you accurately?

Focus

1 ▶01 Watch three people talking about environmental issues in their workplace. Make notes about their answers in the table.

	Speaker 1	Speaker 2	Speaker 3
Would you describe your company as 'environmentally friendly'?			
Does your company have to follow any environmental laws?			
How important is it for your customers to know you are environmentally friendly?			

2 Work with a partner. Take turns to ask and answer the three questions in **1**.

An environmental consultancy

3 You are going to watch an interview with Miles Keeping who talks about his environmental consultancy Hillbreak. Before you watch, match words and phrases from the interview 1–10 to definitions a–j.

1 sustainability _a_
2 drivers ___
3 legislation ___
4 regulations ___
5 jurisdiction ___
6 comply with ___
7 green appeal ___
8 building codes ___
9 refurbish ___
10 urban design ___

a producing or providing goods or services in a way that is good for the environment
b the layout and appearance of a city or town
c reasons that make businesses do something
d when something is attractive because it is environmentally friendly
e the power of an official organization to decide or control something
f to do something because it is the law
g make a building look new again
h a law or laws from the government
i official rules that control something
j rules that control the construction of new buildings

4 ▶02 Watch the interview with Miles Keeping of Hillbreak environmental consultancy. As you watch, number the parts of the video A–F in the correct order 1–6.

A Knowing about the law and environmental regulations ___
B An example of a building with 'green appeal' ___
C Hillbreak consultancy services _1_
D A project in the retail sector ___
E Market drivers and 'green appeal' ___
F Urban development and 'branding' a city ___

5 ▶02 Watch the video again and answer questions 1–11.

1 What type of services does Hillbreak offer?
2 There are two drivers that make companies use Hillbreak's services. What is the first one?
3 Which two sectors use Hillbreak consultancy because they need to comply with regulations?
4 What is the second driver which makes companies use Hillbreak's services?
5 When someone is interested in moving into a building, what might affect their choice?
6 Why did the builders of the Shard want 'green' certificates?
7 In Miles' example of a client, what did the global retailer sell?
8 What aspects of the refurbishment did Hillbreak work on?
9 Which shops were refurbished?
10 According to Miles, how can cities brand themselves?
11 Which example does Miles give of branding through urban development?

6 Complete these sentences with words from **3**.

1 In recent years, online shopping has been a key _____ in the retail sector.
2 To _____ the new government legislation, we pay all our staff a minimum wage.
3 The European Union has no _____ over our company because we are based outside of the EU.
4 This year, we plan to _____ all our shops so they look more modern.
5 In the past, it was easier to start a business but nowadays there are too many rules and _____.
6 They are replacing the old town centre with a new _____ that has lots of green appeal with parks, trees and places outside to relax in.

Branding with 'green appeal'

7 Do you think your company needs more 'green appeal'? How could you brand your business in this way?

8 Work in groups. Imagine your city needs modernizing and wants to brand itself as a city with 'green appeal'. Discuss the pros and cons of these five ideas. At the end, choose the best idea or think of a new one.

• Build a new shopping area that only uses renewable energy such as solar panels.
• Ban all private transport from the city centre and introduce cycle paths, trams and more pedestrian-only areas.
• Build a new bridge over the river with trees and flowers on it. As people walk across the river they can also sit and enjoy nature.
• Knock down the old housing in the middle of the city and create a new park with a play area for children and places for new 'green' businesses to promote their products and ideas.
• Build a tall tower with offices. Only rent the offices to companies and businesses with 'green appeal'.

9 Give a group presentation to the class. Present your choice to the class and give reasons for your decision.

Working with words

1 Match 1–8 to a–h to make sentences.

1 Our firm specializes   *b*
2 I'm responsible   ___
3 Both our roles consist   ___
4 We work   ___
5 I work as   ___
6 She works in   ___
7 They're in   ___
8 He deals   ___

a for the company accounting and general finance.
b in furnishings and household design.
c the areas of pharmaceuticals and hospital supplies.
d with all the enquiries from clients in our northern region.
e of leading small teams of people on projects.
f charge of dealing with after-sales and client services.
g a sales assistant for an engineering firm.
h with each other most of the time.

2 Complete 1–6 in the email with a verb from A and a preposition from B.

A
charge   responsible   consist   specialize   work   deal

B
in   of   with   for   of

Hi Burcu,

Thanks for your email and congratulations on the new position! They couldn't pick a better person to be in ¹_____ _____ their sales team in Ankara. It'll be hard to be ²_____ _____ all those different people at first but I'm sure you'll manage.

With regard to your request for a good translator, I do know someone based in London. Most of her work tends to ³_____ _____ translating technical documents, and I think she might ⁴_____ _____ English-German translations. However, she's also fluent in Turkish, so I'm sure she could ⁵_____ _____ your type of sales literature.

Let me know if you'd like me to contact her. I'm sure you'd find her easy to ⁶_____ _____.

Best

Gerald

Business communication

1 Rick Parry is a buyer for a supermarket chain. He is introducing a colleague, Marcel Grover, to Patti Kline, the representative of a key supplier. Complete their conversation with words from the list.

this is   I want you to meet   what do you do
I'm very pleased   really   here's my   nice to meet you
it was nice

Rick Marcel, ¹____*I want you to meet*____ one of our guests. Marcel, ²_____ Patti Kline. She works with Longridge, one of our biggest suppliers.
Marcel ³_____ to meet you, Patti.
Patti ⁴_____, too. So Marcel, ⁵_____ exactly?
Marcel Well, I'm in charge of all our stores in the south of England.
Patti ⁶_____? That must be very demanding. You know, a lot of responsibility.
Marcel Well, I don't do everything alone. I've got a good team.
Rick Sorry, I need to talk to someone over there. ⁷_____ seeing you, Patti. Keep in touch.
Patti Sure. ⁸_____ card.

2 Read the beginning and end of another conversation. Put the words in *italics* in the correct order.

Greg Good afternoon.
met / I / think / we've / don't / before
¹*I don't think we've met before*. I'm Greg Wilkes from the National Bank.
Jen *to / delighted / meet / I'm / you*
²_____, Mr Wilkes. My name's Jen Mills.
Greg *call / please / Greg / me*
³_____. I see you're from Research and Development.
Jen *are / which / of / you / from / the / US / part*
⁴_____?
Greg Boston, though I spend a lot of time in Europe these days. Anyway, *have / to / I'm / I / now / afraid / go* ⁵_____.
Jen Sure. *to / meet / nice / you / it / very / was*
⁶_____.
Greg It was very nice to meet you, too. I'd like to keep in touch. *have / you / a / card / do* ⁷_____?
Jen Here you are. *I / hearing / forward / from / to / look / you* ⁸_____.

Language at work

Present simple and present continuous

Form

Present simple

	I/you/we/they	She/he/it
Positive	I **work** for Ford. I**'m** French.	It **works** really well. It**'s** fast.
Negative	They **don't** know. They **aren't** here.	He **doesn't** know. She **isn't** here.
Question	Where **do** you work? **Are** you Swedish?	**Does** it **cost** a lot? **Is** she French?

When the verb after *he/she/it* ends in *consonant + -y,*
change the *-y* to an *-i* and add *-es.*
   *He **relies** on financial information.*
With verbs ending in *-ch, -o, -s, -ss,* and *-x,* add *-es.*
   *It **reaches** new levels every day.*

Present continuous

	I/you/we/they	She/he/it
Positive	I**'m waiting** for a call back.	Delia **is emailing** her business partner.
Negative	They **aren't coming.**	Thomas **isn't** **listening** now.
Question	**Are** you **making** progress?	How **is** he **getting** on?

Use

Present simple	Present continuous
To talk about regular or repeated actions. *In my job I **speak** to customers every day on the phone.*	To talk about actions happening now and current projects. *Joel can't help you right now because he**'s speaking** to a client.*
To talk about general facts. *We **employ** over 300 people.*	To talk about trends and changing situations. *The price of fuel **is falling** in many countries.*
With state verbs such as *understand, know, like,* etc. *She **knows** a lot about this area of business.*	To talk about temporary situations. *Kim works at the York office, but she**'s working** at home today.*

Adverbs of frequency and time

We use adverbs of frequency (*always, often, sometimes, never,* etc.) to talk about how often we do something.
1 With *be,* put the adverb after the verb.
   *I**'m never** late for work.*
2 With other verbs, put the adverb before the verb.
   *I **often work** late.*
We use adverbs of time (*now, at the moment, currently,* etc.) to talk about when we do something.
   *I**'m currently** finishing off a project.*

1 Complete the sentences with the present simple or the present continuous form of the verbs in brackets.
1 Carlos usually _____*sits*_____
(sit) in the main office, but today he
_____*is working*_____ (work) at home.
2 What time _____
(you / have to) leave home to get to work?
3 Look at the woman over there. Why
_____ (she / sit) at John's
desk?
4 What _____ (you / work on)
at the moment? Anything interesting?
5 What _____ (Nadia / think)
about her new boss?
6 You're very quiet today! _____
(you / think) about your presentation?
7 How much _____
(a successful salesperson / earn) each year?
8 Excuse me, what _____
(you / do) in this room? This is for staff only.
9 A Whose is this briefcase?
   B I _____ (think) it
   _____ (belong) to one
   of our visitors.
10 They _____ (have) lots of
problems with the new lifts these days.

2 Rewrite the sentences using an adverb from the list.
~~always~~   currently   never   often   normally
nowadays
1 Every Monday morning, we have a team meeting.
   We always have a team meeting on Monday morning.
2 At the moment I'm working on plans for a new shopping centre.
   _____
3 Once or twice each week, I have lunch with clients.
   _____
4 Most Friday afternoons, she leaves at 4.00.
   _____
5 All our customers expect free Wi-fi these days.
   _____
6 I don't take work home at the weekends, even if we're really busy during the week.
   _____

Working with words

1 Complete the sentences with the phrases from the list.

flexitime   overtime   home-working   core hours
lunch break   public holiday   paternity leave
unpaid leave   annual leave   statutory pay

1 I work _flexitime_ , so I can start and finish my working day whenever I like.

2 Our employees' _____ _____ are between ten and four, when they have to be in the office.

3 Last week, I worked for 55 hours, so I did 20 hours _____.

4 I work from home once a week because my company has a system of _____-_____.

5 With maternity leave, the first 12 weeks are fully paid and then you receive 27 weeks' _____ _____, which is less.

6 I rarely take a _____ _____. I usually keep working and eat my sandwich at my desk.

7 In many countries, 1st January is a _____ _____.

8 Nowadays, more fathers are taking _____ _____ to help with a new baby.

9 Last year, I took six months _____ _____ to travel round the world. It was a great experience but I missed receiving a salary!

10 I need to take the rest of my _____ _____ before the end of the year or I'll lose it.

2 Choose the correct words (a, b or c) to complete 1–6 in the text.

> According to research by Peran Kandola, a business psychology firm, 86% of employees also see a link between their moods and how well they do their work. How can this help us at work?
>
> • Take control. If you don't like the terms and [1]_____ at your company, do something about it. Talk to someone or maybe even change jobs.
>
> • Don't work late every day or be the person who always says, 'I'll work [2]_____!' It'll only end up with you needing to take [3]_____ leave.
>
> • Keep your body healthy as well as your mind. Try cycling to work or do exercise during your [4]_____ like a walk round the building.
>
> • Aim for a good work-life [5]_____. Make time for your family and friends. Make sure you take time off when you need it and always take your full [6]_____.

1	a conditions	b agreements	c employment
2	a core hours	b overtime	c unpaid
3	a annual	b statutory	c sick
4	a holiday	b lunch break	c unpaid leave
5	a balance	b day	c flexible
6	a paternity leave	b annual leave	c flexitime

Business communication

1 Put the words in the correct order to make questions in a phone conversation.

a last **name** / what / his / 's
  What's his last name _____?

b say / can / that / you / again
  _____?

c his / have / number / can / I
  _____?

d that / is / case / lower /all
  _____?

e GSA / or / that / was / GSI
  _____?

f me / you / give / that / could
  _____?

2 Now complete 1–6 in the conversation with the questions a–f from **1**.

Katja Hello, Katja speaking.
Niki Hi, Katja. It's Niki.
Katja Oh, hi.
Niki You know the man we met yesterday?
Katja Paul?
Niki Yes. [1]_____
Katja Bicknell. Paul Bicknell.
Niki Thanks. [2]_____
Katja Sorry, I don't have it but I do have his email.
Niki That's great. [3]_____
Katja Yes, sure. It's p dot bicknell at …
Niki Sorry, [4]_____
Katja P dot bicknell at GSI dot org.
Niki [5]_____
Katja I as in India.
Niki Thanks. [6]_____
Katja GSI is upper case.
Niki So that's p dot bicknell at GSI dot org.
Katja That's right.

3 Write the email addresses, URLs and phone numbers.

1 It's g, e, c at hotmail dot com.

_____

2 My number's double zero, double four, three one nine, double four, oh one oh.

_____

3 My email's Lydia underscore forty-nine, at yahoo dot d for dog, t for Turkey.

_____

4 The new website is www dot, about dash, me, dot com, slash courses, underscore online.

_____

Language at work

> **GRAMMAR REFERENCE**
>
> ## The infinitive form
> ### Form
> The infinitive is formed with *to* + base verb (e.g. *to meet, to change, to save*).
> ### Use
> Use the infinitive form of the verb
> - after an adjective:
>   *It's **important to know** the truth.*
>   *We're very **pleased to meet** you.*
> - to express purpose:
>   *I always check with everyone **to make sure** they are happy.*
>   ***To save energy** around the offices, we use timers.*
> - after verbs about plans and decisions:
>   *We **intend to change** the policy.*
>   *They've **decided to stop** buying from us.*
>
> ## The *-ing* form
> ### Form
> The *-ing* form is formed with the base verb + *ing* (e.g. *meeting, changing, saving*).
> ### Use
> Use the *-ing* form of the verb
> - after verbs about likes / dislikes:
>   *I **like playing** sport at the weekends.*
>   *We **enjoyed meeting** you all.*
> - after a preposition:
>   *I need to work **on improving** my IT skills.*
>   *I look forward **to seeing** you all next week.*

1 Complete the sentences with the phrases from the list.

*difficult to know   sad to see   important to be
right to ask   afraid to leave   nice to see*

1 It was so _____ you again. You look so well.
2 It's really _____ what we should do next. There isn't an easy solution.
3 With staff who aren't working hard enough, it's _____ firm but fair.
4 I'm _____ my current job in case I can't get another.
5 On behalf of everyone here, we are _____ you go but want to wish you luck in your next job.
6 I think you're absolutely _____ for a pay rise. It's long overdue.

2 Complete the sentences with the infinitive or *-ing* form of the verbs in brackets.

1 They want _____ (change) to a system of flexitime.
2 Would you like _____ (join) us for dinner?
3 I really dislike _____ (be) late for anything.
4 Do you think he'd be interested in _____ (apply) for this vacancy?
5 Thanks very much for _____ (invite) us to look round.
6 When do you plan _____ (take) your annual leave this year?
7 This team is responsible for _____ (develop) a new product.
8 I'd be happy _____ (help) you with this.
9 When did you decide _____ (requalify)?
10 We look forward to _____ (see) you on the 21st.

3 Complete the introduction to a meeting with the infinitive or *-ing* form of the verbs from the list.

*spend   arrive   interview   keep   make   talk
offer   sum up*

Hello, everyone, and thank you all for [1]_____ on time today. I realize you're all busy, so I hope [2]_____ this meeting brief. As you know, we have been looking at ways of [3]_____ employees the opportunity to work more flexible hours, and I think we have finally come up with a solution [4]_____ sure everyone can achieve a better work–life balance. The process has involved [5]_____ a large number of different people in every department and I have to say that I've really enjoyed [6]_____ time talking to many of you. Anyway, I'd like [7]_____ by presenting the overall feedback and then I plan [8]_____ about the main points of our proposal.

Working with words

1 Put the letters in brackets in the correct order to make words that match the definitions.

1 something available to exploit and use: _resources_ (ESCRORUSE)
2 timetable of activities: _____ (CSEHDLUE)
3 news on how something is progressing: _____ (UTEPAD)
4 money spending plan: _____ (BDTUGE)
5 the last day for finishing a piece of work or project: _____ (ADENDELI)
6 working together: _____ (EAWKTMRO)
7 practical abilities: _____ (LSIKLS)

2 Match 1–8 to a–h to make sentences.

1 It's always difficult to allocate _a_
2 You need to learn how to delegate ___
3 What I like about my boss is she always lets me get ___
4 We're falling ___
5 It's difficult to stay within ___
6 If we continue like this, we should meet ___
7 Hi, Melinda, it's Hanna, I need to get an ___
8 I'm sure we'll be able to catch ___

a resources – skilled staff are in short supply.
b behind schedule, so we all need to work this weekend.
c update on how the project is progressing.
d tasks – you can't possibly do everything yourself.
e up – there are three more weeks left.
f on with my work on my own.
g budget – we always overspend.
h the deadline without too much trouble.

3 Complete the email with the correct form of words from **2**.

Dear Jan,

I'm afraid it looks like we are not going to be able to meet the [1]_____ next Friday. We've fallen behind [2]_____ because we were not [3]_____ sufficient [4]_____. We need more [5]_____ with the appropriate skills to be put on the project immediately. Of course, this does mean that we won't be able to stay within our [6]_____ either. I will send you an [7]_____ after our team meeting this afternoon to let you know what is decided.

Very best wishes,

Graham

Business communication

1 Complete the conversation with the words from the list.

~~on track~~   happening with   anyone else   so far
we're currently   let's check   help with   update me
let's meet   where are

Henry Right, so everything's [1] _on track_ with accommodation. What's next on the list? Ah yes, before I forget, Melinda, can you contact the car hire people for the VIPs?
Melinda I'd prefer not to if that's OK. I'd do it but I'm really busy with the caterers.
Henry Oh really? What's [2]_____ them?
Melinda The usual problems with menu changes – which is why I can't take anything else on.
Henry As Melinda's busy, is that something you can [3]_____, Martin?
Martin Sure, no problem.
Henry Thanks, Martin.
Martin You're welcome.
Henry And [4]_____ we with replies to the invitations, Rebecca?
Rebecca I've sent them out but [5]_____ waiting for replies from 70 people.
Henry That many? Can [6]_____ help you check if they're coming?
Rebecca No, I can manage. I'll ring them individually over the next two days.
Henry Thanks, Rebecca. OK Ralph. Can you [7]_____ on briefing the media?
Ralph [8]_____ so good. I've sent out a press release and a few journalists have already confirmed.
Henry Good, so [9]_____ we all know what we're doing. Melinda is dealing with the caterers, Rebecca is handling the invitations, Martin is handling the car hire firm and Ralph has volunteered to deal with the media. OK, if that's everything, [10]_____ again in a week to review progress.

2 Put the words in *italics* in the correct order to complete the conversation.

Kevin Express Printers, Kevin speaking.
Ludo Hi Kevin, it's Ludo here. *everything / going / 's / How* [1]_How's everything going_ with our brochures?
Kevin So far so good. *almost / we / finished / 've* [2]_____.
Ludo Great, so *track / everything / on / is* [3]_____?
Kevin Yes, but we need somebody to deliver them.
Ludo Well, *something / I / is / can / that* [4]_____ help with? Call me when they're ready and I can come and collect them.
Kevin OK. Great.
Ludo Good. So to sum up, you're going to make sure they're completed *I / going / 'm / to / and* [5]_____ collect them.

Language at work

GRAMMAR REFERENCE

Present perfect and past simple
Form

Present perfect	Past simple
has/have + past participle I **have worked** here for five years.	verb + -ed I **worked** here two years ago.

Use
Use both the present perfect and the past simple to talk about the past in different situations.

Present perfect	Past simple
To talk about finished actions or events when the speaker does not say, ask or know when it happened. (The time is not specified.) We've already **done** this. I **haven't seen him**, I'm afraid. ???	To talk about finished actions or events when the speaker says, asks or knows when something happened. (The time is specified.) I **met** him last Saturday. When **did** he **leave**? last Saturday
To talk about actions or events that took place in a time period that has not finished, e.g. up to now, today, this year. We've **manufactured** this product for over three years. How long **have you been** here?	To talk about actions or events that took place in a finished time period. She **worked** here for five years, from 1999 to 2004. five years 1999 2004
We often use the adverbs just, yet and already with the present perfect. We use **just** to show an action happened in the very recent past. We use **yet** in negative sentences and questions to talk about something that hasn't happened but you expect will happen. We use **already** to emphasize an action happened sooner than expected or planned.	We usually use time words and phrases with the past simple, e.g. yesterday, last week, last year, in 2011, three years ago, when I arrived.

1 <u>Underline</u> the correct words in *italics* to complete the sentences.
1 I *booked / have booked* the hotel yesterday.
2 *Have / Did* you ever been to India?
3 I live in London now, but I *have lived / lived* in Paris from 2010 to 2012.
4 I *haven't seen / didn't see* him recently.
5 Last year, I *have changed / changed* jobs.
6 *Have / Did* you go to the meeting last week?
7 He *hasn't arrived / didn't arrive* yet.
8 *I asked / I've asked* for this report three times already this week!

2 Complete the sentences with the past simple or present perfect form of the verbs in brackets.
1 Anna _____*has worked*_____ (work) here for ages. She still does the same job.
2 The sales office _____ (close) down over a month ago.
3 The Managing Director _____ (just / organize) a meeting with all line managers.
4 _____ (you / call) him back yet?
5 What time _____ (she / arrive)?
6 I don't think we _____ (ever / meet) before, have we?
7 We _____ (not / take) the opportunity when we had the chance.
8 Things _____ (not / improve) that much since he took over.
9 _____ (you / ever / speak) to the CEO?
10 You know a lot about this company. How long _____ (you / work) here?

3 Complete the conversation with the words from the list.
already   just   yet
A The presentation is in two minutes and I still haven't seen Caroline [1]_____.
B Actually, she's [2]_____ arrived – I saw her car arrive a few minutes ago.
A Great. And our speaker has [3]_____ set up in the conference room, so I think we're ready to start once Caroline comes up …
C Sorry I'm late. The traffic was terrible!

Working with words

1 Replace the words in *italics* in 1–8 with the words from the list and rewrite the sentences.

secure   ~~user-friendly~~   handy   up-to-date   accurate
time-consuming   poor quality   efficient

1 Everything about this app is really *easy to understand and operate*.
   Everything about this app is really user-friendly.
   _____

2 The new café round the corner is a bit expensive, but it's so *convenient* for lunch.
   _____
   _____

3 How *correct* are these figures? They don't appear to add up.
   _____
   _____

4 All your information is stored on state-of-the-art servers, so it's very *safe* from identify thieves.
   _____
   _____

5 You take a numbered ticket at the bank now instead of queuing. It's really *good for reducing the time*.
   _____
   _____

6 I'd like a report on the situation which is detailed and *says what's happening now*!
   _____
   _____

7 This new software seems to have made doing the monthly payroll *take up more of my day* compared to the old system.
   _____
   _____

8 The graphics on this new version are really *not very good given the price*.
   _____
   _____

2 Complete the sentences with the phrases from the list. Then <u>underline</u> the correct verbs in *italics*.

Having a financial adviser   *Flying business class*
Hiring a consultant   *Online banking*

1 _____ *helps / allows* the company look at problems objectively and consider all the possibilities.

2 _____ *makes / allows* me to concentrate on earning the money and not on what to do with it.

3 _____ *lets / makes* it so much faster than going to a building and waiting with everyone else.

4 _____ *lets / allows* me get a decent night's sleep and saves the cost of a hotel room.

Business communication

1 Complete the sentences with words from the list.

allow   convinced   find   happens
problems   question   seem

1 One of the biggest _____ is that the Wi-fi signal is very weak.

2 That's a good _____.

3 What _____ if I press this flashing button?

4 I'm not _____ that the new motor is faster. To me, it seems slower.

5 Even though it's automatic, will it _____ me to save my work manually?

6 It might _____ complicated now but, in fact, it'll become clear when you start using it.

7 I'm sure you'll _____ it much easier to use once you get used to it.

2 Complete the conversation with the phrases from the list.

another useful feature is   it'll let
the main benefit is   it's also a lot less
makes things easier   make your life easier
will it let   that's probably true

A So, this is the new photocopier.
   ^1_____ that it's faster and can do larger amounts at one time.
   ^2_____ time-consuming to use because it's programmable.

B ^3_____ me copy on both sides of the paper?

A Yes, of course. ^4_____ you copy on two sides, put two pages on one side and reduce and enlarge pages. Everything really. I'm sure you'll find it will ^5_____.

B ^6_____, but it still looks rather complicated.

A It might seem like that at first but, in fact, it's very user-friendly and ^7_____.

B What happens if I select this button that shows a double-sided option with a staple?

A Well, ^8_____ that the photocopier can staple pages together.

B Really?

A Yes, try it.

Language at work

> **GRAMMAR REFERENCE**
>
> ## Comparative forms and modifiers
> ### Form
> 1 Add -er to one- and some two-syllable adjectives and to adverbs with the same form as adjectives.
>> small → smaller
>> fast → faster
>
>   If the adjective or adverb ends in -y, change the -y to an -i and add -er.
>> happy → happier
> 2 Double the consonant after a vowel at the end of short adjectives.
>> hot → hotter
>> big → bigger
>> thin → thinner
> 3 Some adjectives and adverbs are irregular.
>> good/well → better, bad/badly → worse
> 4 Add more to adjectives and adverbs with two or more syllables.
>> accurate → more accurate
>> quickly → more quickly
> 5 Add than after the comparative form to compare two things.
>> Carole is more sociable **than** Vincent.
>
> ### Use
> 1 Use the comparative to compare two or more things or people.
>> This new system is **better** than the old one.
> 2 To say something is the same, use as + adjective + as.
>> It's **as accurate as** the old system.
> 3 To say something is different, use not as + adjective + as.
>> It **is not (isn't) as efficient as** the old system.
>
> ## Modifying comparative adjectives and adverbs
> Use modifiers to talk about differences in the size of the comparison.
> 1 Big differences: much, far, a lot, a great deal.
>> Sales are **far bigger** this year than last year.
>> We sold out **much more quickly** this year.
>
>   Before as + adjective + as, use not anything like.
>> Sales weren't **anything like as** big as last year's.
> 2 Small differences: a bit, a little, slightly, marginally.
>> Sales were **a bit better** this year.
>> Overall, we did **a little better** this year.
>
>   Before as + adjective + as, use nearly or almost.
>> There were **nearly as** many customers last night **as** there were at Christmas.

1 Complete the guidelines for designing a website with the correct form of the adjectives in brackets.

To be effective, websites must always score much [1] _higher_ (high) in what 'usability guru', Jakob Nielsen, calls 'the three Fs'.

Functional

First of all, a website must be as [2] _____ (easy) to use as anyone else's. Badly-designed sites don't function as [3] _____ (good) as their competitors' and so they lose a lot more business. Another point is that sites which are successful are continually looking at how they can be even [4] _____ (friendly) to the user.

Fast

The second F is to be [5] _____ (fast) than the rest. Customers won't want to use the website if downloading pages on the site is [6] _____ (slow) than on other sites.

Familiar

The final F is familiarity. A site which is [7] _____ (original) than its competitors' may look good, but in the end it will be [8] _____ (popular) if it's similar to other websites and users know how it works and what it does.

2 Adrian Sewell's company is looking for a new website designer. He is discussing the options with two members of his team. Read this information and underline the correct words in italics in their conversation.

Fritz Neff	Experience: 5 years Salary expectation: very high Style: modern Sickness record: 1 day last year
Maria Mendes	Experience: 4 years, 6 months Salary expectation: medium Style: traditional Sickness record: 0 days last year
Jean Petit	Experience: 2 years Salary expectation: medium / low Style: experimental Sickness record: 11 days last year

Adrian So, Katie, Guy – what do you think of our candidates?

Katie Well, I think we should choose Maria. She is [1]a lot / _more_ experienced [2]as / than Jean, and she didn't take any days off due to sickness last year.

Guy Yes, but I think Jean would be better [3]than / that Maria. He's more dynamic and his salary expectations are also [4]a bit / a lot lower than hers.

Adrian Well, I disagree with both of you. I think we should go for Fritz. His designs are [5]slightly / more up-to-date than Maria's and that's important for our image. And his sickness record is [6]a little / much better than Jean's and only [7]a bit / a great deal worse than Maria's.

Katie Yes, but Maria is [8]almost as / not nearly as experienced as Fritz, and her salary expectations are [9]far / a bit lower.

Adrian I think we can talk to Fritz about salaries …

Working with words

1 Complete the sentences with the correct form of the words from the list.

care   serve   require   ~~loyal~~   expect   satisfy

1 Once you've built good customer __loyalty__, they keep coming back year after year.
2 First of all, I need to find out about your _____. What exactly do you need?
3 I'll just put you through to customer _____. They should be able to help you.
4 In this company we really _____ about our customers and we're always thinking of how we can keep them happy.
5 The results show that we're not always matching up to people's _____.
6 We regularly do market research to find out about levels of customer _____ with our products.

2 Underline the correct words in *italics* to complete the sentences.

1 It's a *caring / loyal* company which wants to make customers happy.
2 Our aim is to exceed your *expectations / satisfaction* every time.
3 Whatever you *require / satisfy*, we can supply it within 24 hours.
4 Is there a way to *produce / deliver* this in a smaller size?
5 If you are not 100% *expected / satisfied* with the item, we will replace it or give you your money back.
6 Note that *delivery / care* times may vary during the holiday period.
7 I've had a highly *required / productive* week and done everything on my list.

3 Match the words from the list to definitions 1–6.

expect   loyalty   satisfy   require   services   care

1 something companies supply – not products
   _____
2 giving or showing strong support for a company or brand _____
3 to believe something will happen _____
4 to need something for a particular purpose
   _____
5 looking after somebody or something _____
6 to make someone feel pleased and contented
   _____

Business communication

1 Underline the correct words in *italics* to complete the conversation.

A It's ¹*about / around* our IT seminar next year. I'd like to ²*do / fix* a date for it.
B Didn't we ³*attend / arrange* it for January?
A Yes, we did, but not many of our staff can ⁴*arrive / come* then. They say it's too soon after Christmas.
B OK. Well, the second half of February is ⁵*well / good* for me. How does that ⁶*suit / convenient* you?
A Actually, can we ⁷*make / bring* it later in the year?
B Of course. But when?
A Most people seem to think that late in March is ⁸*any good / OK*. How about Friday 27th?
B I'm not ⁹*confirmed / free* on that day. Can we ¹⁰*fix / bring* it forward to the Wednesday of that same week?
A The 25th? Sure.
B So that's the IT seminar arranged for Wednesday March 25th.

2 Complete the sentences with the prepositions from the list.

about   at   back   for   forward   in   on   ~~to~~

1 Hello, I'm calling __to__ arrange a meeting at your hotel.
2 It's _____ our appointment at four today. Something's come up.
3 Is Tuesday any good _____ you?
4 Sorry, but I'm not free _____ one. Maybe later in the day?
5 I'm afraid I can't come _____ Thursday.
6 I'm busy next week, so can we move it _____ to the week after?
7 Instead of the afternoon, why don't we bring it _____ to the morning?
8 Can we make it later _____ the week?

Language at work

GRAMMAR REFERENCE

Present tenses for future reference

Form
See page 107 for the present simple and present continuous.
See page 109 for verbs + *to* + infinitive.

Use

Present simple
We often use the present simple with the verbs *arrive, leave, come back, go, start, finish* to talk about a scheduled or timetabled event in the future.
> The flights **arrives** at six in the evening.
> **Does** this train **leave** at midday?
> No, it **doesn't leave** until three in the afternoon.

Present continuous
We often use the present continuous to talk about an arrangement for the future.
> She's **joining** us at one for lunch.
> We **aren't meeting** anyone until later this afternoon.
> What time **are you arriving** at the conference centre?

Verbs + *to* + infinitive
We use present tense verbs such as *plan, hope, intend, want, expect* + *to* + infinitive for future plans, hopes and expectations.
> Let's **plan to meet** everyone at the airport and take a taxi together.
> I **hope to schedule** the presentation for three so that everyone can attend.
> He **doesn't intend to let** the discussion last too long.
> Do you **expect to be** late home tonight?

***be* + adjective**
We use the present tense of *be* with adjectives such as *free, busy, available, tied up* to talk about future availability.
> We're **busy** next week but the week after **is good** for everyone.
> I'm afraid I'm **not available** until the fifth.
> Are you **free** for a breakfast meeting tomorrow?

1 Complete the phone call with the present simple or present continuous form of the verbs in brackets.

Enrico Hello, Sophie. It's Enrico. I'm calling to check the details for tomorrow's visit.

Sophie Hello, Enrico. Yes, everything's organized. What time [1] *does your flight arrive* (flight / arrive)?

Enrico It [2]_____ (get in) at 9.15 a.m.

Sophie Oh yes, that's what I have written here on the schedule, and John [3]_____ (meet) you at the airport. Then he [4]_____ (bring) you back to the office.

Enrico Oh good. And [5]_____ (we all / have) lunch together?

Sophie Yes, and then we [6]_____ (show) you around the factory.

Enrico Great. And what [7]_____ (we / do) after that?

Sophie Then we [8]_____ (have) a meal at an Italian restaurant and after that you have to go back to the airport. What time [9]_____ (your flight / leave)?

Enrico It [10]_____ (leave) at 10.30 p.m.

Sophie Oh, that's fine. We can order a taxi to pick you up at 8.00 p.m.

2 Complete the email using the prompts in *italics*.

Dear Maria,

1 *you / free / on / Thursday / evening?*
   Are you free on Thursday evening?

2 *Our team / go out / to celebrate / Torsten's birthday.*
   _____

   Would you like to come?

3 *We / plan / meet / in reception / around five.*
   _____

4 We haven't booked anywhere yet, but
   I / hope / try / that new Greek restaurant.
   _____

5 We could go home together afterwards.
   The last train / leave / at midnight.
   _____

6 *If you / not / busy,* it'd be great to see you.
   _____

All the best,
Mounir

Working with words

1 Complete the review of a hotel. Use the answers to complete the puzzle and find the European city where the hotel is located.

> ### HOTEL REVIEWS
>
> This first-class hotel and conference centre welcomes guests from all over the world. Its ¹_facilities_ are second to none. There are 300 en-suite rooms and five apartment suites. For business guests, it has ten meetings rooms, two of which are big enough to be used as ²_____ halls.
>
> The hotel can also organize events such as guided ³_____ around the town centre for conference ⁴_____ and hotel guests who enjoy a bit of ⁵_____. For food-lovers, the four-star restaurant serves regional ⁶_____ every evening. All in all, this is a top-class ⁷_____ for business and for pleasure.

```
                          A
                    1 f a c i l i t i e s
                2 [ ] [ ] [ ] [ ] [ ] [ ]
                          3 [ ] [ ] [ ] [ ] [ ] [ ]
                    4 [ ] [ ] [ ] [ ] [ ] [ ]
            5 [ ] [ ] [ ] [ ] [ ]
                6 [ ] [ ] [ ] [ ] [ ] [ ]
                          7 [ ] [ ] [ ] [ ] [ ] [ ]
```

2 Replace the words in *italics* (1–8) with the phrases from the list. Add a pronoun if necessary.

*look around   freshen up   eat out   pick someone up
meet up with   check in   ~~drop someone off~~
show someone around*

Pedro It's difficult to park here. Can I ~~stop and leave you~~ ¹___drop you off___ in front of the hotel?

Sabrina Sure, I'll *register* ²_____ and then I'd like to *have a wash, and change my clothes* ³_____.

Pedro If you like, tonight I can *give you a tour of* ⁴_____ the old city. We could *eat in a restaurant* ⁵_____ by the port.

Sabrina That sounds great! I'd rather *walk about and see* ⁶_____ the city than stay in my hotel room.

Pedro I'll *collect you* ⁷_____ at 8.30 p.m. We'll *see* ⁸_____ Alberto and Maite in the main square.

Business communication

1 Put the words in the correct order to make expressions.

1 meet / person / it's / nice / to / you / in
   It's nice to meet you in person.
2 have / did / finding / you / any / trouble / us?
   _____?
3 worry / signing / don't / about / in
   _____.
4 through / programme / I'll / run / today's
   _____.
5 this / my / come / way / to / office
   _____.
6 need / building / you'll / this / enter / badge / the / to
   _____.
7 reception / sure / make / in / at / you / sign
   _____.

2 Raymond Roberts has an appointment with Janet Rose. He has just arrived at HBG premises. Complete their conversation with the phrases from the list.

*let me take your bag   how was your journey
can I get you a drink   You'll need this
~~Welcome to HBG publishing~~   Make sure you
I thought you could   catch up again*

Raymond Good morning, I'm here to see Janet Rose.
Janet Hello, I'm Janet. ¹_Welcome to HBG publishing_.
Raymond It's nice to meet you in person.
Janet Likewise. So, ²_____?
Raymond Well, there were traffic jams on the motorway and I got a little bit lost in the industrial park.
Janet Don't worry. That happens to everyone. Anyway, ³_____ – I'll store it in my office.
Raymond I'll hang on to it it if you don't mind. It's got all my stuff in it.
Janet Well, if you change your mind just tell me. And ⁴_____?
Raymond Thanks. I'll have a cup of tea, please.
Janet Sure, I'll just get that for you in a second. First of all, I'll run through the schedule. ⁵_____ start by meeting Karen Rankin this morning and then we'll ⁶_____ at lunchtime.
Raymond OK. And will I see Malcolm Briscoe?
Janet Yes, in fact he's joining us for lunch. One other thing. ⁷_____. It's your security pass. ⁸_____ wear it at all times.

Language at work

1 Complete the sentences with *a, an, the* or no article (–).
  1 Is there ___ bus to the airport from my hotel?
  2 Our centre is equipped with ___ latest facilities.
  3 How long have you been learning to speak ___ Chinese?
  4 Could I have ___ cup of tea, please?
  5 Sorry, but he isn't at ___ work today.
  6 ___ main exhibition centre is over there.
  7 He's ___ person I mentioned during dinner. You should meet him.
  8 Is this ___ information you wanted?
  9 What time's my flight to ___ USA?
  10 I normally travel by ___ bicycle.
  11 I love ___ vegetarian food.
  12 The greatest innovation of ___ twentieth century was the Internet.
  13 Are we meeting again on ___ Thursday?
  14 Hi. My name's Elaine Keevey and I'm ___ accountant.

2 Read eight rules and guidelines for staff working at a conference centre. Add the correct article(s).
  1 All staff must be polite and helpful to *the* trade fair delegates.
  2 Remember to wear ID badge at all times.
  3 Check visitors' names on registration list when they enter main venue.
  4 If you see visitor who looks lost, immediately offer to help.
  5 Staff not wearing uniform will be sent home.
  6 Exhibition centre is always closed to visitors on Mondays.
  7 For information, direct visitors to Central Registration Desk.
  8 If you travel by car, please park in Staff Car Park.

Working with words

1 Read the news report. Replace the words in *italics* (1–7) with the words from the list.

was down   ~~*victims*~~   *prevent*   *vulnerable*   *hackers*
network   *encrypted*

More than five hundred Canadians have been notified that they may have been the ¹*people who suffered* _victims_ of a major security breach at a large consumer-credit reporting agency. According to reports, staff noticed the problem when the whole ²*connected system of computers* _____ ³*stopped working* _____ for an hour. During that time, unauthorized access was gained to personal, detailed credit files containing customers' banking details and home addresses. Although, the ⁴*people who tried to steal the information* _____ weren't able to access all the information because some of it was ⁵*unreadable because it needed a password* _____, the company wasn't able to ⁶*stop* _____ them from stealing details on around 500 customers. This is the second time this month that a major business has found that its customer records are ⁷*weak and easily attacked* _____ to identity theft.

2 Match 1–7 to a–g to make sentences.

1 Last night, we upgraded ___
2 Don't forget to back up ___
3 Businesses need to encrypt ___
4 It's a good idea to create ___
5 Double-click this icon to open ___
6 This tool lets you share ___
7 Try running ___

a the attachment on your email.
b sensitive data so no one else can read it.
c all your files so you have a copy.
d documents with colleagues while working on them.
e the software, so you'll notice some changes.
f a scan to check for a virus.
g a new password at least once every three months.

Business communication

1 Read the first part of a teleconference. Number the lines in the correct order 1–10.

___ Is that any better?
___ Yes. Loud and clear. Hi, Natasha.
___ Yes, it is. Hello, Ryan. Natasha is here with me, too. Can you hear me OK?
_1_ Hello? Is that Michael?
___ Me neither. Ryan, your line isn't very good. Can you speak up?
___ Hi, Ryan.
___ We're just waiting for Liza. She's calling from Rome.
___ Yes, much better.
___ Sure. I haven't spoken to her for ages.
___ Hello? This is Liza.

2 Read two more parts of the teleconference. Complete the missing words (1–8).

Michael OK, let's ¹b_____. Thank you everyone for coming. We have myself and Natasha in Manchester, Ryan in Boston and Liza in Rome. Today, I want to ²d_____ our online security. You've all seen copies of Liza's report and proposal but Liza, can you ³s_____ first? I'd like you to give a brief summary of the main points.

Liza Sure.

Michael And then Ryan, you can speak next. I'd like to hear the views from your team in Boston.

Natasha Can I ⁴s_____ something before we begin?

Michael Go ahead.

Natasha. Ryan and Liza? Can I ask you both a ⁵q_____? I sent out two drafts of the report and I want to check that you are looking at the second version …

[Later]

Ryan So I think that ⁶c_____ everything from my team. And of course, I'll ⁷s_____ up the main points in an email.

Michael Great. Thanks for that Ryan.

Liza Michael, can I ⁸c_____ in here? Ryan, at the beginning you said most of your team are happy with the existing system but …

Language at work

GRAMMAR REFERENCE

Verbs of obligation, prohibition and permission

Form

Verbs of obligation, prohibition and permission
(e.g. *must, have to, can't, can*) come before the main verb.

> Customers **must pay** *for the product within 30 days.*
> *Do I* **have to** *check out before 12.00?*
> *We* **can't take** *our phones into meetings.*
> *You* **can make** *short personal calls at work.*

Use

1 Use *must, have to, need to* for talking about
obligations (e.g. rules) and necessity.
> *You* **must** *wear your uniform during working hours.*
> *They* **have to** *start work at three.*
> *She* **needs to** *update her password by the end of the week.*

2 Use *don't have to, don't need to* when there is no
obligation or necessity to do something.
> *Employees* **don't have to** *wear an ID badge.*
> *With flexitime,* **no one needs to** *start or end at a fixed time of day.*

3 Use *mustn't, can't, (be) not allowed to* for prohibition
(stopping somebody from doing something).
> *You* **mustn't** *leave the designated area.*
> *Employees* **can't** *use the Internet during work time for personal use.*
> *Visitors* **are not allowed** *to enter this area of the building without a pass.*

4 Use *can, (be) allowed to* for talking about and asking
for permission.
> *We* **can** *make personal calls from our workstations at lunchtimes.*
> *You'***re allowed to** *bring your mobile phone into the lab.*
> **Am I allowed to** *log in to the server from home?*

5 *Must* has no past form. Use *had to* instead.
> *They* **must** *sign in at reception.* (Present)
> *He* **had to** *show his passport at the security desk.* (Past)

6 With question forms about rules, use *Do I have to …?*
or *Do I need to …?* We rarely use *must* to ask about
rules.
> **Does he have to** *lock up every day?*
> **Do I need to** *ask for permission to leave early?*

---

1 Underline the correct verbs in *italics* to complete
the sentences. In two sentences both verbs are
correct.

1 You *need to / are allowed to* get a parking permit if
you want to use the car park.

2 Employees *mustn't / have to* attend at least three
training days per year to receive a certificate.

3 She *doesn't have to / can't* work with us if she doesn't
want to. I just thought she might like to.

4 *Can I / Am I allowed to* call my family on this phone?

5 You *mustn't / don't have to* drink the water from this
tap. It's only for washing hands.

6 The room over there is for having a coffee and
taking a break. Anyone *can / needs to* use it.

7 You *aren't allowed to / mustn't* smoke anywhere on
the premises. Go outside if you need a cigarette.

8 Do we *have to / must* wait outside until the security
guard arrives with the key?

2 Rewrite the sentences starting with the words
given. Use *must, have to, need to*, etc.

1 My job is to welcome guests and answer the phone.
I ___*have to welcome guests*___ and answer the
phone.

2 It isn't necessary to bring your laptop – we have
one you can use.
You don't _____ – we have
one you can use.

3 This is a no-smoking area.
We aren't _____ in this area.

4 It is forbidden to take these documents out of the
building.
You _____ these documents
out of the building.

5 In theory we can't talk in the library, but everyone
does.
We're _____ in the library, but
everyone does.

6 You're obliged to wear a helmet on the construction
site.
You _____ a helmet on the
construction site.

7 Can I use your password to log in?
Am I _____ to log in?

8 Is it the law to drive on the right or the left in this
country?
Do I _____ the left in this
country?

Working with words

1 Complete the sentences and use the answers to complete the crossword.

ACROSS

1 _____ is a new way of raising money online for a business idea without giving away lots of equity.

2 You often need plenty of _____ to start a new business.

6 If you have _____ in a company, you own part of it.

7 _____ are the units a company is divided into and sold on the stock market.

8 Budding _____ need lots of energy and passion in order to succeed in business.

9 Your financial _____ are rather optimistic. Do you really think you can make this much money by next year?

DOWN

1 _____ is the money you pay someone for helping to sell your products or service.

3 If you need financial help to start a business, you could consider having some _____ who will give you the money in return for a share in the business.

4 Some businesses start with a bank _____, but be careful about how much interest you might pay.

5 With investors and shareholders, you'll have to pay them some _____ once you start making a profit.

```
1
c r o w d f u n d i n g
      2     3
      4         5
         6
7
8
         9
```

2 Complete the sentences with the prepositions from the list.

towards   for   out   back

1 How much did you pay _____ your new car?

2 If you lent them the money, why didn't they pay you _____?

3 Hans is retiring next week, so would everyone like to pay something _____ the cost of a present?

4 How often do they pay _____ dividends to the shareholders?

Business communication

1 Look at the four slides and read their descriptions 1–4. <u>Underline</u> the correct words in *italics*.

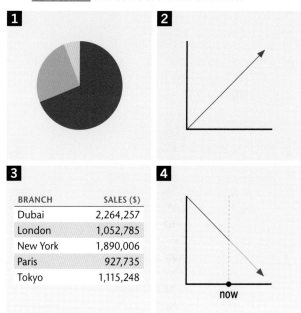

BRANCH	SALES ($)
Dubai	2,264,257
London	1,052,785
New York	1,890,006
Paris	927,735
Tokyo	1,115,248

now

1 This *table / graph / chart* shows you the main findings.

It's *based on / divided into / shown from* three sections.

2 The *upward / flat / downward* trend shows positive results.

3 These *tables / graphs / figures* are the sales results of each of our branches.

4 This decrease will definitely *stop / continue / change* into next year.

2 Complete the presentation with the prepositions from the list.

to   at   into   from   in   over   on

Take a look [1]_____ this chart. It's based [2]_____ data from our research department and it shows the average number of visitors to our website. It's broken [3]_____ two parts: the green side indicates the number of visitors who visited but didn't buy and the red side indicates the number who purchased something. As you can see [4]_____ this, around a third of the visitors actually bought something. You might think that's low but in fact 30% is normal for most online retailers. Now I'd like to draw your attention [5]_____ another slide. It's a graph which compares visitors and purchases in each month of the year. Over the last 12 months, the number of visitors and purchases has increased. That's good news. And notice [6]_____ particular that the number of purchases per visit has also increased. So the conversion rate rose from 26% to 34% over the year. This upwards trend is positive and will continue [7]_____ the next year if we build on this.

Language at work

GRAMMAR REFERENCE

Going to

Form

am/is/are + *going to* + verb

I'm going to work late tonight.

Use

1 To make a strong prediction based on evidence.

He's going to be late for the meeting because he's still on his way to the office.

2 To talk about things we intend to do, or have already planned.

I'm going to start my own business once I've completed this training.

Will

Form

will + verb

I think the new product will be successful.

Use

1 To talk about future facts.

Next year the call centre will be in Bangkok.

2 To talk about predictions.

The price of gold will continue to rise.

3 To make decisions at the moment of speaking.

A Can I call for a taxi? I need to get to the airport.

B No need to do that. I'll drive you there myself.

4 To make promises.

I'll finish it tomorrow, don't worry.

Will + adverbs of certainty

Adverbs of certainty come <u>after</u> *will*.

I'll probably take the job.

Adverbs of certainty come <u>before</u> *won't*.

I probably won't take the job.

Modal verbs: *might*, *may*, *could*

Form

might/may/could + verb

The new offices might be ready by the end of the year.

Use

Use *might*, *may* or *could* to talk about something that is possible in the future but not certain.

This clause in the contract may give us problems later.

might not, *may not*, *could not*

Use *might not* and *may not* to say that something is unlikely to happen in the future.

They might not accept our offer.

Do not use *could not* in the same way. It has a different meaning in its negative form.

They could not accept our offer. (Refers to past ability. They weren't able to accept the offer.)

1 Some guests are visiting Patrick Wilson's company. Complete the conversation with *will* or *(be) going to*.

Angie Why are you wearing a tie today, Patrick? You're not usually so smart.

Patrick I [1]_____*am going to*_____ meet the Russian visitors today and I want to make a good impression.

Angie Oh, of course. I'd forgotten about that. What are your plans for them?

Patrick Well, I [2]_____ bring them to the office and show them around, but there are no plans after that, so I need some suggestions from you both.

Sasha We should probably take them out for a meal tonight.

Angie Yes, that's a good idea … I know, I [3]_____ book a table at that new French restaurant.

Sasha That sounds good, and I [4]_____ try and organize something for after the meal.

Patrick Great. Let me know when you've arranged it. Oh, look at the time! I [5]_____ be late. I'm supposed to be at their hotel in five minutes!

Sasha Don't worry, Patrick, I've got my car with me today. I [6]_____ give you a lift.

Patrick Thanks, Sasha. That's great.

2 Choose the best option (a, b or c) to complete the sentences.

1 A Would you like to join us for dinner after the meeting?

B That's kind of you, but I _c_ have an early night. I'm tired after the journey.

a will   b could   ~~c am going to~~

2 A How do I get to your place from the airport?

B Don't worry, I ___ definitely be there to pick you up.

a could   b might   c 'll

3 A Is Marika coming to the meeting?

B I think so, but there are some new roadworks near her house, so she ___ be a few minutes late.

a might   b is going to   c 'll definitely

4 We have to think carefully about signing their contract, as it ___ be a big mistake.

a is going to   b will   c could

5 These new trading laws ___ not affect us as much as we think. We'll have to wait and see if they really change anything.

a may   b could   c will

6 Making this decision without Michael here ___ make him angry, but you never know with Michael.

a will definitely b will possibly c is going to

Working with words

1 Complete the sentences with the words in **bold**. Change the form of the word in **bold** or add another word to it.

supply

1 It's important to build good relationships with different _suppliers_ .

2 Our _supply chain_ begins with the manufacturer in India and ends in our UK shops.

transport

3 The cost of air _____ is much higher but it's faster.

show

4 Customers from all over Europe visit our _____ in Paris and Milan.

invent

5 Every item in our _____ is unique, so we keep photographic records of each of them.

middle

6 The problem with using _____ is that it adds to the final cost of products because we have to add on their fee.

ship

7 We have a large _____ arriving in three days.

track

8 We use barcodes to _____ _____ of the stock coming in and out of the warehouse.

made

9 All our pots are _____, which makes them expensive, but our target customer doesn't want anything mass-produced.

original

10 The _____ of the products is printed on the bottom of the box.

2 Underline the correct words in *italics* to complete the sentences.

1 The book is currently out of stock, but it is *on / out of* order, so we'll have it soon.

2 We need to *stock up on / run out of* headed paper. Could you put an order in?

3 I ran *low on / out of* ink, so I couldn't print out the report.

4 We can keep *track of / on track* our order by satellite.

5 Let's stop at the next service station. We are running *low / out* on petrol.

Business communication

1 Complete the phone call between Virginie, a customer, and Kevin, a call handler. Put the words in *italics* in the correct order.

Kevin Good afternoon, you're speaking to Kevin. How can I help you?

Virginie Hello, I am ~~up / chasing / an / order~~
¹___chasing up an order___ I placed three weeks ago.

Kevin *account / take / I / your / details / Can*
²_____, please?

Virginie Yes. The account number is 572638.

Kevin OK. If you bear with me a moment, I'll *into / look / it* ³_____.
Let me see. Well, *my / to / information / according*
⁴_____, it is still on order.

Virginie I really need to know *happened / to / has / it / what* ⁵_____.
Could *check / me / you / it / for / out*
⁶_____?

Kevin Certainly. I'll *back / you / to / hour / within / get / the* ⁷_____.

Virginie Thank you.

2 Kevin calls Virginie back. Complete their conversation with the phrases from the list.

~~put the order straight through~~   asap   charge it to
was dispatched on   check it out   as quick as we can
must have gone wrong

Kevin Hello, this is Kevin from DYK calling. I've got some information about your order.

Virginie Oh, thanks for calling back. So, what's happened to it?

Kevin Well, we ¹_put the order straight through_ to the warehouse, and it ²_____ the 25th.

Virginie But I haven't received it yet.

Kevin I'm sorry about that. Can you confirm the delivery address?

Virginie We wanted it delivered to our Brussels office.

Kevin Oh, something ³_____.
It looks like it might have gone to your Paris office instead. I'll ⁴_____ straightaway.

Virginie I've already been waiting three weeks. Could you just send it again ⁵_____?

Kevin OK, no problem. We'll resend it
⁶_____.

Virginie Thank you. And please
⁷_____ the Brussels account, not the Paris one.

Language at work

GRAMMAR REFERENCE

Direct and indirect questions

Form
We use a question word (e.g. *what, when, how*) + auxiliary verb (e.g. *be, do, can*) + subject + verb to form direct questions.

> **What are** you doing tomorrow?
> **When did** she arrive?   **How can** he get there?

Yes/No direct questions
For a direct question which needs a 'yes' or 'no' answer, we just use an auxiliary verb at the beginning.

> **Are** you free tomorrow?   **Did** she arrive on time?
> **Can** he get there?

We use the following phrases before indirect questions.

> *I'd like to know/ask …   Do you know …*
> *Can/Could you/anyone tell me …   I was wondering …*
> *Do you have any idea …   Would you mind telling me …*

Use a question word after each indirect question phrase, but use the same word order as an affirmative sentence and don't use an auxiliary verb.

Direct question	Indirect question
What time **does** the train leave?	I'd like to know what time the train **leaves**.
How often **do** trains to London **leave**?	Do you know how often trains to London **leave**?

Yes/No indirect questions
For an indirect question which needs a 'yes' or 'no' answer, use an *if* statement after each phrase.

> A *I was wondering **if** this train goes to London?*
> B *Yes*, it does.
> A *Do you know **if** it leaves at three?*
> B *No*, it doesn't. It leaves at four.

Writing indirect questions
Some indirect questions need a question mark and some just need a full stop. If the phrase starts with a question word, use a question mark. If the phrase is a statement, use a full stop.

> **Do you know** how often trains to London leave?
> **I'd like to know** what time the train leaves.

Use
1 We use indirect questions instead of direct questions to sound more formal, polite and less direct.
> **I was wondering if you could** meet me at 3.00?
> **Can you** meet me at 3.00? (more direct)

2 We use indirect questions at the beginning of an enquiry followed by a series of direct questions.
> A **Can you tell me how much it costs** to send a package to the USA?
> B *It depends on the size.*
> A **How much does a five kilo box cost**?

1 Put the words in the correct order to make direct or indirect questions.

1 was / if / could / I / order / an / place / I / wondering
   _____*I was wondering if I could place an order*_____?

2 much / a / does / it / magazine / cost / how / to / send
   _____?

3 idea / do / you / how / any / it / long / have / takes
   _____?

4 would / mind / arrived / if / a / telling / me / has / package / you
   _____?

5 has / visitor / yet / my / arrived
   _____?

6 tell / the / where / is / me / could / post / anyone / office
   _____?

7 do / for / you / a / if / know / left / message / they / me
   _____?

8 will / my / what / arrive / day / order
   _____?

2 Complete the indirect questions so that they have the same meaning as the direct questions.

1 What would you like to drink?
   I was wondering ___*what you'd like to drink*___.

2 Why didn't you call to say you'd be late?
   I'd like to know _____.

3 Where is the next conference?
   Could you tell me _____?

4 Which flight is Mr Stoppard on?
   Do you have any idea _____?

5 Are they arriving tonight?
   Do you know _____?

6 How often does the bus come?
   Would you mind telling me
   _____?

Working with words

1 Read these comments from people talking about their places of work. Match the adjectives from the list to the comments.

fully-equipped   ~~open-plan~~   *comfortable*   *spacious*
old-fashioned   *state-of-the-art*   *futuristic*   *fun*

1 'With the old offices everyone was in separate rooms with closed doors. Now you can see everyone.' _____*open-plan*_____

2 'The architect must have liked science fiction. The new headquarters looks like a spaceship has just landed!' _____

3 'Our new factory has the most modern equipment in the world.' _____

4 'Since we replaced the old computers with laptops, there's so much more room to work in.'
_____

5 'I complained about my chair because I kept getting a sore back. This new one is so much better for sitting in for long periods.'
_____

6 'I have everything I need in my office. A computer, a photocopier, a fax and a coffee machine.'
_____

7 'We have a room for staff with lots of computer games, a pool table and even a trampoline. I believe that adults need to behave like children sometimes.' _____

8 'We don't have many computers in our office. A lot of work is still done using pens and paper!'
_____

2 Underline the correct words in *italics* to complete the sentences.

1 That bright red colour on the walls *isn't exactly / is very* relaxing. I was thinking of a light green or something instead.

2 It's going to be difficult to change the dates. They're *fairly / not very* flexible.

3 My flight was 12 hours overnight. I'm *really / exactly* tired.

4 We've had some *extremely / pretty* good ideas so far but I think we can do better. Let's keep brainstorming.

5 The negotiations went *fairly / extremely* well. We didn't get everything we wanted, but neither did they. I still think we might get what we want in the end, though.

6 This new software is *very / not very* easy to use. I learnt all the basic functions in less than an hour.

7 We're all *not exactly / extremely* happy with your performance this year, so I see no need for you to make any changes.

Business communication

1 Complete the second sentences so that they have the same meaning as the first sentences.

1 I'm not sure it's a good idea to do this.
I have a few reservations
_____*about doing this*_____.

2 How about changing the colour?
Why don't we _____?

3 Let's ask them to make a better offer.
I think we should consider
_____.

4 I don't think we'll be able to convince them of our proposals.
It might prove _____.

5 Perhaps we could provide some chairs.
Couldn't _____?

6 We could always have music in the factory.
Have you thought about
_____?

7 Do you mind if I don't come?
I'd rather _____.

8 I'd recommend looking at this again tomorrow morning.
I'd recommend that _____.

2 Complete the missing words in the conversations.

1 A What do you think of this idea?
B Great. I r<u>eally</u> l<u>ike</u> it.

2 A It seems like a bad plan to me.
B No! It's a g_____ i_____.

3 A Maybe we should change the office round so that everyone shares desks.
B Sorry, but I don't think that w_____
w_____.

4 A This new system seems slower than the old one.
B I agree. Replacing the old one m_____
p_____ to be a bad idea!

5 A These new meeting rooms are very large but I don't like the colour.
B We c_____ a_____ repaint them.

6 A Let's cancel the order for new desks.
B Yes, I like the old ones. B_____, we can't really afford them.

Language at work

GRAMMAR REFERENCE

Quantifiers

Form

Quantifiers (e.g. *much, many, some, any, a little, a lot of, a few*) come before nouns.

> There are **a few problems** with the order.
> We don't have **much time**.

Use

The quantifier you use depends on the type of noun (countable or uncountable) that follows it.

1 Countable nouns have a singular and plural form (usually ending in *-s*, but some plurals are irregular). Uncountable nouns only have one form.
   Countable nouns: *chair (chairs), employee (employees), man (men), child (children)*
   Uncountable nouns: *time, money, information, coffee*

2 Use *some, any, a lot of* with countable AND uncountable nouns.
   > There are **a lot of** employees in this factory.
   > There's **a lot of** money in my bank account.

3 Use *many* and *a few* ONLY with plural countable nouns.
   > **How many** employees are there? Only **a few**.

4 Use *much* and *a little* ONLY with uncountable nouns.
   > **How much** information do you have? Only **a little**.

5 *Any, much* and *many* are mostly used in questions or negative statements.
   > How **much** money do you need?
   > Do you have **any** problems?
   > There aren't **many** employees in this company.

6 *Some* is mostly used in questions or positive statements.
   > Could you give me **some** help?
   > I've got **some** work for you to do.

7 *A lot of* can be used with questions, negative statements and positive statements.
   > He gets / doesn't get **a lot of** support in his job.
   > Do you get **a lot of** emails every day?

8 To make a comparison with countable or uncountable nouns you can use *more*.
   > I need **more** time to work on this!
   > We need **more** clients!

9 To make the comparative of *little / not much* with uncountable nouns, use *less*.
   > My new boss has **little** time for my questions.
   > My new boss has **less** time for my questions than my old boss.

10 To make the comparative of *few / not many* with countable nouns, use *fewer*.
   > The company does**n't** deal with **many** clients.
   > The company deals with **fewer** clients than ours.

---

1 Correct the sentences which have mistakes. Tick (✓) the correct sentences.

1 Do you have any ~~informations~~ about these people? *information*

2 How many people do you employ? _____

3 Sorry, I don't have much time. Let's be quick. _____

4 A little customers have complained about the increase. _____

5 I'm afraid we don't have many paper in stock. _____

6 There isn't much demand for this line any more. _____

7 Give him any more time to finish this. _____

8 I've got fewer space in my new office than in my old one. _____

9 A lot of people said they preferred the taste of this one. _____

10 I'd like a little help with that, please. _____

2 Two people are checking the store cupboard at work. Complete their conversation with a suitable quantifier.

A So, how ¹_*many*_ boxes of paper clips do we have in stock?

B Well, we only have a ²_____, so we should probably order some more.

A How about ink cartridges? I don't think there are ³_____ left.

B Well, there's an extra box of them here, but we'll need ⁴_____ more, sooner or later.

A OK. What about the coffee machine? How ⁵_____ coffee is there?

B There's a ⁶_____ of that, but there aren't ⁷_____ packets of tea.

A Right, so that's paper clips, ink cartridges and tea. Anything else?

B Well, we don't have ⁸_____ at the moment, but a ⁹_____ people in the office have asked me if we can have biscuits for the tea breaks.

Working with words

1 Match 1–7 to a–g to make sentences.

1 I wish you'd make _c_
2 It's important to evaluate ___
3 If you don't like doing the task, ___
4 That new employee seems to avoid ___
5 If you ignore ___
6 I'd like to invite ___
7 With long lists, I'd prioritize ___

a delegate it.
b doing anything manual.
c up your mind!
d everyone to comment on the new website designs.
e the different options before deciding.
f the problem, it rarely goes away.
g tasks in order of importance.

2 Complete the sentences with the correct form of the words in **bold**.

democracy

1 Our company is very _____ because we vote on every decision we make.

consult

2 We've had a _____ meeting with our accountants and the future doesn't look great.

confront

3 There was a _____ between management and the trade union but I think they've avoided a strike.

hierarchy

4 Most decisions are made at the top and passed down, so I'd describe my company as very _____!

cooperate

5 You aren't being very _____. Why do you have to disagree with everything I say?

3 Put the letters in brackets in the correct order to make words that match the definitions.

1 something you need to do quickly: (REGUNT) _____ _urgent_
2 general agreement between people: (OENSCSNUS) _____
3 a person who is part of a club, society or cooperative: (MBREME) _____
4 assess/judge: (EVELAUAT) _____
5 an argument or open conflict: (AOTONROFNCNTI) _____
6 final conclusion after thinking about or discussing something: (NIODICES) _____

Business communication

1 Put the words in the correct order to make expressions for negotiating.

1 me / you / offer / let / make / an
   Let me make you an offer .
2 concerns / do / any / this / you / have / about
   _____ ?
3 halfway / meet / 'll / you / I
   _____ .
4 would / I / think / fair / that / be
   _____ .
5 10% / if / offer / more / I / agree / you / will / years / to / two
   _____ ?
6 issue / with / discuss / you / to / an / I'd / like
   _____ .
7 not / in / to / position / I'm / that / accept / a
   _____ .

2 Read a conversation between a manager and one of their team. Complete the missing words 1–7.

A Hello. Please, sit down. There's something we need to ¹d_iscuss_____. I have an ²i_____ with your work.

B Really? What's that?

A The ³c_____ I have is that you are not doing regular hours and I never know when you are in the office.

B But we have a system of flexitime and home working. When I'm not here, I'm working from home.

A I understand that. But you still need to be here at certain times for meetings and so on.
The ⁴p_____ is that we need to agree some core hours.

B That's fine, although sometimes I get so much more done at home.

A I can imagine there are distractions in the office. Especially with your kind of work, where you need to concentrate a lot. ⁵S_____ we agree on three days when you are here for a full eight hours?

B Three days? I think that's unnecessary with the type of project I'm doing at the moment. Most of it is research and report writing.

A But you're still part of a team and your team members need to see you. How ⁶a_____ if I offered you the chance to do two fixed days in the office and then you choose a flexible third office day?

B OK, though I'm afraid it isn't always possible to do two fixed days. What happens when I have to travel?

A That's true. OK, let's review your schedule at the beginning of every month. It's really just a case of knowing when you are going to be here and when you absolutely have to be here.

B Right. I ⁷c_____ agree to that.

Language at work

GRAMMAR REFERENCE

First conditional

Form

if + present simple (= condition), *will/can/may/might* + infinitive (= result)

> *If we **change** our supplier, we**'ll reduce** costs.*

Use

To talk about likely or possible future situations and their likely results.

> *If they **close** the factory down, we**'ll have to** look for another job.*
> (It is possible that the factory might close down in the future.)

Second conditional

Form

if + past simple (= condition), *would/could* + infinitive (= result)

> *If we **changed** our supplier, we **would reduce** costs.*

Use

1 To talk about events that are unlikely to happen.
> *If you **wasted** less time chatting on the phone, you **would get** more work done.*
> (But I think you will continue to waste time.)
2 To talk about impossible (or highly unlikely) situations.
> *If I **were** taller, people **would take** me more seriously.*
> (But I'll always be short.)
> *If I **ran** the company, I **would make** a lot of changes.*
> (But I am just an 18-year-old office clerk.)
3 To talk about an imaginary situation.
> *If we **took over** their company, we**'d have** access to the South American market.*
4 To be more polite, or achieve more 'social distance'.
> *What **would** you **say if** I **asked** you to be CEO?*
5 We can use the second conditional structure *If I was* ... or *If I were* ... to give advice. We often use *were* instead of *was* to sound more formal.
> *If I **was/were** the manager, I **would improve** working conditions.*

unless, when, as soon as

1 We can use *unless* to mean *if not* or *except*.
> *They won't let you into the restaurant **unless** you're wearing a tie.*
2 Use *when / as soon as* instead of *if*, to show you are sure that something will happen.
> *Liz will call me **when** the client arrives.*
> (You are sure the client will arrive.)
> *Liz will call me **if** the client arrives.*
> (Maybe the client will arrive, but you are not sure.)

---

1 Complete the sentences with the most appropriate form of the verbs in brackets.

1 I know it won't ever happen, but what <u>*would we do*</u> (we / do) if our restaurant suddenly <u>*became*</u> (become) famous?

2 Unless you _____ (have) good financial planning, your expansion plans _____ (end) in disaster.

3 Every new recruit starts with the same opportunities. If you _____ (work) hard, you _____ (be) promoted.

4 If I _____ (know) the answer to that question, I _____ (be) a very rich person!

5 If you _____ (have) three wishes for your career, what _____ (they / be)?

6 Unless your work _____ (improve), you _____ (have to) start looking for another job.

7 I'm not saying it's going to happen, but how _____ (you / feel) if we _____ (ask) you to work in our Lagos office?

8 Just imagine what you _____ (do) if the firm suddenly _____ (go) bankrupt.

9 If you _____ (can) change just one thing about your working environment, what _____ (you / change)?

10 When they _____ (arrive), we _____ (be able to) start the meeting.

2 <u>Underline</u> the correct words in *italics* to complete the sentences.

1 We will start working on the project *as soon as / unless* the budget is agreed.

2 *If / When* we know more about our competitor's plans, we will make our final decision.

3 *If / Unless* you make the decision, I *will have / had* to make it for you.

4 *When / Unless* we improve the design, it *will look / looks* too old-fashioned.

5 She *will have to / has to* accept being unpopular *unless / if* she becomes the boss.

Working with words

1 Put the letters in brackets in the correct order to make words that match the definitions.

1 something that gets in the way: (OSALTBCE) _____obstacle_____

2 often changing in an exciting way: (MICANDY) _____

3 an idea for something new: (OCNEPCT) _____

4 something which you can depend on: (ELREIBLA) _____

5 not complicated: (EMSLIP) _____

6 new and original: (NNAIOVIVTE) _____

7 something which can change the way things are done or thought about: (AEVYROONLTUIR) _____

8 new and interesting in a way that is different from anything that has existed before: (GORILINA) _____

9 a new idea based on something that already exists: (VIRONTENINE) _____

10 clever and complicated: (THISDETOPICAS) _____

2 Choose the correct words (a, b or c) to complete 1–8 in the text.

In many ways, the company Doherty Preserves looks like your typical food company, with a simple ¹____c____. It sells a ²_____ range of marmalades, jams and fruit preserves, based on old recipes, to delicatessens and local markets. And like every other food business these days, the company is aiming to reach a more health-conscious consumer, so not a ³_____ idea.

What is surprising is that the company was the ⁴_____ of a 14-year-old. Now aged 16, Fraser Doherty first ⁵_____ with the idea of selling preserves when his grandmother taught him the secret recipe for her marmalade. This was the ⁶_____ for Fraser's business idea, and within weeks he'd begun selling to the neighbours. From there, he employed friends to sell door to door on a commission basis.

Such ⁷_____ from one so young might be put down to a good education, but Fraser says, 'It's a million miles away from what I learnt at school.' In addition, money doesn't seem to be an ⁸_____. 'I don't concern myself so much with profits and productivity – what's important to me is improving quality and customer satisfaction.'

	a	b	c
1	a reinvention	b catalyst	c concept
2	a traditional	b revolutionary	c up-to-date
3	a revolutionary	b reliable	c simple
4	a obstacle	b brainchild	c invention
5	a came across	b came out	c came up
6	a challenge	b solution	c catalyst
7	a breakthrough	b innovation	c reliability
8	a obstacle	b prototype	c brainchild

Business communication

1 Underline the correct words in *italics* to complete the sentences.

1 Good morning, and thanks *for / to / at* coming.

2 I'm going to tell you *of / about / for* my new concept.

3 I'd like to begin *from / at / by* outlining the main problems.

4 I'll take questions *by / at / to* the end.

5 Let's look *at / by / from* this chart.

6 The main reason *of / for / about* this is the drop in demand.

7 The best thing *of / for / about* this is its simplicity.

8 That brings me *by / at / to* the end of my presentation.

9 We *think / notice / take* it's a good idea.

10 That's everything I want to *end / tell / say*.

2 Complete the introduction to a presentation with a suitable word.

¹_____ afternoon, everyone. I am ²_____ today to tell you about an exciting new way of choosing your holiday. I'd like to ³_____ by giving you an overview of my talk. ⁴_____, I'll tell you about how the concept was developed. ⁵_____, we'll have a look at how it was launched. And ⁶_____, we'll have a look at the website and I'll show you how it works. Please feel ⁷_____ to ask questions at any time.

3 Number the lines of the final part of the presentation in the correct order 1–12.

a bring immediate results. So, to ___

b we need to listen. Then ___

c for listening. Are ___

d see from this ___

e summarize, there are three ___

f brings me to the end of my presentation. Thanks ___

g ways to respond to our customers. First, ___

h So, as you can ___1___

i we need to be seen to be listening and reacting. OK, that ___

j there any questions? ___

k diagram, thinking about our customers can ___

l we need to act. And finally, ___

Language at work

1 Correct the mistakes with the superlative form in each sentence.

1 Face-to-face communication is still the ~~most~~ best way of doing business. ___*best*___
2 I think quickest way to send it is by courier.
    _____
3 Microsoft must still be the more influential company in the whole world.
    _____
4 It's one of the most beautiful place in the world.
    _____
5 Since taking this job, I'm the boredest I've ever been. _____
6 We don't want to be a second most successful. We want to be number one!
    _____
7 What's the biggest order you ever received?
    _____
8 My boss is the most busiest person in the company.
    _____

2 Complete the article with the words from the list. If necessary, change the word to a superlative form.

bad   good   few (x2)   flexible   second   ~~the~~   one

Age at work

They forget things. They don't work in teams. They can't adapt to [1] ___*the*___ latest technology. These are often the reasons given for not employing older people. But research shows that the [2] _____ workers are not necessarily the slowest and in fact slower workers often make the [3] _____ mistakes.

Jutta Kray of Saarland University in Germany, who specializes in this area of research, did find that when it comes to being the most [4] _____ and quickest at decision-making, older people come [5] _____ best to their younger counterparts. In the 21st century, where speed of thought is [6] _____ of the most important business skills, this is clearly a disadvantage. But Kray also found in other tests that the 'inflexible old' made the [7] _____ mistakes in certain tasks, so for some jobs the older employee may be the [8] _____ suited.

Working with words

1 <u>Underline</u> the correct words in *italics* (1–10) to complete the texts.

In the case of product [1]*injury / failure*, please contact the number below to obtain a returns code. Then return the defective unit to us in its original packaging in order to receive a [2]*refund / recall*.

All our computer systems are [3]*down / defect* and we are unable to deal with customer enquiries. Please call again tomorrow.

If your order has a manufacturer's [4]*complaint / defect* or it is [5]*misunderstood / damaged* in some way, we will pay for any returns postage.

When using this machinery, wear protective goggles and gloves at all time to avoid personal [6]*injury / defect*.

Due to a fault in the steering system, the vehicle manufacturer is [7]*resolving / recalling* all cars made in the year 2008.

Over the last three days, we have received over 1,000 [8]*complaints / faults* from viewers of this TV programme. It was inappropriate to broadcast this before 9 p.m. and we would like to apologize for our [9]*mistake / damage*.

The technical problem with our online ordering system has now been [10]*resolved / refunded*. We apologize for any inconvenience caused.

2 Match 1–6 to a–f to make sentences.
1 A machine fault caused _f_
2 As a result of a machine fault, ___
3 A machine fault lead ___
4 There was product damage because ___
5 A machine fault resulted ___
6 The product damage was due ___

a to product damage.
b in product damage.
c to a machine fault.
d there was product damage.
e of a machine fault.
f ~~product damage.~~

Business communication

1 Complete the conversation with the words from the list.

do you mean by   should solve the problem   won't
think you should   keeps on   if I were you
sounds as though   ~~can I help~~   have you tried

Gareth Hi, Blanka. How [1]_____*can I help*_____?
Blanka It's my printer. It [2]_____ give me clean print-outs of anything. It just messes them up.
Gareth What exactly [3]_____ 'messes them up'?
Blanka Well, it [4]_____ missing lines and you can hardly read it.
Gareth Don't worry, it [5]_____ it could simply be a printing-head problem. [6]_____ cleaning them?
Blanka No. I didn't know I had to.
Gareth Yes, I [7]_____ clean the heads regularly so that this doesn't happen again. I'll show you. There, that [8]_____.
Blanka Oh, that's much better, Gareth. Thanks!
Gareth You're welcome. Although from now on, I'd clean the heads regularly [9]_____.

2 <u>Underline</u> the correct words in *italics* to complete the sentences.
1 It looks *like / though* you'll have to buy a new one.
2 It's extremely annoying – she *always borrows / 's always borrowing* my calculator without asking.
3 I'm really annoyed. Ludo keeps on *taking / take* biscuits from my desk.
4 What's *matter / wrong* with it exactly?
5 There we are, that *should / must* fix it.
6 I'd *advise / say* you not to use it again – best to call the engineer first.
7 It *smells / sounds* like something must be loose – it's so noisy.
8 That *should / mean* solve the problem.
9 So what *appears / looks like* to be the problem with your computer?
10 Have you tried *put / putting* it in a different position?

Language at work

1 Match 1–5 to a–e to make sentences.
  1 She's the inventor _d_
  2 This is the discovery ___
  3 Nine o'clock on a Monday is the time ___
  4 He's the person ___
  5 That's the same place ___

  a when we have our weekly team meeting.
  b where you went on holiday last year, isn't it?
  c who has just been fired.
  d whose last idea made her a millionaire.
  e which changed the world of telecommunications.

2 In which two sentences above can you use *that* as the relative pronoun?

  _____

3 Complete the conversation with the correct relative pronouns.
  A Look at this photograph. It's the place ¹_____ we could build a new factory.
  B Is it for sale?
  A Yes, the person ²_____ land it is, wants to sell as soon as possible.
  B Do we have permission to build on it?
  A I have a meeting with the person at the local council ³_____ deals with planning permission. He sounded positive on the phone.
  B Great. But is there a town or city nearby ⁴_____ employees could relocate to? After all, a new factory needs a workforce.
  A The nearest town is about two kilometres away, with a population of ten thousand people. There are plans to expand the town into a city, so the government is building a new railway through the region. That will be the time ⁵_____ land will become more expensive, so we should buy it sooner rather than later.

4 Join the two sentences with a relative pronoun.
  1 I'm the person. I deal with technical issues round the office.
    I'm the person who deals with technical issues round the office.
  2 They are the people. Their company went bankrupt last year.

    _____

  3 Palo Alto is a city. It has lots of tech businesses.

    _____

  4 The lunchbreak is a time. You should relax at lunchbreak.

    _____

  5 Tennis is a sport. A lot of employees play tennis after work.

    _____

Working with words

1 Make multi-word verbs with the words in the table and match them to the synonyms 1–10.

drop	up	of
pick	down	on
set	out	
make	into	
sign	away	
cut	off	
turn		
take		
throw		

1 reduce _____
2 discard _____
3 transform _____
4 remove (to another place)
  _____
5 start (a new business) _____
6 deliver and leave _____
7 select _____
8 collect _____
9 create from _____
10 register (for something) _____

2 Complete the sentences with the correct multi-word verbs from **1**.

1 I was trying to _____ _____ a new dress for work but I can't find anything suitable in this shop.
2 Don't _____ _____ that office chair! We can use it somewhere else.
3 He's the sort of person who, one day, will leave here and _____ _____ his own company.
4 I'm trying to _____ _____ _____ cigarettes at the moment.
5 We _____ all our products _____ _____ recycled plastic.
6 What time does the truck normally _____ _____ the finished products at the warehouse?
7 Our production process creates lots of waste by-products. I wonder if we could _____ them _____ something useful.
8 The courier is coming at twelve to _____ _____ this package. Can you make sure he collects it on time?

Business communication

1 Put the words in the correct order to make questions and sentences.

1 questions / are / any / there
  _Are there any questions_____?
2 have / questions / does / any / anyone
  _____?
3 quite / understand / question / I / the / don't
  _____.
4 let / correctly / understood / me / check / I've / you
  _____.
5 for / you / question / that / thank
  _____.
6 that / question / an / 's / important
  _____.
7 to / are / two / parts / question / your / there
  _____.
8 answer / that / your / does / question
  _____?
9 have / question / I / answered / your
  _____?

2 Complete the conversation with the pairs of words from the list.

asking + if   questions + answer   ~~brings + end~~
check + correctly   that + your   quite + question
hear + repeat

A That [1]_brings_ me to the ___end___ of the presentation, so if anyone has any [2]_____, I'm happy to try and _____ them.
B Yes, with regard to your final point, how long do you think the process of change will take?
A Sorry, I couldn't [3]_____ you. Can you _____ that?
B I was asking how long you think the process of change will take.
A Sorry, I don't [4]_____ understand the _____.
B I mean, are all the changes you outlined in the near future or are some of them long-term?
A Let me [5]_____ I've understood you _____. You're [6]_____ me _____ all the changes I've outlined need to happen sooner or later?
B Yes, I suppose I am.
A All of them need to happen as soon as possible. If we don't change, we won't survive. Does [7]_____ answer _____ question?

Language at work

Passive forms

Form

Verbs in sentences can either be active or passive.
The passive is formed with the verb *be* + past participle of the main verb.

Tense	Passive form	Active form
Present simple	*The post **is opened** in the morning.*	*David **opens** the post in the morning.*
Present continuous	*The report **is being written** right now.*	*Christina **is writing** that report right now.*
Past simple	*I **was given** your name by a colleague.*	*Joe Langley **gave** me your name.*
Present perfect	*We've **been asked** to speak at the event.*	*The CEO **has asked** us to speak at the event.*
Modal	*It **mustn't be changed** in any way.*	*Nobody **must change** it in any way.*
Infinitive	*The waste is taken **to be turned into** fuel.*	*The company takes the waste **to turn it into** fuel.*

Use

1 To talk about processes or how something is done.
   *First of all, the bottle **is washed** and sterilized. Next, it **is filled** …*
2 To emphasize the result, rather than the person or thing causing it.
   *We **have been forced** to change our plans because …*
3 When the person who does the action is unknown, unimportant or obvious.
   *Hello, I **was advised** to talk to you about purchasing …*
4 Passive forms tend to be written down more than they are spoken. For example, we often use passives in formal business writing such as memos and reports.
   *It **is recommended** that all staff arrange an appointment with their line managers.*

1 Underline the correct words in *italics* to complete the sentences.
   1 The Kabul Star football *manufactures / is manufactured* in Afghanistan.
   2 Employees *make / are made* the footballs in a large house in Kabul.
   3 The process starts in the garage where pieces of leather *cut and paint / are cut and painted*.
   4 The workers then *sew / are sewn* the leather pieces together to make the balls.
   5 After that, the balls *wash / are washed* in the bathroom and packaged in the largest bedroom in the house.
   6 The factory only *employs / is employed* women.
   7 A charity called Humanitarian Assistance for Women *supports / is supported* the factory.
   8 The female workers *encourage and train / are encouraged and trained* to set up their own businesses.

2 Complete the sentences with the correct form of the verbs from the list.
   use   ~~know~~   turn   locate   hold   win
   1 The Tate Modern _____*is known*_____ as one of the best modern art galleries in London.
   2 It _____ on the banks of the River Thames in the heart of the city.
   3 An old power station _____ into the gallery in the year 2000.
   4 An international competition _____ to find a suitable proposal for transforming the power station into an art gallery.
   5 It _____ by Herzog & deMeuron, a Swiss architectural practice.
   6 This unique space _____ to display the large collection of art since its opening.

3 Rewrite the sentences in either the passive or active form.
   1 Most business these days is done over the phone.
      People *do most of their business over the phone these days*.
   2 The company is opening three more new branches this year.
      Three more branches _____.
   3 The manager must give employees a warning if they are late.
      Employees _____.
   4 It has been agreed to extend the hours of work.
      We _____.
   5 People in this culture regard punctuality as a sign of politeness.
      Punctuality _____.

Working with words

1 Match the adjectives in the list to comments 1–7.

confident   *hard-working*   *enthusiastic*   ~~*creative*~~
punctual   *patient*   *ambitious*

1 'I like his original ideas and new ways of approaching things.'   _creative_

2 'She doesn't seem to have any doubts about her abilities.'   _____

3 'She wants to be CEO of this company by the time she's twenty-five.'   _____

4 'It's important, as a manager, to spend time listening to your employees and not expect them to always get things right the first time round.'
_____

5 'He's always the first one in and the last one out, at work. You never see him resting.'
_____

6 'Whatever the plan, she's always happy to try it out.'   _____

7 'Workers in this country are never late for work. It's considered very bad.'   _____

2 Complete the words in the sentences with the correct ending.

1 People such as doctors and nurses must be so dedicate_d_ to their work.

2 Sorry to keep you waiting. Thank you for your patien_____.

3 We don't have much confiden_____ in this new product, because the initial sales figures have been very disappointing.

4 You need a lot of motivat_____ when you're self-employed.

5 We've been very impressed with your creativ_____ in coming up with solutions to problems.

6 They say that women are able to do more than one job at a time and are more flexib_____ than men.

7 He's young and has lots of enthusias_____, so we should probably spend time and money on training him.

8 My biggest ambitio_____ is to climb Mount Everest.

Business communication

1 Complete the conversation with suitable words or phrases.

A In [1] _general_, we're very
[2] _____ with your performance. You seem to be doing very well since you started. How do you
[3] _____ about the last six months?

B I'm really [4] _____ with my work and the staff seem to like me.

A Yes, one of your key [5] _____ is motivating your team. You
[6] _____ to be doing very well. However, one [7] _____ I wanted to discuss was a complaint we had from one employee.

2 Underline the correct words in *italics* to complete the conversation.

A How are you getting [1] *on* / *off* / *out* with these late orders?

B I think we've dealt with most of them.

A That's great. Have you thought [2] *with* / *about* / *for* how we can avoid delays like this in the future?

B Personally, I think communication between purchasing and the warehouse is an area [3] *at* / *with* / *for* improvement.

A You might be right. I think we should have another meeting next week. Is that OK [4] *to* / *from* / *with* you?

3 Complete the conversation with the verbs from the list.

~~*summarize*~~   *intend*   *add*   *do*   *sound*

A So let's [1] _summarize_ what we've agreed. One thing you're going to [2] _____ is talk to your line manager about your idea for a new system. And you also [3] _____ to join the English classes at lunchtime. How does that [4] _____?

B Fine.

A Is there anything else you'd like to [5] _____?

Language at work

GRAMMAR REFERENCE

Past perfect

Form

had + past participle

Use

1 To say that one event happened before another completed past event.

   *The meeting **had ended** when he arrived.*

2 The past perfect often appears in sentences with conjunctions such as *when, by the time, because, so.* The other verb in the sentence is often in the past simple.

3 Words often used with the present perfect are also often used with the past perfect, e.g. *for, since, yet, just, never, recently, already.*

   *The email had **already** been sent when John noticed the mistake.*

Past continuous

Form

was/were + *-ing* form

Use

1 To talk about something in progress at a particular time in the past. It often appears with the past simple in the same sentence.

   *We **were talking** when he arrived.*

   Note that the past action might happen whilst the continuous action is in progress (a), or it might interrupt and stop the continuous action (b).

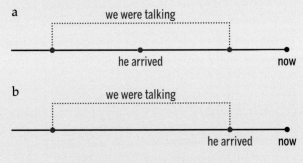

2 To give background information in the past.
   *We **were phoning** customers all day.*

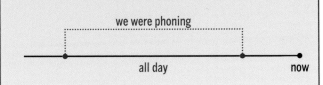

1 <u>Underline</u> the correct words in *italics* to complete the information.

'Several years ago I [1]*have worked* / <u>*was working*</u> as the quality technician with a new company. Well, I [2]*hadn't been* / *wasn't* there many weeks when, one day, while we [3]*were all finishing* / *all finished* off – it was around 5.00 p.m. – the supervisor came by. He [4]*was saying* / *said* he was going round the factory and asking everyone for feedback on a new idea of his to improve a process on the production floor. He [5]*was asking* / *hadn't asked* me up to this point, so I said I'd have a look. But while I [6]*was suggesting* / *had suggested* reversing a couple of steps in the process, he suddenly [7]*stopped* / *had stopped* me and explained why my suggestions weren't possible and walked off. Anyway, six months later, I was reading my annual appraisal report from the same supervisor when I [8]*was coming* / *came across* this line. "He is unable to accept other people's opinions." He obviously [9]*wasn't liking* / *hadn't liked* the feedback on his idea six months before and he [10]*has waited* / *had waited* all that time to criticize me!'

2 Complete the interview with the past perfect or the past continuous form of the verbs in brackets.

Journalist You opened your first clothes shop in 1998, Mary. So, did your interest in fashion begin there or [1]_____*had you been*_____ (be) interested before that?

Mary Yes, I suppose so. I [2]_____ (have) a number of jobs in the Hong Kong fashion industry long before I opened my own shop. And that was all at the time when clothes with a Chinese look [3]_____ (quickly / become) very fashionable around the world. Although, even as a child, while I [4]_____ (grow) up in America, I knew that working in fashion was something I wanted to do.

Journalist So why didn't you stay in the USA, where there was already an established industry?

Mary Well, when my boyfriend, now my husband, was offered a job in Hong Kong, I [5]_____ (just / graduate), so I was free to go anywhere.

Journalist And was it while you [6]_____ (run) your own shop that Tiger Retro approached you?

Mary That's right. Actually, they [7]_____ (ask) me once before.

Journalist So why [8]_____ (you / not take) the job previously?

Mary At the time, my own business [9]_____ (do) really well and I wanted to see how far we could go with that …

Communication activities

Unit 1 | Talking point, task 1

Speed networking cards

JOB Property developer

COMPANY ELB (Elite Building International): builds and sells property in the UK, France, Italy and Spain.

REASONS FOR ATTENDING NETWORKING EVENT
PROFESSIONAL: Look for business partners. Want to find a printer for your brochures and promotional literature.
PERSONAL: Arrange a study tour for your daughter.

INTERESTS Collecting modern art, golf.

JOB Hot-air balloon pilot

COMPANY Hot Air Experiences – offers flights over castles, forests and famous landmarks across Europe. Also arranges trips to African game parks. Great as incentives and prizes to customers and sales staff.

REASONS FOR ATTENDING NETWORKING EVENT
PROFESSIONAL: Find new partners. Find a sponsor for your next expedition.
PERSONAL: Meet some interesting people.

INTERESTS Photography, music.

JOB Event organizer

COMPANY Instant Events – organizes conferences and hospitality events (venue, catering, photographers, printed invitations).

REASONS FOR ATTENDING NETWORKING EVENT
PROFESSIONAL: Make contacts and find potential customers. Find partners who can offer exciting events and motivational prizes.
PERSONAL: Organize your next holiday.

INTERESTS Extreme sports, languages, travel.

JOB Marketing manager

COMPANY Speakeasy, a chain of language schools with centres in all the major European capitals. Also runs holiday courses for young people in different countries.

REASONS FOR ATTENDING NETWORKING EVENT
PROFESSIONAL: Find new partners and customers.
PERSONAL: Buy a property in Spain.

Interests Eating out, travel, walking, cycling.

JOB Travel agent

COMPANY Romano Travel – specializes in exciting and unusual holidays, e.g. sledging with dogs in the north of Canada, eco-tourism in the Brazilian rainforest.

REASONS FOR ATTENDING NETWORKING EVENT
PROFESSIONAL: Sell your holidays. Find new partners.
PERSONAL: Make friends. Improve your social life.

INTERESTS Sport, travel, cooking.

JOB Cook and caterer

COMPANY EPG – specializes in international cuisine. Has cookery schools for young people in Florence and Lyon.

REASONS FOR ATTENDING NETWORKING EVENT
PROFESSIONAL: Expand the business into gastro-tourism. Looking for partners in the travel industry and people who can take care of promotional material and packages.
PERSONAL: Find people who share your hobbies.

INTERESTS Languages, sport, exotic travel.

JOB Customer services manager

COMPANY Paper Solutions – hi-tech printers specializing in promotional literature and company prospectuses for prestigious organizations.

REASONS FOR ATTENDING NETWORKING EVENT
PROFESSIONAL: Make new business contacts.
PERSONAL: Meet some interesting people.

INTERESTS Golf, tennis, travel.

Unit 2 | Business communication, exercise 7

Student A

Call 1:
You met Keiran at a meeting last week in Dublin. You can't find his contact details. Call Student B and ask for Keiran's last name, mobile number and email.

Call 2:
Answer Student A's phone call. Give the information on this contact:
Marianne Chiew
00 86 10 6957 8699
www.KALglobal.org.hk

Unit 3 | Business communication, exercise 5

Student A

You are in charge of Project 1. Your partner is in charge of Project 2. Call your partner. Give an update about Project 1 and delegate two tasks to your partner. Then ask your partner for an update about Project 2.

Project 1
Organizing a two-day training session for staff
- Venue for training session – room booked.
- Hotel for trainers – Victoria Hotel has available rooms. Trying to negotiate discount.
- Lunch – none so far. Need someone to book caterers and negotiate payment. Delegate this to your partner.
- Information pack for trainees – need to ask trainers to send schedule and summary of training session.
- Need to organize transport between hotel and office. Delegate this to your partner.

Project 2
Raising money for a local children's charity
- Posters and leaflets?
- 10 km sponsored run?
- Charity sale?
- Anything else?

Unit 6 | Language at work, exercise 6

Student A

1 You are going to a trade fair. Read some sentences about it and write in *the*, *a* or no article (–).
   - The annual Garden Trade Fair in [1]___ Cologne attracts over 40,000 visitors who come from all over [2]___ world.
   - [3]___ exhibition centre is 200,000 square metres with [4]___ outdoor and indoor displays.
   - All exhibitors must reserve [5]___ stand by May 5th to guarantee [6]___ place.
   - For overseas visitors, there is [7]___ regular shuttle bus leaving from [8]___ airport every 15 minutes.

2 You are going to ask your partner for more information about the trade fair. Prepare these questions with the correct article (or no article) and ask your partner for the information.
   How many / exhibitors attend / trade fair?
   Which parts of / world do exhibitors come from?
   What opportunities does / exhibition offer?
   Why should you go sightseeing in / Cologne?

3 Your partner is also going to the trade fair. Answer his/her questions using the information in 1.

Unit 8 | Language at work, exercise 8

Pair A

You are in charge of setting up a new company office in another country. You have asked the Finance Department for a budget of $100,000 (not including wages) to set it up.

1 Brainstorm all the expenses you think you'll need to budget for and write these down. Then discuss how to divide the $100,000 between the expenses. Write a figure next to each expense.

2 Meet with Pair B. Present your budget with the expenses and figures to the Finance Department and answer their questions.

Viewpoint 2 | exercise 13

What was happening in each situation?

1 In some cultures, it is normal and polite to listen to your partner, to wait and then to speak. In other cultures, it's normal to interrupt when you want to speak.

2 In some cultures, including Thai culture, it is not acceptable to criticize someone in front of their colleagues because they cannot 'save face'. The woman feels she has no choice but to resign.

3 The German approach to discussion is more direct and to the point than it might be in the USA. The American mistakes this directness as aggressive.

Unit 8 | Business communication, exercise 6

Student A

You are going to present a slide from a presentation to UK building investors. Prepare and then take turns to present the information to your partner. Decide with your partner if UK property is a good investment for the future.

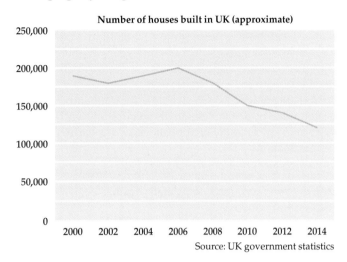

Number of houses built in UK (approximate)

Source: UK government statistics

Unit 8 | Talking point, task 4

What happened to the crowdfunding ideas?

Fish on wheels

This idea failed to raise €40,000. In fact, some critics were surprised that there were 89 people who offered a total of €5,250. After all, would the fish crash? And what happens when two fish are in at the same time? Nevertheless, Studio Diip, the company who made it, is still in business today.

MiRing

Twin brothers Zach and Max Zitney only raised around $8,000 for their ring, so failed to get crowdfunding. However, there is a positive end to the story. A UK-firm working on a similar product contacted the brothers as a result of their attempt at crowdfunding and now they are collaborating.

New York City Opera

The opera company only raised $301,019 through crowdfunding, so failed to meet its $1million target. New York City Opera went bankrupt and closed in 2013.

Form1

This was successful! In fact, Form1 received much more than its $100,000 goal. Over 2,000 investors offered $3 million dollars in funding. Nowadays, the Form1 (manufactured by Formlabs) is used by designers, engineers and artists around the world.

Unit 4 | Business communication, exercise 5

Student A

You think the new system is a good idea but your partner has some concerns. Talk about the benefits of the new system to Student B and handle any questions and concerns. Try to convince Student B that it's a good system.

Unit 9 | Language at work, exercise 7

Student A

Think about what questions you might need to ask to get the information you need. (Use a mix of indirect and direct questions).

Call 1:

You work for a shipping company. Use this information to answer your partner's questions about a shipment from Singapore to New York.

Size of containers	Price	Time for shipment
67 cubic metres	£5,000	6 weeks (approximately)
33 cubic metres	£3,500	

Warehouse storage: First seven days free. After that, minimum of $100 a week (depending on size of order).

Note: For insurance enquiries, please contact our agent on 0044 235 4756.

Call 2:

You want to transport some handmade goods from Istanbul to London by road. Call the transport company for a quote. Find out about:
- price for up to 1,000 kilos
- delivery time
- any additional costs
- warehouse storage for two days
- insurance for goods

Unit 11 | Business communication, exercise 6

Student B

Negotiate an agreement between a manufacturer of car parts and a regional distributor. Agree upon some details of the new contract.

You are the regional distributor for the southern region of the country. You would like a contract with exclusivity for three years. If the manufacturer wants to have a shorter contract or to introduce sales performance reviews, then you will need to negotiate. You also know that the manufacturer wants distributors in the western and northern regions of the country and you would like this business. Spend a few minutes preparing your position, then begin the negotiation.

Unit 9 | Business communication, exercise 5

Student A

Take turns to role-play two situations on the phone. In one situation you will be a customer, and in the other situation a call handler. In each situation you will have two conversations.

Situation 1

Conversation 1

You are the customer. You work for an oil company.
- Call the supplier (S1 Engineering).
- Give your account number HK568 and order two drill pieces.

Conversation 2

You urgently need the pieces you ordered five days ago. You are very unhappy with the delay.
- Call S1 Engineering again. Explain the problem.
- Give your account/order details again.
- Ask for a solution.

Situation 2

Conversation 1

You are a call handler for Haddows Trading, a fashion distributor.
- Answer the call from a customer.
- Ask for the account number and details of the order.
- Give this order reference: HTGS899.

Conversation 2

You receive another call from the customer two days later.
- Answer the call.
- Ask for the account details and order reference. Find out what the problem is.
- Invent an excuse and explanation.
- Promise to send a delivery van with the order today at no extra charge.

Unit 10 | Working with words, exercise 10

Look at this website with offices to rent. Take turns to choose a property and describe it to your partner. Use different adverbs and adjectives to describe it. Your partner must guess which property it is.

TOP OFFICE RENTALS

Property 1
Fallows Court Offices

5 individual offices on 3rd floor of four-floor building.

Location: Off motorway. Excellent parking. 1 km from mainline station.

Built: 2015

Facilities: Conference room, Reception area, Shared kitchen on 2nd floor. No shops or cafés near.

Property 2
High Towers

Open plan office for approximately 15 staff. 3 individual offices.

Location: City centre. Bus stop outside. No parking.

Built: 1998

Facilities: Shops and cafés nearby. Membership of local gym.

Property 3
Watson's Wharf

50 cubical offices with 2 large breakout areas on 5th floor. Previously used as call centre.

Built: 2002

Location: 3 km from city centre with cycle path. Parking and bus stop.

Facilities: Canteen on ground floor. Also use of locker room and showers.

Property 4
The Old Warehouse

2 open plan areas with 5 offices and conference room.

Built: Original warehouse built in 1910, renovated in 2003.

Location: 0.5 km from airport. Shuttle bus from city centre (25 minutes). Parking.

Facilities: Canteen. Small shared gym and changing rooms with showers. Fitness classes held three evenings a week.

Unit 10 | Business communication, exercise 6

1 An architect is redesigning your office space. Look at these two styles of office and read about some advantages and disadvantages for each in the table. Can you add any more?

	Style A	Style B
Advantages	friendly, easy to communicate	good for concentration, private
Disadvantages	noisy, harder for private conversation	not as social, old-fashioned

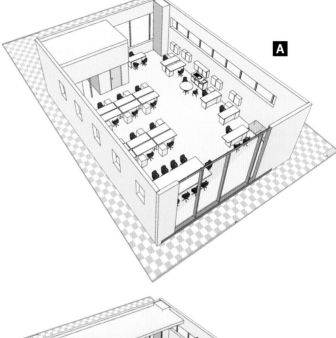

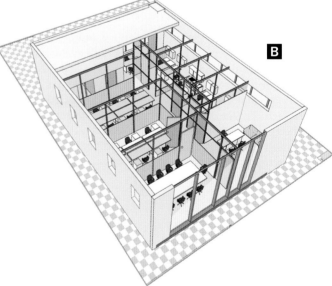

2 Now prepare and give your recommendation for one of the office styles using the expressions from **4**. Student A, promote style A. Student B, promote style B. Respond to the recommendation you hear. Try to come to an agreement with your partner.

Example: **A** *I'd recommend having an open-plan office because …*

B *I think we should consider building closed offices because …*

Unit 10 | Talking point, task 3

Frederick Herzberg (1923–2000) researched motivation in the workplace over many years. After different studies, he developed his theory that satisfaction and dissatisfaction at work were caused by two sets of factors.

- In general, there are factors which workers like but do not provide long-term satisfaction. These include: a company car, job security, new company policies, relationship with boss, salary, relationship with colleagues, your personal life.

- Then there are long-term factors which are the true motivators in the workplace. These include: achievement, recognition of good performance, the nature of the work, level of responsibility, advancement.

Unit 11 | Business communication, exercise 6

Student A

Negotiate an agreement between a manufacturer of car parts and a regional distributor. Agree upon some details of the new contract.

You are the manufacturer. You would like a contract lasting two years with reviews of sales performance every 12 months. If the distributor doesn't reach a target, you have 90 days to end the contract. The distributor will have exclusivity to distribute in the southern region of the country. Currently, you also have a distributor in the western region, though the contract ends in 12 months, and you are currently looking for a distributor in the northern region. You could offer the southern distributor these two other regions also in return for something. Spend a few minutes preparing your position, then begin the negotiation.

Unit 15 | Business communication, exercise 5

Imagine you have a performance review. Complete this form for your job.

Part A

Please answer the questions on this form and return to your line manager before your performance review.

1 Have the last six months been good/bad/satisfactory? Why?

_____

_____

2 What do you consider are your most important achievements of the six months?

_____

_____

3 Which parts of the job interest you the most? And the least?

_____

_____

4 How could your performance be improved in your current position?

_____

_____

Unit 2 | Business communication, exercise 7

Student B

Call 1:

Answer Student A's phone call. Give the information on this contact:

Keiran Geraghty
00 353 1 657 4770
K_geraghty@iol.ie

Call 2:

You met Ms Chiew at an exhibition stand in Hong Kong. You can't find her contact details. Call Student A and ask for her first name, office number and company website.

Unit 3 | Business communication, exercise 5

Student B

Your partner is in charge of Project 1. You are in charge of Project 2. Your partner will call you. Ask your partner for an update about Project 1. Then give an update about Project 2 and delegate two tasks to your partner.

Project 1
Organizing a two-day training session for staff
- Venue for training session?
- Hotel for trainers?
- Lunch?
- Information pack for trainees?
- Anything else?

Project 2
Raising money for a local children's charity
- Posters and leaflets – printing now.
- 10 km sponsored run – need to contact council about using sports stadium. Delegate this task to your partner.
- Charity sale – all staff have received a memo.
- Need someone to organize collection boxes for charity sale. Delegate this task to your partner.

Unit 6 | Language at work, exercise 6

Student B

1 You are going to a trade fair. Read some sentences about it and write in *the*, *an* or no article (–).
   - Every year, 2,000 exhibitors attend [1]___ annual Garden Trade Fair in [2]___ Cologne.
   - There are exhibitors from over [3]___ 50 countries in Europe, North and South America, and [4]___ Asia.
   - [5]___ exhibition offers opportunities to show [6]___ latest trends in plants and garden products.
   - Cologne is [7]___ ancient and beautiful city, so you should go [8]___ sightseeing while you are here.
2 Your partner is also going to the trade fair. Answer his/her questions using the information in 1.
3 You are going to ask your partner for more information about the trade fair. Prepare these questions with the correct article (or no article) and ask your partner for the information.
   How many / visitors attend / trade fair?
   How large is / exhibition?
   By what date do you need to book / stand?
   How do I get from / airport to / trade fair?

Unit 8 | Language at work, exercise 8

Pair B

You are the Finance Department. Before you give Pair A a budget of $100,000, you would like more details.

1 Discuss what you think Pair A might need the budget for. Then prepare any questions you have for them.
2 Meet with Pair A. Listen to their presentation and ask questions about their expenses and figures. Make sure they are going to spend the budget correctly.

Unit 4 | Business communication, exercise 5

Student B

You have some concerns about the new system. Talk to Student A and listen to the benefits. Ask questions and express your concerns.

Unit 8 | Business communication, exercise 6

Student B

You are going to present a slide from a presentation to UK building investors. Prepare and then take turns to present the information to your partner. Decide with your partner if UK property is a good investment for the future.

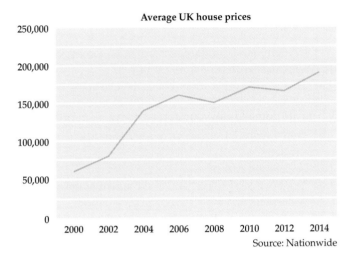

Average UK house prices

Source: Nationwide

Unit 9 | Business communication, exercise 5

Student B

Take turns to role-play two situations on the phone. In one situation you will be a customer, and in the other situation a call handler. In each situation you will have two conversations.

Situation 1

Conversation 1

You work for S1 Engineering, a company which provides spare parts for the oil industry. A customer calls you to place an order.

• Answer the call.
• Ask for the account number and details of the order.
• Give this order reference: 965/LQ and say goodbye.

Conversation 2

Five days later you receive another call from the customer.

• Answer the call.
• Ask for the account details and order reference.
• Explain that the order was delayed by two days because of a strike.
• Tell the customer the order will arrive later this afternoon.

Situation 2

Conversation 1

You are a customer from the fashion trade.

• Call the supplier (Haddows Trading, a fashion distributor).
• Give your account number VX890 and order 15 green skirts.

Conversation 2

You have just received the order from Haddows Trading. Unfortunately it contained 50 green shirts. You are very unhappy.

• Call and complain.
• Ask for a solution.
• Agree and say goodbye.

Audio scripts

Unit 1

1.1

Emrann Good morning, everyone, and welcome to your first day of what I hope will be an interesting and useful course in online marketing. As you know, my name's Emrann Bhatt and I'm your trainer for the next two days. However, you don't know each other, so before we begin I'd like everyone to give a short presentation about themselves. OK? Veronique, you can go first.

Veronique Sure. Good morning, everyone. My name's Veronique Denvir and I work for a medical charity. In my job, I often deal with fundraising projects and advertising campaigns. So, for example, I'm currently running a campaign to raise over a million euros for a water project in central Africa. I'm mainly based in Paris though I'm living and working in London for three months.

Emrann So why are you taking this course today?

Veronique Well, my organization usually advertises in traditional media such as newspapers and TV. That means most of our sponsors tend to be older people. But these days, more and more people are reading text and watching video online, so we aren't reaching a large part of the population. My problem is that I don't know enough about online marketing and I need to learn about it quickly. So that's why I'm doing this course.

Emrann Great. Thank you, Veronique, and I'm sure this course can help you with that. Now, who's next?

1.2

Joel So you're … Veronique.

Veronique That's right. And you're Joel. Where are you based?

Joel I'm a freelance consultant, so I work from my home in Bruges. But at the moment, I'm doing a lot of work in the USA.

Veronique Really? How often do you travel there?

Joel Err, I probably go about once a month. It's a project for a pharmaceutical company.

Veronique Is that right? My company works with pharmaceutical companies, too. But we're usually looking for sponsorship on the projects we run.

Joel Yes, well this one gives money to charities and non-profit organizations.

Veronique That sounds interesting! It would be good to keep in contact. Do you have a card?

1.3

Really?
Is that right?
That sounds interesting!

1.4

1

Hannah Hi, Luc.

Luc Hi, Hannah.

Hannah Luc, I want you to meet Jo Johansson. Jo is from the Bloomfield Foundation. Jo, this is Luc Akele, one of our area managers.

Jo Nice to meet you, Luc.

Luc Nice to meet you, too. So tell me, what do you do at the Bloomfield Foundation?

Jo Well, I deal with fund applications.

Luc That's interesting. I sometimes have to apply for funding.

Jo Really? What do you do, exactly?

Luc Well, I'm in charge of our sub-Saharan Africa operations.

Jo Sub-Saharan Africa?

Luc Yes, I oversee projects and make sure that the money is well spent. So I report to our main sponsors.

Jo I see. So, how much time do you spend in the field?

Luc Well, I usually do five or six trips a year, sometimes more.

Jo Wow! That's a lot of time away from home …

Luc Well, I'm afraid I have to go now, Jo, but it was very nice to meet you.

Jo Yes, it was nice meeting you, too. The work you are doing is fascinating.

Luc Well, I'd like to keep in contact. Do you have a card?

Jo Sure. Here you are.

Luc And here's mine.

Jo Thanks. Goodbye.

Luc Goodbye.

2

Hiroko Can I join you?

Dr Mayer Sure. Have a seat.

Hiroko Thanks. Let me introduce myself. I'm Hiroko Watanabe from Head Office.

Dr Mayer Well, I'm delighted to meet you, Ms Watanabe. My name's Dr Walter Mayer. But please, call me Walter.

Hiroko I'm very pleased to meet you, too, Walter. I see from your badge that you're with FPR Pharmaceuticals.

Dr Mayer Yes, that's right. Here's my card. I'm responsible for their medical donations programme. I handle all the inter-government work.

Hiroko That sounds very rewarding, knowing that you're helping so many people.

Dr Mayer Yes, it is, although it involves a lot of negotiation, which can be quite slow.

Hiroko Yes, I can imagine.

Dr Mayer So which part of Japan are you from?

Hiroko Actually, I'm from Brazil. I'm a third-generation Brazilian.

Dr Mayer Oh, I'm sorry. I thought … well …

Hiroko Please, don't apologize. I'm proud of my Japanese heritage … Well, it was nice meeting you.

Dr Mayer It was nice meeting you, too. And thank you for your interest in our donations programme. I look forward to hearing from you.

Hiroko You're welcome. Goodbye, Walter.

Unit 2

2.1

1

I think, overall, employees at my company have a fairly good work–life balance. A lot of us have to work long hours and sometimes we work through the weekends, but we have a system of time off in lieu. So if you work a day at the weekend, you can take an extra day off some other time. Last month, I worked over two whole weekends so I have four extra days. This really works well for me because I can add them to my annual holiday. The only bad thing about this system is that there isn't any paid overtime. I often work late but I don't receive any extra money. I think that's OK if you're a manager but not if you're an ordinary employee. I think they should pay us for working late or they should give us extra time off.

2

We have flexible working hours, which is good for me because I have children. I can start work at eight in the morning and finish at around three thirty to meet them after school. And I also work from home one day a week, so that helps. Having flexitime and spending more time at home helps me feel like I have a life outside of just working. There is one problem with flexitime, though. It means that I tend to work through lunch and I don't always take a break. Sitting at my desk all day probably isn't very good for me, and most of my colleagues do the same. Maybe the company should tell us to take an hour off at lunchtime. Also, because so many people work from home on different days, it makes it very difficult to organize project meetings, as there is always somebody not in the office. I think we need some core days in the week when everybody is in the office for meetings.

2.2

1

A Hi. You know a few people are off sick this week. Well, it means we're behind with some of the deliveries. Would you be interested in doing some overtime this weekend? It'd be paid of course.

B Yes, absolutely! What time do you want me here?

2

A Hi. Sorry to interrupt your lunch break, but can you find this order for me? We were supposed to deliver it yesterday but I think there was a mistake.

B Yes, sure.

A Thanks. Finish your sandwich first, though.

3

A Hi. Can you help me with something? I know you're about to go home but this order just came in and the other driver is sick. Can you deliver it on your way home?

B Well, I'm actually going out this evening but … OK … Yes, I suppose so.

A Thanks. I really appreciate it.

4

A Hi. I know you have the day off tomorrow, but I've made a small mistake. I've given the day off to Mark as well. There's a big delivery tomorrow, so we need someone here. I asked Mark but he's arranged to take his children somewhere. Could you take your day off next week instead?

B Yes, no problem.

A Thanks. That really helps. Let me know which day you want to take off instead.

2.3

Mirella Hello, Mirella Lyrio speaking.
Raul Hi, Mirella. It's Raul.
Mirella Oh, hi.
Raul You remember Leif Gunnarson? We met him in Stockholm last month.
Mirella Yes, he's with Skidbladnir Shipping.
Raul That's right. I thought I had him in my contacts list but I don't. Could you give me his details?
Mirella Yes, sure. One moment. I've got his card here.
Raul Great. Can I have his number?
Mirella His mobile or his office?
Raul His office.
Mirella It's double 0 46. 967. Double 5 6745.
Raul Sorry, can you repeat that?
Mirella Yes, it's double 0 46 for Sweden. And then 967 double 5 6745.
Raul So that's 967 55 6745.
Mirella Yes, that's it.
Raul And do you spell his last name with one N or double N?
Mirella Double N. So that's G-U-N-N-A-R-S-O-N.
Raul Sorry, was that E-R or A-R?
Mirella A as in apple. So it's Gunnarson.
Raul Sorry. Can you say that again?
Mirella A not E in Gunnarson.
Raul OK, thanks. Do you have his email?
Mirella It's leif dot gunnarson at SBN shipping dot SE. You know you can find all his information online?
Raul Right, of course. What's his company's web address?
Mirella It's www dot SBN shipping dot SE slash sales. The SBN is in upper case letters.
Raul OK, thanks, Mirella.
Mirella No problem. Is there anything else?
Raul No. That's everything. Thanks for your help.

Unit 3

3.1

So this is my project – a centre for senior citizens. We have to finish by the end of the week and I think we'll meet the deadline. We fell behind schedule because of Thanksgiving, but we managed to catch up last week and we're back on track now – we might even finish ahead of schedule.

…

It was hard at first, knowing how to allocate resources – you know – who does what, when, how much it will cost, etc. I have managed to stay within budget, but only just!

…

I think the key thing I've learnt is the importance of delegation. I try as much as possible to delegate tasks and trust people to get on with them. If I tried to do everything myself, we'd never finish on time. Teamwork is essential and I get updates from people every two days, so that I don't lose control of the project.

…

I'm very happy with the project – so far, things are going according to plan. So, fingers crossed for the last few days.

3.2

Judith Hi, Dawud. Have a seat.
Dawud Thanks.
Judith I'd like to get an update on the project and check all the deadlines so far.
Dawud Sure. Well, I've agreed the approximate equipment costings with finance.
Judith. That's good. And did you place the order for the equipment yesterday?
Dawud No, I didn't. As I said, the figures are only approximate. That's because some departments haven't sent their requirements yet. We can't order until we have their final requirements.
Judith Which departments?
Dawud Marketing and IT.
Judith But they've had three weeks to decide!
Dawud I know. I've just emailed them another reminder.
Judith OK. And what about the plans? Has anyone given their feedback?
Dawud Yes, I've already received it.
Judith What? From everyone?
Dawud Yes. Everyone replied before the deadline and overall they were very positive …

3.3

Dawud Hello?
Judith Hi, Dawud. Just calling to see how things are going. Has the new equipment arrived yet?
Dawud No, it hasn't but I've just called the supplier and the truck left the warehouse this morning. It'll be here around four o'clock.
Judith Did they deliver everything else on schedule?
Dawud Yes, they did. We've unpacked most of the boxes already.

3.4

1 Are you back on track again?
   Yes, I am. In fact, the whole project is ahead of schedule now.
2 Did you email me the schedule?
   Yes, I did. I sent it two minutes ago.
3 Have you returned your feedback?
   No, not yet. Sorry, but I've been really busy this week.
4 Can we meet for an update?
   Yes, OK. I'll come to your office right now.

3.5

Ramon OK. The last thing we need to discuss is Xavier. As you know, Xavier could be away on sick leave for a few weeks, or even longer. Xavier is project managing the opening of the new branch, so for the time being I need everyone to help out. Sue, you've already done some work with Xavier on recruitment. Can you update me on that?
Sue Sure. We've recruited all the frontline staff but we're currently looking for someone to fill the post of manager. The interviews are next week. I can do the interviews on my own but I prefer to interview with someone else.
Ramon Eloise, is that something you can help with?
Eloise Yes, no problem. What are the dates exactly?
Sue It's next week.
Eloise Next week! What? All week?
Sue Yes. Though we won't interview on the Friday because we need a day to review all the candidates.
Ramon I'd like you to help if possible, Eloise.
Eloise OK. I'll do it. But I need to postpone a few other things, though.
Ramon Thanks, Eloise. It really is very important.
Sue Ramon, there is also the induction training for the new frontline staff.
Ramon OK. What's happening with that?
Sue Well, Xavier scheduled it for the week after next. I'm afraid I'm on holiday that week. I'd postpone it, but I've booked my flight and everything.
Ramon I'd do it, but I'm away as well that week. Can anyone else help you or do we need to cancel it?
Eloise Sorry, but I've never run induction training before.
Ramon Derek. Would you like to help with that?
Derek Sure, I'll do it. I've run that training before, so it should be OK.
Ramon Great, thanks, Derek. Can you speak to Sue afterwards about the details?
Derek Sure.
Ramon So, let's check we all know what we're doing. Eloise is going to interview with Sue all next week. And Derek is going to run induction training the week after. Let's meet again in three weeks' time to review the situation. I might know more about Xavier by then.

Unit 4

4.1

1

The new system is quite well designed. You log in and look at a calendar for each room. The system of colour coding helps you see if a room is free. Then you reserve the room. There's also the option to invite people to the meeting, which is a useful idea but it isn't always accurate. I had to email one person again because they didn't receive the invitation.

2

Last week, I spent over 90 minutes in the queue. The whole system is so time-consuming. They've even introduced a new self-service system which enables you to put your passport on a screen and walk through. It looks fairly user-friendly, but guess what happened when I used it? It wouldn't recognize my passport and I had to wait for someone to come and let me through.

3

I work at a university and we're lucky to have some new childcare services. Parents can drop their children off in the morning and pick them up later in the day. Plus you can see your children at lunchtime. The staff are so friendly, and it's a very secure environment for the children. It's great because it allows employees to keep working full-time.

4.2

A Well, the real reason I'm calling is just to check how you are getting on with the new version of the warehouse management systems software. Do you think it's better?

B Oh, it's very good. Overall, it works a lot more efficiently than the old version.

A That's great to hear! How about the new customer-profile system? Have you noticed any improvements there?

B Err, yes, a little. Though I didn't think there was anything wrong with the old version. You could find a profile almost as easily.

A Well, you should be able to add more details and the options are a lot more useful.

B Ah. There is one small difference I don't like, and that's the new order form page. It requires more information, so staff are filling it in a little more slowly. I'm sure they'll get faster with practice, but is it possible to delete some of the options because we really don't need them all?

A Yes, that's easy to do. You need to click on main settings and press the edit function, then …

4.3

When we asked businesses about software installation, we received well over one hundred responses. They gave the following answers. Nearly a third uses the company which supplied the software. Then, about half of them have an in-house person or an IT department to do the job. And the number of respondents who employ an external IT company, but do not use the software supplier, was a little under 15%.

4.4

A Hi, everyone. I'm here to talk about the new software. Well, the main benefit is the payroll feature. It's a lot more accurate because it automatically knows how many hours you've worked each month. With the current system, one of the problems is that your manager has to fill in a form for each of you. It's very time-consuming and it's easy to make mistakes. But with this new software, it's better for everyone.

B What happens if I forget to log on in the morning when I start work? It means I won't get paid.

A That's a good question, but you can choose between two systems. Either you log on and log off or you can set your computer to do it when you switch on or switch off.

B But wouldn't that require us to have to adjust the settings on our computers? It's not ideal for those of us who aren't so good with computers.

A It might seem that you'd need to adjust your settings, but in fact the software can do this automatically if you tell us which system you would prefer, so you don't have to do anything different to what you usually do.

B I see. I suppose that makes it easier.

C I have a question, too. When I'm overseas, will it let me log on from a hotel? Because otherwise my manager won't know if I'm working or not.

A That's true, but there's a mobile app. So you log in on your phone and it sends a message.

C I'm not convinced that it's possible to do that every time you're abroad.

A Of course, I understand that sometimes there might be a problem, but you can still talk to your manager and let them know you had a problem. After a few weeks, I'm sure you'll find it much easier to use than the current system …

Unit 5

5.1

Giray Hi, Anita. This is Giray. I'm sorry, but I'm busy next Monday evening, so I can't meet you personally at the airport. When your flight arrives, a driver will meet you. Let's plan to meet in your hotel reception on Tuesday morning at around eight thirty, because we're meeting the first client at nine thirty instead of eleven. By the way, do you intend to check out in the morning or are you staying another night in Ankara? I'm afraid I'm not free in the evening, but I can book you an excellent restaurant near the hotel for dinner if you are staying. It opens around eight, I think. Anyway, let me know your plans.

5.2

1 I'm sorry, but I'm busy next Monday evening.
2 I'm sorry, but can you repeat that?
3 I'm sorry to keep you waiting.
4 I'm sorry, but the traffic was terrible this morning.
5 I'm sorry, but can I say something at this point?

5.3

1 I'm sorry, but I'm busy next Monday evening.
   No problem. How about Tuesday instead?
2 I'm sorry, but can you repeat that?
   Sure. It's A as in Alpha.
3 I'm sorry to keep you waiting.
   Not to worry. We haven't started yet.
4 I'm sorry, but the traffic was terrible this morning.
   That's OK. There was a problem with my train as well.
5 I'm sorry, but can I say something at this point?
   Of course. Go ahead.

5.4

Sergio Hello, Sergio Boccherini speaking.
Elena Hello, Mr Boccherini. You probably don't remember me but we met at the trade show in Geneva last month. I visited your stand and I have your card here.
Sergio OK, great. Sorry, what's your name?
Elena It's Elena Schenker. I'm Head of Facilities for the Altenhof hotels in Switzerland.
Sergio Oh yes. I remember. You were interested in some of our gym equipment.
Elena That's right. As I told you at the time, we've recently received mixed feedback on some of our hotel fitness facilities. In particular, some of the machines need updating. Is that something you can help us with?
Sergio I'm sure we can. Where are you based exactly?
Elena I'm at our head office in Bern, but what I need first of all is some idea of prices.
Sergio Well, I can email you a brochure and some details but it's difficult to give an exact price without a meeting. One moment. I just want to check something … I am actually coming up to Switzerland next month.
Elena Really? Can we arrange a date to meet?
Sergio Yes, I have a meeting with some other clients in Geneva who I met at the same trade show. It's on 31st January. That's a Monday …

Elena On Monday? I'm afraid I'm always busy on Mondays … I can't make it that day. How about Tuesday?
Sergio The 1st?
Elena Yes.
Sergio Sure. That suits me. Is two o'clock convenient?
Elena Err, can we make it later? At three?
Sergio Fine. So that's Tuesday the first at three. I'll confirm it by email.
Elena And I'll send you some more details about us with a map of where we are. In fact, there's one on our website. It's www dot …

5.5

On Monday?
The 1st?
At three?

5.6

Elena Hello. Elena Schenker speaking.
Sergio Hello, Elena. This is Sergio from FTF Fitness.
Elena Oh, hi. Nice to hear from you again.
Sergio Sorry for calling so late in the day.
Elena That's OK. I've only just got back to the office.
Sergio Is this a busy time for you?
Elena It's our busiest season with all the skiing.
Sergio Of course. Anyway, it's about next Tuesday. I'm afraid I can't make it. Can we move the meeting back a day?
Elena To Wednesday?
Sergio Yes, that's right.
Elena Erm. The afternoon is free.
Sergio Great – there's a train that arrives at one thirty. So after lunch? At two?
Elena OK. So that's Wednesday the second at two o'clock then.
Sergio Thanks. And sorry about that.
Elena No problem. See you then.
Sergio Bye.

Unit 6

6.1

A Hello?

B Hi. It's Joel. I've just received an email from Doctor Doyle. He's changed his flight from the morning. He's landing at six thirty on Tuesday evening now, so we need a driver to pick him up.

A That's fine. We can take him straight to the hotel.

B Actually, he wants to see the main auditorium and check the facilities before his talk on Wednesday morning, so the driver needs to collect him from the airport and drop him off at the exhibition centre first. I'm there all day helping delegates with their stands, so I can meet up with him and show him around. Then we'll walk over to the hotel afterwards to check in.

A OK. But what about the excursion on the Tuesday afternoon? Should we cancel it?

B No, because Ms Cruz lands on Tuesday morning and has the whole day free. Besides, she would like to look around the old city and do some sightseeing.

A Right. Normal check-in is after two o'clock but I'll call the hotel and try to arrange an early check-in.

B Yes, she'll want to freshen up after the flight.

A Is someone taking her in the afternoon?

B The hotel tour guide service offers an afternoon excursion, so I'll book it with them. It also includes eating out at a traditional restaurant and trying a few local specialities.

A Sounds perfect. Do you think that's something Doctor Doyle would like to do on Thursday?

6.2

Doctor Billah	Mr Cardoso
Ms Walker	Professor Halsdorff
Sir James Logan	Madam Sargie
Miss Pfaner	Mrs Ludwig

6.3

1

A Hello, Madam. Can I help you?

B Thank you, I'm looking for Ms Wei.

A That's me. And you must be Mrs Cruz. Please, call me Hanna.

2

C Are you Doctor Doyle?

D That's right. Miles Doyle. How do you do.

C How do you do. My name's Ken and I'm organizing the conference. How would you like me to address you? As Doctor Doyle or Miles?

D Oh, please, call me by my first name.

3

C Miles, let me introduce you to Hanna Wei. She's the other organizer.

D Nice to meet you. Can I call you Hanna?

A Sure. Nice to meet you, too, Miles.

6.4

Marvin Hello, I'm Marvin Bernstein. I have an appointment with Ms Jacinta Ross.

Jacinta Hi, I'm Jacinta Ross. And on behalf of HYB Electronics, welcome to our new facility.

Marvin Thank you very much, Ms Ross.

Jacinta It's nice to finally meet you in person at last. And please, call me Jacinta.

Marvin OK.

Jacinta So, how was your journey?

Marvin It was fine, thanks. Though there was quite a lot of traffic.

Jacinta Ah. And did you have any trouble finding us?

Marvin No, not at all, your directions were excellent.

Jacinta I'm glad to hear it. Here, let me take your coat.

Marvin Oh, that's OK, I'll hang on to it for now.

Jacinta Of course. Can I get you a coffee?

Marvin That sounds nice.

Jacinta OK. Come this way and I'll run through today's programme.

Marvin Great.

…

Jacinta Here you are. Have a seat.

Marvin Thanks.

Jacinta So, first of all, I thought you could take a tour of the facility this morning.

Marvin Sounds interesting.

Jacinta My colleague Aruna Singh is taking you round. Then, we'll catch up again at lunchtime and, after that, I'll introduce you to the team.

Marvin And will I be seeing Dilip Patel today?

Jacinta He has another appointment this morning, but you'll get a chance to meet up with him over lunch.

Marvin Great.

Jacinta Now, you'll need this ID card to get around the site. Make sure you keep it on you at all times.

Marvin No problem. And what about my car? Am I allowed to leave it in the staff car park?

Jacinta Yes, don't worry about that. I'll clear it with Facilities. Ah, what's your registration number?

Marvin It's …

6.5

As hotel guests, we probably all have the same basic requirements: a friendly welcome, a comfortable bed for a good night's sleep, not to mention the all-important free Wi-fi connection. But beyond these basics, visitor expectations of the hotel experience will vary from culture to culture.

For example, would you be happily surprised to find a bowl of fruit in your room? Or are you from a culture where you'd complain if there wasn't one? Ice machines are another good example of this. No hotel in the USA would be without an ice machine on every floor, but for many Europeans an ice machine seems like a wonderful extravagance.

Like ice machines in the USA, vending machines can also surprise foreign guests in Japanese hotels. It's estimated that there's one vending machine for every 23 people in Japan and your hotel vending machine can dispense everything from an evening meal to a change of underwear. The Japanese love of technology even extends to their hotel-room toilets which may have up to 20 different settings – a challenge for any visitor.

At a more basic level, most hotels in Asia will provide a pair of slippers in your room. That's because most of the people living in these countries wouldn't wear shoes inside their homes and the same is true for their hotel room. Visitors also tend to notice how welcoming staff can be in Asian hotels; probably because hotel staff tend to greet you by name.

Unit 7

7.1

1

Finance is so behind with their figures this month. They're in the process of upgrading the accounting software and backing up all their files. It's taking ages to do but in the future all the data can be encrypted and made more secure.

2

After we had a cyberattack at our company, they introduced the policy of creating a new password every 12 weeks. To make the password stronger, it has to be eight characters including at least one number and one capital letter. It can be annoying trying to remember your new password all the time, but it's probably for the best.

3

I often open attachments and share documents for my job. Sometimes I don't know the person they came from, so it's important to run regular scans on my computer in case of viruses.

7.2

A Right. So this is your desk with a phone and your laptop. I think there are a few pens in the top drawer, but if you need anything else the stationery cupboard over there has everything else you'll need.

B Great. Do I have to use a password with the laptop?

A Oh, yes. I nearly forgot. This is your temporary password. Log on with it and then you need to choose a new one.

B Am I allowed to choose my own?

A Yes, and you have to change it every 24 weeks. And IT get very angry if you forget it.

B Right. Oh, one other thing. Can I make personal calls from this phone?

A Err, no, not really. You have to use your own mobile phone unless it's an emergency or something. You know, like a family problem …

7.3

A Do you know how I can register with this website?

B Sure. OK, so begin by filling in these details first and then click 'register'. Next, it'll email you a temporary password which you can change to something personal. Once you've done that …

A One moment. Let me fill it in first … OK, I've done that.

B So, now you've changed the password, you can log on.

A That's what I thought, but it isn't working.

B Let's have a look. OK. You need to click this box before you finish. It's to say you agree to all the terms and conditions on the site.

A Oh. Should I read them first?

B If you want to. I never bother.

A OK.

B There. It's registered you. You can start.

A Great. Thanks a lot.

7.4

Vance Hello?

Helmi Hi, Vance. This is Helmi.

Vance Hi, Helmi. How are you?

Helmi Fine, thanks. A bit cold in Helsinki this evening. What time is it with you?

Vance Two o'clock. Lauren is here with me.

Helmi Hi, Lauren.

Lauren Hi, Helmi.

Vance We're just waiting for Raymond.

Raymond Hello? Hello? Can you hear me?

Vance Hi, Raymond. Yes, but your line isn't very good. Can you speak up?

Raymond Hello. Is that better?

Vance Oh, yes, much better. And Lauren and Helmi are also here.

Raymond Hi, Lauren. Hi, Helmi.

Helmi/Lauren Hello, Raymond.

Vance OK, let's begin. Today, I want to discuss the new fingerprint technology for company security. We've trialled it here in our New York facility and the system works really well. Anyway, Lauren has been in charge of it so, Lauren, can you speak first please?

Lauren OK. Well, as Vance said, the new fingerprint readers have been very successful and the feedback has been excellent. So now we'd like to introduce them in all our overseas facilities.

…

Lauren The other really big advantage of introducing the same system worldwide is that any employee can enter any of our buildings by pressing their fingerprint on the pad to enter.

Raymond/Helmi Sorry, but can I say something here? / I have a question.

Vance One moment. Raymond, can you speak first? And then Helmi, you can speak next.

Raymond Thanks. So does that mean if we see a new person enter one of our laboratories, they don't need to wear their ID?

Lauren Ah, good question. I'm not quite sure yet.

Vance I can answer that Lauren. That's right. Of course, we'll advise everyone to wear ID at all times, but with so many staff working internationally now it isn't practical to check everyone.

Raymond Yes, I suppose so. OK.

Vance And Helmi? Would you like to comment now?

Helmi Actually, I had the same question as Raymond. Especially for the Helsinki office. As you know, we're quite a small office so …

…

Vance OK. Well, I think that covers everything. Are there any questions before we finish?

…

Vance Good. And of course, I'll sum up the main points in an email. So thank you everyone for coming.

All other participants Thanks/Goodbye/Bye.

Unit 8

8.1

1

Thierry OK, so let's begin with these figures for wages and overtime. You're under budget with the wages but you've spent too much on overtime.

Adriana Yes, but that's because two people resigned last month, so I asked everyone to help out by doing some overtime. We're going to spend even more if we don't employ someone else.

Thierry That might be OK, but let me check with HR first. Besides, you still have some budget for recruitment, so you can afford it. But, in the meantime, try not to give out any more overtime …

2

Adriana The other thing I'm worried about is travel. I'd like some of my staff to go on a course next month in Milan but we're over budget on travel. I told them it may not happen but that I'd try to find the money from somewhere.

Thierry Well, to be honest, that budget for travel seems very low. Next year, we'll probably increase the travel budget, but for this year I don't think it's a problem, because you've got lots of budget left for training. Why don't you put their travel expenses under training?

Adriana That's what I thought, but …

3

Thierry OK, so that's everything for this year. Have Finance asked you to send them estimates for next year yet?

Adriana No, not yet. But everything could go up by about 5%. What do you think?

Thierry I agree. You'll definitely need more for travel and maybe more for recruitment and wages as well.

Adriana Why's that?

Thierry Well, it isn't confirmed yet but we'll possibly expand your department next year, so you may need a much bigger budget.

8.2

1

A I'm wondering whether to sell my shares. What do you think?

B I'd keep them. I'm sure they'll go up again.

2

A Is there any way you can bring down the price?

B If you pay before the end of the month, I'll give you a 10% discount.

3

A Would you like to order?

B Yes, I think I'll have soup for starters and steak for my main course.

4

A Have you finished that report yet?

B No, sorry. I'll get it to you tomorrow at the latest.

8.3

OK. Now I'd like to present our proposal in a bit more detail. Take a look at this chart. It illustrates the growth in student numbers in the last five years. Each line is split into two, with the increasing number of domestic students in green. Also notice in particular this grey line. That's the increase in international students. And nearly all these students need accommodation …

… As you can see on this chart, forecasts show this upward trend will definitely continue for both domestic and international students, which means the demand for student accommodation is going to increase over the next few years. And many investors already know this …

… This chart shows you the returns on different property investments for the previous year. It's based on data from one of the country's leading estate agents. I'd like to draw your attention to the first line, which shows the average return on an investment in student accommodation. It's higher than every other type of property investment …

… So to sum up, with a minimum investment of $70,000, this slide shows a forecasted annual return of 19%. That's based on 10% for the annual rental income and, in addition to that, we think your investment will rise annually by 9%. I can't think of many other investments that are currently giving that level of return.

Unit 9

9.1

Interviewer So you're quite specialized?

Steve That's right. Our customers like the personal touch. We spend a lot of time discussing their needs and the type of machine they need. And if there's a problem, they don't have to send the machine away, they just come to the shop.

Interviewer But that means you have to keep a lot of components in stock. How do you make sure that you don't run out?

Steve Well, everything has its own bar code which shows up on the database. It tells us what we have left, if it's on order, and so on – see.

Interviewer So will it order automatically if you're running low on something?

Steve No, it just warns us if we're low on stock. You don't want to stock up on components which are not going to sell.

Interviewer Now, a lot of your components come from Asia, don't they?

Steve That's right. They're usually sent by an international carrier.

Interviewer So, do you take advantage of the tracking facility?

Steve It depends, really. I mean, if something's not particularly urgent, then I don't bother. But if there's an essential package, then I make sure I keep track of it.

9.2

A Hello. FHS Deliveries. Can I help you?

B Hi. My name's Sean Steen and I was wondering if I could get a quote.

A Sure. Go ahead.

B I'd like to know how much it costs to send a package to São Paolo.

A That depends. Could you tell me how big the package is?

B It's just documents in an A4 envelope.

A Oh, I see. The standard airmail rate to Brazil is £45.50.

B How long does that take?

A Three days maximum. Or express delivery guarantees arrival within 24 hours.

B What's the price for express delivery?

A £71. …

9.3

A Can you tell me how the meeting went?

B Very well! He says that he's looking for a long-term agreement but with some kind of exclusivity clause.

A Sounds promising. Did it sound like he'll order with us?

B I couldn't tell. But he has suggested that the three of us should meet to discuss it further.

A Did he say when?

B One day next week.

A I can't next week. Let's say the week after.

B Hmm. That might be too long. I don't want him to lose interest.

A OK, I'll tell you what. Let's meet next week on Friday. Tell him that and let's see what he says.

9.4

Linda Composource Components. Linda speaking. How can I help?

Gisele Good morning. My name is Gisele Kern from Abracomp in Germany. I'm calling about an order I placed two weeks ago. I'd like to find out what's happened to it.

Linda Of course. Can you tell me your account number?

Gisele Yes, it's P-G-2-7-8.

Linda I'm sorry, was that B-J?

Gisele No, P for Peter, G for George.

Linda OK, thanks. If you'll bear with me a moment, I'll call up your details. Let me see … Do you have any idea when you placed the order?

Gisele On the 11th February.

Linda Right, I've got it here. It was a repeat order for 2,000 motherboards. We put it straight through to our warehouse. It says here that it was dispatched that afternoon.

Gisele Something must have gone wrong because we haven't received it. This is a real problem for me.

Linda I'll look into it immediately. Would you like me to call you back, or will you hold while I contact the warehouse?

Gisele I think I'd better hold.

Linda I'll be as quick as I can. One moment.

Unit 10

10.1

1

I can't believe it. Your new offices are really spacious. In your old headquarters you couldn't move for people and furniture, but this is great. It's all very hi-tech and extremely relaxing.

2

My trip was fine but I see what you mean about their factory. It's not exactly state-of-the-art, is it? It feels fairly old-fashioned and the facilities aren't very up-to-date. Having said that, the whole working environment felt pretty stress-free, so they must be doing something right.

10.2

1

A So this area is for staff to leave their things. For example, a lot of employees cycle to work and get changed in here.

B I see. So how many people use this facility?

A Maybe 20.

B There isn't much space for 20.

A Well, they don't all arrive at the same time. And we also have some lockers along the wall outside …

2

B Are there any places for staff to go during their breaks? You know, so they can get away from their desks.

A Yes, this room has a table and a few chairs. Though, to be honest, not many staff use it.

B I'm not surprised. It doesn't have any windows. It's very dark.

A I know, but there aren't any other free rooms. Perhaps a little paint on the walls might improve it.

B Yes, that would probably help.

10.3

A And what's this room for?

B It's for all our employees. They can leave personal belongings here and they are free to use it during breaks.

A But you said there are about 25 people working in this factory. This room isn't big enough, is it?

B Well, they never use it all at the same time because they are on different shifts. Although, I agree, at the moment we don't have enough lockers, so we're ordering more.

A Also, the room is too dark.

B Yes, it's because two of the light bulbs have blown. I've reported that.

A So how many people actually use this room at one time?

B Err, it's hard to say. Maybe five?

A Five? So there are too few chairs. And one of them looks like it's broken. That needs to go on your list as well.

B Of course.

10.4

Architect So that's the plan for the main offices.

Manager I really like it. Now, there's just one other thing. What about the idea of a crèche and relaxation area?

Architect Well, it might prove difficult to have both. I'm afraid there isn't much space for both of them.

Manager OK. Well, I think we should consider having the crèche first. Besides, I have a few reservations about having an 'Anarchy Zone'!

Architect You might be better off without it if employees spend too long in there!

Manager Exactly. I'd rather not have it.

Architect Well, just say the architect said it wasn't possible.

Manager Good idea. So where can we put the crèche? We thought about … here, next to the canteen.

Architect Sorry, but I don't think that would work. I'd recommend putting it here – in this area behind reception. Then employees leave their children as they arrive. And also, it's quite a long way from the factory area, which is good for health and safety.

Manager Great!

Unit 11

11.1

When you're busy at work, you probably make a list of all the jobs you have. That's the easy part. The hardest part is to make up your mind which job to do first. Let me show you a tool which might help you decide. It's called a Priority Matrix and it has two axes. The vertical axis is urgent and not urgent and the horizontal axis is important and not important. So this gives you four squares to put the jobs in. Let's look at this section first. Look at your list of jobs and prioritize any job which is urgent and important. Do it straightaway.

This next square is for anything which is important but not urgent. So it's for longer-term decision-making. Spend some time thinking about this kind of job before you reach a final decision. It might be useful to invite suggestions from colleagues and evaluate their opinions before making a final plan.

Now let's look at the other side of the matrix. This is for the jobs that people often find harder to categorize. This square is for jobs which are urgent but not important. These are the types of jobs you can often delegate to others. And if you can't delegate them, then do them quickly and get them out of the way.

Finally, this square is for anything on your list which is low priority. Avoid dealing with those kinds of jobs for a while. And you never know. If you ignore them, they might disappear altogether.

11.2

1

A Oh, it's such a difficult decision.

B Not really. They're offering more money, a company car and your own department. If I were you, I'd take it.

A But what about loyalty? I've been with this company since I left school.

2

A They said if we can't pay them by the end of the week, then we'll have to move out of the shop.

B If only we had more time.

A More time *and* more money.

3

A Right. Thank you all for coming. Now the purpose of today … Yes, Walter?

B If you don't mind, I'd like to leave a bit early today. I have a doctor's appointment.

A Err, yes, OK. So as I was saying, the purpose of …

4

A I just don't think they'll agree to it. It's nearly 20% more than they were paying last year.

B What if we gave them after-sales support for free?

A Hmm, that would help but I still don't think they're going to like it.

11.3

Version 1

Patricia OK, Laszlo, so I'm happy to tell you that we're all very happy for you to be our distributor in Hungary. But I'd like to discuss an issue with you on the draft contract.

Laszlo Sure, Patricia. Go ahead.

Patricia So the agreement is for three years but we have an issue with the exclusivity clause.

Laszlo Why's that? It's fairly standard, isn't it?

Patricia The concern we have is that in the wording of the contract it's for the full length of the contract. Do you have any views on it?

Laszlo Well, obviously I need exclusivity in the region because your brand is virtually unknown in Hungary. It will take time to build a customer base.

Patricia Yes, we understand that. But supposing we link it to performance. How about if we review the sales every 12 months of the contract with an option to end the contract if you don't achieve a certain target?

Laszlo I'm sorry, but I can't agree to that. I think three years is a perfectly reasonable length of time. If we spend one or two years building the brand and then you offer distribution rights to our competitors, it isn't fair.

Patricia I see your point. It's just that we feel we need some kind of clause that—

Laszlo No, I'm sorry. If the contract has such a clause, then I'm not in a position to accept it.

11.4

Version 2

Patricia OK, Laszlo, so I'm happy to tell you that we're all very happy for you to be our distributor in Hungary. But there's something we need to discuss on the draft contract.

Laszlo Sure, Patricia. Go ahead.

Patricia So the agreement is for three years but we have an issue with the exclusivity clause.

Laszlo Why's that? It's fairly standard, isn't it?

Patricia The concern we have is that in the wording of the contract it's for the full length of the contract. So there's no time limit.

Laszlo Well, I need exclusivity in the region because your brand is virtually unknown in Hungary. It will take time to build a customer base.

Patricia Yes, we understand that. But imagine if we link it to sales performance. How about if we review the sales targets every 12 months of the contract with an option to end the contract if you don't achieve a certain target?

Laszlo I'm sorry, but I can't agree to that. I think three years is a perfectly reasonable length of time. If we spend one or two years building the brand and then you offer distribution rights to our competitors, it isn't fair.

Patricia I see your point. It's just that we feel we need some kind of clause that—

Laszlo Look. I can't accept every 12 months but maybe after the first two years we could agree upon a sales target.

Patricia OK. I'll meet you halfway on this. If I offer a review after 18 months, will you agree?

Laszlo Yes, I think that would be fair.

Patricia Great. So in principle, it's a deal. There is one other thing I'd like to talk to you about which could also change things. We're currently looking for someone to distribute in Slovakia. Now, I know you don't have an office there at the moment but what if …

Unit 12

12.1

1

A Are you really thinking of leaving your job?

B I'm not sure. I like everyone here and the pay is OK. The company is fine, a bit traditional, but they've always been very reliable. But I really need a change. You know, a job that's more exciting and dynamic.

A Maybe you need to come at this differently.

B How do you mean?

A Well, why not try to make the company you work for a bit more up-to-date. Make it a place you really want to be at.

2

A So why are you at this trade fair?

B Well, I've come up with a revolutionary idea for cleaning the house and I'm looking for investors, or even a partner. You know, someone who knows how to take it to market.

A That's interesting. I'm in the sales business. What's your product?

B Well, it's a sophisticated piece of technology that allows you to monitor dirt in the home. It all came about when my wife was cleaning the carpets one day …

3

A You know, I've always wanted to set up my own business, but I always come to the conclusion that I can't do it.

B What kind of business were you thinking of?

A Well, I had this idea the other day when I came across an article in the paper. It's simple really – and not very original – but this person had started a home-catering company from their own kitchen – you know, cooking for dinner parties or preparing buffets at weddings. That kind of thing. The article said there's a lot of money in it.

B It's funny, but I think I read the same thing. I even thought to myself, one day I should do something like that.

A Really?

12.2

1

So, as the employee with the longest career history at the company, it only leaves me to say that, on behalf of everyone here, I'd like to thank you for all your hard work over the last 30 years. Your work is always of the highest quality and you really are an example to us all. And I know that everyone appreciates you both as a colleague and also as a friend.

2

Trevor, do you have a moment? Thanks for all your hard work on this. I'm very impressed by the results on this project. You've done an excellent job. Well done.

3

I realize this is quite hard to learn how to do, but you're doing really well. But feel free to ask me again if you need any help. Good job! Keep at it!

12.3

Good morning, everyone, and thanks for coming. We have a lot to do, so let's start. I'd like to begin by explaining the basic concept behind the meeting this morning. First, I'm going to talk for a few minutes about where this company is. Then, we'll try to define how we want our customers, clients, and even our competitors to view Bertran RL. And of course, the main reason for this meeting is to come up with a new mission statement, so finally we'll start brainstorming ideas. OK? Great. Oh, and feel free to ask questions whenever you want.

12.4

Right. First of all, let's look at this slide. As you can see, it has a number of words that describe our company. These aren't my words but they are answers from some of our oldest and newest customers to the question, 'What words describe Bertran RL?' You'll notice that some words are in blue and some are in red. So, which words do you think represent the views of our oldest customers? Which ones are the most pleased with our products?

12.5

OK. That's everything I want to say for the moment. Thank you all for listening. So now we've come to the main part of the morning: to try and create a new, innovative company mission statement. But before I ask you to brainstorm ideas in small groups, are there any questions? Yes, Rudi.

12.6

Short extracts of the following types of music:

1 classical
2 pop
3 rock
4 opera
5 Bollywood
6 jazz

Unit 13

13.1

In business, we often do everything we can to avoid making mistakes. After all, mistakes can cost time and money. And yet, mistakes will always happen. And many people would argue that you can't be creative or innovative without making mistakes. Take, for example, Post-it notes. These are the colourful notes which are stuck to office desks and walls all over the world. They were the result of a mistake by Spencer Silver. He was a researcher who worked for 3M and was trying to make a strong adhesive. One day, he made an adhesive that wouldn't stick properly. However, while it wouldn't stick objects together permanently, it was reusable and didn't leave a mark on surfaces.

Another famous example is Alexander Fleming. He's the scientist whose discovery has saved millions of lives. It was a September morning in 1928 when Fleming accidentally discovered penicillin. He had just returned from holiday to the hospital where he worked. While he was away, some mould had grown in the old Petri dishes that had been left on his desk. He noticed the mould had killed the bacteria which was in the Petri dishes. The mould contained penicillin. These are just two of many more mistakes which …

13.2

1

A The team isn't working well together. Do you know what I mean? In particular, there are two people who are making communication a nightmare.

B Absolutely. It's become a real problem. We'll have to discuss this seriously at the next meeting.

2

A All you have to do is fill in this form and pass it to Joanna, who'll put in your request. Then you just have to wait for confirmation. Does that make sense?

B Kind of, but could you explain the first bit again?

3

A It sounds as though you've got a mains problem. You'll need to switch everything off and restart it remotely. Then try to perform the function again when it asks you to. Is that clear?

B I don't get why I have to switch everything off.

4

A I'd speak to the person whose job it is to deal with this kind of thing. After all, you aren't paid to worry about what other employees do with the company's money. And if you tell someone in management, at least they'll be aware of the problem, do you see?

B Yes, I see what you mean. I just don't feel comfortable about reporting on a colleague.

13.3

1

Ruth Hi, Magda. What's the matter?

Magda It's this report. I just can't do it.

Ruth Why? Is it too difficult?

Magda No, it's not that. I just don't have enough time. My boss keeps on giving me extra work and I don't know when I'll be able to do it all.

Ruth What do you mean by 'extra work'?

Magda Well, she gives me things to do on top of my normal workload and I can't do it. What shall I do?

Ruth Well, it looks like you've got a communication problem to me. Have you tried talking to her? She might not even know that you're too busy.

Magda No, I haven't.

Ruth Well, I'd ask to speak to her if I were you. She needs to know you feel overworked.

Magda OK. But in the meantime, what about this report?

Ruth Well, if you really don't have enough time, I think you should ask for an extension on the deadline. That should sort it out temporarily. But you have to get it approved by management first. It's easy enough to do – there's a simple form to fill out. I'll email it to you.

Magda Thanks, Ruth.

2

Help desk Good afternoon. How can I help?

Customer It's my laptop. It keeps on going wrong all the time.

Help desk Oh. What's wrong with it exactly?

Customer Well, it's always crashing and it won't remember the time or date. It's so frustrating. Until now it's been completely reliable.

Help desk When you say 'it's always crashing', do you mean it stops working or it switches off?

Customer It switches off after about 20 minutes.

Help desk Well, it sounds as though it could be a battery problem. How old is your laptop?

Customer About three and a half years.

Help desk Well, basically, you could just use the electrical cable, but the best thing would be to buy a new battery. That should fix it.

Customer OK. How much would that cost?

Unit 14

14.1

Tom Szaky is always looking for ways to cut down on waste and help the planet both at home and also in his job. Tom is the founder and Chief Executive of a company called TerraCycle which specializes in finding waste and turning it into something useful. Tom set up the company in 2002 in a basement. Now it operates in 21 countries, with a turnover of 20 million dollars.

TerraCycle will pick up waste from special collection points. The waste can include anything that people throw away such as cigarette stubs, coffee capsules or biscuit wrappers. Then it processes the material so it can be sold to a manufacturer. Alternatively, it will pick out a type of rubbish and try to make something new out of it; for example, it turns rubbish into new TerraCycle products like bags, benches and dustbins.

TerraCycle's ability to balance profit with doing something good for the planet is another key to its business success. Whilst it relies on contracts with large businesses such as Kenco, which pay TerraCycle to take away its waste, it also works with individual consumers who can drop off rubbish at collection points. Any local business can sign up to become a drop-off point and, for every load of rubbish, TerraCycle will make a donation to the company's favourite charity.

14.2

Let me explain how we turn jatropha plants into biofuel. The basic process is fairly simple and has been possible for some time, but it's only in recent years that it's become economical. Essentially, there are two main stages: growing and processing. First of all, jatropha plants can be grown in hot climates such as Central American countries. After the seeds have been harvested, they are taken to a refinery where we feed them into a grinder. Having taken the oil out of the seeds, you're ready to mix it and heat it with methanol. What you end up with is a very good quality fuel which can be put into a diesel engine. It's also worth noting that this kind of fuel produces about half the CO_2 emissions of normal diesel.

14.3

1

Presenter So I think that's everything I wanted to say about the new system. We've looked at how to complete the new forms and you all know who is responsible for these in your team. We have a few minutes left, so if anyone has any questions, I'm happy to try and answer them now. Yes? Over there.

Audience member Err, overall the new forms look like they're easier to fill in than the old ones. My question is about time, and perhaps you said this, but how much time do we have to make a report after the actual injury?

Presenter That's a good question. You need to submit the form within 24 hours but, ideally, it's best to complete the form immediately if you can, though that might not always be possible …

2

Audience member You've assigned a team leader to be responsible. But what if that person isn't at work that day, or even, what if that's the person who's injured?

Presenter I think there are two parts to that question. First of all, every team leader needs to choose a co-team leader to supervise when they are off. If you haven't been told who that is, then ask your team leader. And for your second point, if the team leader is injured, then the co-team leader is responsible.

3

Audience member You talked about different types of injury but I still don't understand when we have to fill this form in?

Presenter Sorry, I don't quite understand the question.

Audience member Well, is it necessary to fill in the form for any kind of injury or just for a serious injury? For example, what if I just cut my finger or something?

Presenter Let me check I've understood you correctly. You're asking me if it depends on the level of the injury? The answer is no, it doesn't depend on how serious the injury is. You need to fill the form in for any kind of injury.

Audience member Even for a cut finger?

Presenter Even for a cut finger. That might seem a bit stupid, but what might seem like a minor injury could actually be worse than you think. For example, if you hit your head, you might not realize there is a problem until much later in the day. So, we need a record of any kind of injury. Does that answer your question?

Audience member Yes, thank you.

Unit 15

15.1

Ahmed I was having a few problems with my previous company so I started to look for a new job. It was a very traditional company and I didn't like the town much. Anyway, I heard that one of our competitors had opened a new office a few months earlier and they were recruiting more staff. Unfortunately it was on the other side of the country, but I applied anyway and it worked out really well because they offered me a job with better pay and relocation costs. Of course, the first six months were hard because I was living in a new city, but all my new colleagues made me feel at home, so that really helped. Anyway, I've just had my first annual performance review and the feedback from my line manager was really positive, so it was definitely the right decision.

15.2

1

Helena I was working for a large food company which didn't employ many women. At my first performance review the production manager told me that if I didn't work as part of a team, I'd never get anywhere in the company. It was terrible to hear this, because I had already discussed with him how difficult it was to be the only woman. Anyway, as it turned out, he was wrong because six months later I was transferred to another subsidiary, and six months after that, I was running the factory!

2

Matthias One reason I left my last company was because of a performance review I'd had with our HR manager. We were talking about the usual things, but during all of this, he answered the phone twice and even replied to an email. This annoyed me because I had prepared very thoroughly. Then at the end, he handed me a typed review and asked me to sign it. I asked if I could take it out of the office to read it and he said 'No!'. Anyway, I quickly read it and it didn't match our discussion. One thing was that he'd said I was doing really well, but the review said I would only get a 3% raise. Some weeks later, I heard that he was fired, but I'd already left by then.

15.3

Interviewer Now I'd like to ask you something about your current job. What's one thing about your job that you've found challenging and how have you dealt with it?

Candidate Oh, right. Well err, when I started the job, one of my first tasks was to lead a small team of three people. We were working together on a small project but the problem was we were all quite different characters, so it was quite hard to get everyone to work together well. In particular, I remember that one of the team was very independent.

Interviewer So how did you deal with that?

Candidate After I'd got to know everyone better, I started giving each person tasks which I thought would appeal to their strengths and interest. So, for example, I gave the person I mentioned research tasks to do on his own, and then he had to report back to the group at our weekly meeting. Overall, I found that worked fairly well.

Interviewer So you'd say you dealt with that challenge.

Candidate Yes, in general, I'd say the project was a success. Certainly, I learnt a lot from it.

15.4

Appraiser Come in. Oh, hi Chris. Take a seat. A coffee?

Chris No, I'm OK, thanks.

Appraiser Now, I've got the forms you filled in here. Thanks for getting them in on time. As you know, the main aim of this meeting is to appraise your performance and set some goals for the next six months. So, we'll begin by discussing your comments and then we'll start setting some objectives. I'll also be adding a few notes on the form. OK?

Chris Sure.

Appraiser I would like to say before we begin that, in general, we're very pleased with your performance. You seem to be doing very well.

Chris Well, that's good to know.

Appraiser I know there had been a few problems at the other factory before you moved here, but in the last six months, I've received lots of good reports about all your hard work.

Chris Good. That's nice to hear. I was finding it all difficult when I first came to work here, but it's easier now.

Appraiser Great. Now, one thing I wanted to discuss was this on your form. You mention solving problems with machinery, but is this something you like or dislike and is it an area you'd like to develop?

Chris No, it's something I like. I like challenges.

Appraiser OK, good. So, is there anything you don't like about the job?

Chris No, not really.

Appraiser No?

Chris Well, I think maybe we have too many meetings. And I like it when I'm given a job and can get on with it.

Appraiser How do you feel about working with other people?

Chris It's OK, but I think I'm someone who likes working alone. I think maybe that's something I need to work on.

Appraiser Right …

15.5

Appraiser … So, let's summarize what we've agreed. You're interested in more technical training, so one thing I'm going to do is speak to the Head of Engineering about the possibilities.

Chris That sounds good.

Appraiser And one thing you're going to do is look at the questionnaire I've given you on teams and team working. Is that OK with you?

Chris Yes. Fine.

Appraiser Now, is there anything else you'd like to add? We've still got five minutes.

Chris No, I don't think so.

Irregular verb list

Verb	Past simple	Past participle	Verb	Past simple	Past participle
be	was/were	been	let	let	let
become	became	become	light	lit	lit
begin	began	begun	lose	lost	lost
break	broke	broken	make	made	made
bring	brought	brought	mean	meant	meant
build	built	built	meet	met	met
burn	burnt/burned	burnt/burned	pay	paid	paid
buy	bought	bought	put	put	put
catch	caught	caught	read	read	read
choose	chose	chosen	ride	rode	ridden
come	came	come	ring	rang	rung
cost	cost	cost	rise	rose	risen
cut	cut	cut	run	ran	run
deal	dealt	dealt	say	said	said
do	did	done	see	saw	seen
dream	dreamt	dreamt	sell	sold	sold
drink	drank	drunk	send	sent	sent
drive	drove	driven	set	set	set
eat	ate	eaten	shine	shone	shone
fall	fell	fallen	show	showed	shown
feed	fed	fed	shut	shut	shut
feel	felt	felt	sing	sang	sung
fight	fought	fought	sit	sat	sat
find	found	found	sleep	slept	slept
fly	flew	flown	speak	spoke	spoken
forget	forgot	forgotten	spell	spelt/spelled	spelt/spelled
freeze	froze	frozen	spend	spent	spent
get	got	got	stand	stood	stood
give	gave	given	steal	stole	stolen
go	went	gone/been	swim	swam	swum
grow	grew	grown	take	took	taken
have	had	had	teach	taught	taught
hear	heard	heard	tell	told	told
hide	hid	hidden	think	thought	thought
hold	held	held	throw	threw	thrown
keep	kept	kept	understand	understood	understood
know	knew	known	wake	woke	woken
lead	led	led	wear	wore	worn
learn	learnt/learned	learnt/learned	win	won	won
leave	left	left	write	wrote	written
lend	lent	lent			

OXFORD
UNIVERSITY PRESS

Great Clarendon Street, Oxford, OX2 6DP, United Kingdom

Oxford University Press is a department of the University of Oxford.
It furthers the University's objective of excellence in research, scholarship,
and education by publishing worldwide. Oxford is a registered trade
mark of Oxford University Press in the UK and in certain other countries

© Oxford University Press 2017

The moral rights of the author have been asserted

First published in 2017
2022
10 9

ISBN: 978 0 19 473890 3   (book)
ISBN: 978 0 19 473886 6   (pack)

Printed in China

This book is printed on paper from certified and well-managed sources

ACKNOWLEDGEMENTS

The authors and publisher are grateful to those who have given permission to reproduce
the following extracts and adaptations of copyright material: p.65 Adapted extracts
from "Guitars and sci-fi break-out areas: a tour around Google's funky
fourth floor" by Sumant Bhatia, www.telegraph.co.uk, 12 December 2011.
© Telegraph Media Group Limited 2011. Reproduced by permission. p.72
Diagram: 'The Priority Matrix' from *Teach Yourself: Run Your Own Business* by
Kevin Duncan Copyright © Kevin Duncan, 2010. Reproduced by permission
of John Murray Press, an imprint of Hodder and Stoughton Limited. p.92 Logo
and extracts from TerraCycle, www.terracycle.com. © 2015. Reproduced by
permission. p.94 Diagram 'The Olleco Oil Cycle', by permission of Olleco,
www.olleco.co.uk. p.97 Diagram 'Lean Coffee' from "Power your next meeting
with Lean Coffee" produced by Gerry Kirk and created by Jim Benson and
Jeremy Lightsmith , 13 August 2013. Reproduced by permission of Gerry Kirk,
www.gerrykirk.net.

Sources: p.45 Situations adapted from Critical incidents in *Intercultural Business
Communication* by Robert Gibson, 2000, Corenelson & Oxford University Press
GmbH & Co. p.46 "Cover: The Untold Cost of Cybersecurity" by Valentina
Pasquali, www.gfmag.com, 2 May 2013. p.68 "Provide the right workplace
facilities", www.hse.gov.uk p.83 "Beware of Beethoven", www.economist.com,
23 August 2014. p.103 "Why it pays to be an ambivert. (And why you probably
are one.)" by Daniel H. Pink, www.danpink.com.

The publisher would like to thank the following for their permission to reproduce
photographs: 123RF pp.6 (Howard), 8, 19, 26 (phone), 28, 34, 46 (padlock), 47,
60 (freight ship, lorry), 63 (airport), 68, 73 (bulbs), 77, 83, 86 (car), 87, 88 (crisps,
notes), 95, 97, 104; Alamy pp.6 (Emrann/Mint Images Limited), 32 (Zappo
boxes/ZUMA Press, Inc.), 37 (keys/Jonathan Tenant), 48 (IndiaPicture),
50 (Blue Jean Images), 52 (cats/WENN Ltd), 55 (David Sanger Photography),
57 (New York City Opera/age fotostock, 3D printer/David Stock), 58 (weaver/
CTK), 73 (Isabelle Plasschaert), 74 (wonderlandstock), 88 (Alexander
Fleming/Pictorial Press Ltd), 91 (Deepwater Horizon oil rig on fire/US Coast
Guard Photo), 92 (all Terracycle/ZUMA Press, Inc.); Getty pp.6 (building/
EschCollection), 9, 12 (both), 14 (man cooking/Gary Burchell), 15 (Thomas
Barwick), 16 (Tim Robberts), 17, 18 (cranes/Jon Hicks, volunteer/Hill Street
Studios/Eric Raptosh), 21 (Biddiboo), 23 (storm/Don Klumpp), 24 (woman with
laptop and phone/Bloomberg), 25 (office/Bloomberg), 26 (cars/Nigel Treblin),
30 (FPG), 32 (shop/Theodore Kaye), 36, 38 (both), 40 (Sascha Schuermann),
41 (arabianEye), 42, 46 (woman/Erik Isakson), 52 (stockmarket/Mark Joseph),
54 (Frederic Lucano), 58 (freight/xPACIFICA), 60 (cargo plane/Sean Gallup),
61 (Thomas Barwick), 63 (couple/Joe McBride), 64, 66 (office/View Pictures,
Google wall/Brooks Kraft), 69, 70, 71 (factory/Al Moldvay), 72 (Bernd Opitz),
76 (Gary Burchell), 78 (Gardens in the Bay/WIN-Initiative, Cirque du Soleil/
Adrian Dennis), 81, 85 (Universal Images Group), 86 (engineer/Andrew
Brookes), 89, 90 (Nicholas Rigg), 91 (oil on water), 92 (printworks), 96,
98 (both), 100, 102, 105 (Highline/Bruce Yuanyue Bi); Oxford University
Press pp.6 (Tasia, Fey), 14 (runner, women), 49, 51, 57 (dollars), 62,
105 (skyline); PA Photos p.91 (Tony Hayward interview/Patrick Semansky/
AP/Press Association Images); Rex Features pp.23 (oil rig/Action Press/REX/
Shutterstock); Shutterstock pp.11, 31, 43, 84, 88 (printer), 97 (coffee ring
within infographic), 103.

With special thanks to: British Inventors' Society Awards/Cristina Schek
p.80 (both), MiRing p.57, Olleco p.94, Studio Diip p.57 (Fish on Wheels).

Illustrations by: Mark Duffin p.39, Willie Ryan p.95, Liza Whitney pp.43, 51, 97.

Cover image: Getty Images/Gary Burchell

Back cover photograph: Oxford University Press building/David Fisher

The authors and publisher would also like to thank the following individuals for their
advice and assistance in developing the material for this course: Beth Alexander,
Angelica Anastacio Molzahn, Clare Burke, Linda Cox, Louise Dixon, Simon
Drury, Justin Ehresman, Tom Evans, Jane Hoatson, Annie Kavaka, Christen
Kisch, Catherine Mayer, Sean O'Malley, Graeme Romanes, Rachael Smith,
Greg Steven, Edward Taylor.

*Although every effort has been made to trace and contact copyright holders before
publication, this has not been possible in some cases. We apologize for any apparent
infringement of copyright and if notified, the publisher will be pleased to rectify any
errors or omissions at the earliest opportunity.*